l American

Wall Street, 1903

OVER THE LONG TERM...

the story of J. & W. Seligman & Co.

1864-1964

by Ross L. Muir and Carl J. White

OVER THE LONG TERM . . .
the story of J. & W. Seligman & Co.

Library of Congress Catalog Card Number: 64-24580

First Edition

Published By
J. & W. SELIGMAN & CO.
ESTABLISHED 1864
65 BROADWAY, NEW YORK, N.Y. 10006

1964

DEDICATED

To those who helped to build the firm
over the long term
. . . men and women who were
—and are
members of the staff of
J. & W. Seligman & Co.

*But the Images of mens wits and knowledges remaine in Bookes,
exempted from the wrong of time, and capable
of perpetual renouation: Neither are they fitly to be
called Images, because they generate still, and cast their
seedes in the minds of others, prouoking and causing
infinit actions and opinions, in succeeding ages.*

—*Francis Bacon, 1561-1626*

FOREWORD

When a book to commemorate the one hundredth anniversary of J. & W. Seligman & Co. was proposed at a partners' meeting many months ago, the idea had an odd result. It propelled us into a long period of self-examination. Each of us reflected that our business is peculiarly private. Attention seeking plays no part in it. Our function is the management of investments, giving financial advice, and providing the essential brokerage facilities and related services which are a foundation of our business.

Clearly, we are not historians. Our primary goal is making money for our clients and for the firm, and money is made by men who stick to the work they know best. Having achieved some competence in our own field only after generations of experience and development, we were willing to believe that the making of books was not so easy as it might appear. Very likely, it was best left to professional writers and publishers. Moreover, although the story of our firm is interesting to us, we wondered how much general significance it might have.

There were persuasive arguments in favor of the project. One hundred years is a long time for an American enterprise of any kind to have been in successful operation. It is an exceptionally long time for a partnership to survive in the financial field with the same name and in the same form under which it was founded. We felt this fact alone to be significant. Perhaps lessons could be learned from a thorough examination of J. & W. Seligman & Co.'s beginnings and its subsequent evolution. Rediscovering the origins of the traditions within which the firm has operated over so many years and tracing their development might lead to a better understanding of ourselves, and help our friends and associates to understand why we have become what we are.

Telling the firm's story seemed to be a fitting way to pay tribute to the resourceful, energetic men who founded J. & W. Seligman & Co. in 1864 and to those who succeeded them. Like many others of their age, the firm's founders pitted their strengths and wills against the odds of humble background and the hardships of a harsh, young society and won high places in the business world for themselves in the process. Their struggles helped to create the most remarkable economy the world has ever seen, and this, it seems clear, has meaning for people everywhere. For this reason, reviewing the firm's years of trial and accomplishment might provide new inspiration for our faith in the self-reliance and initiative which fired our predecessors, and which, in essence, still sparks great enterprise wherever it is found.

The decision to publish this book – like all others we make – was a group decision, the product of all of our minds working together. We weighed our purposes and we agreed that an account of the firm's first one hundred years would be helpful to our business and would contribute to the business history of the United States. The conditions laid down were minimal, but important. The finished book should reflect truly what J. & W. Seligman & Co. has been in the past and what it is now; it should try to avoid the technical language of finance, and it should strive—with pictures as well as with words—to place the firm's activities over the years within a framework of the age in which they occurred. This is what the authors have tried to do.

Looking back into the second half of the Nineteenth Century during which the practice of banking and finance began to grow in the United States from virtually nothing into what we know today, the rapidity with which the world has changed is breath-taking. It is hard to believe that a small group of men in a single firm could play a major role in Government fiscal policy, finance the westward path of railroads through virtual wilderness, launch urban transit systems, participate in large-scale mining and land ventures, and have a hand in the destiny of a host of less dramatic undertakings and at the same time operate a network of banking houses scattered throughout the United States and Europe. It is impressive to reflect that the firm went on to become a prime mover behind the Panama Canal, loaned a partner to the Federal Reserve Board of Governors, helped to finance great companies which are still leaders in automobile manufacturing, electrical and electronics products, insurance, public utilities, shipbuilding, steel, and a good many other industries, and contributed probably as much to the development and growth of modern investment companies as any other institution.

Such versatility is no longer likely in complex modern business. The world indeed has changed. However, it is reassuring that, even though the firm's business has become more specialized with the passing of time, fundamental requirements for success remain unchanged. We believe that a thorough knowledge of the job at hand and hard, painstaking work are the only proven ingredients in sustained achievement. The firm's founders believed this, too.

In these times of strict regulation in the brokerage and investment fields, we may sometimes envy the pioneer financier the freedom of action he enjoyed in an age when the public interest was honestly believed to coincide with private interest. But on reflection, it is evident that regulation has not basically altered the true nature of our business; the high standards required, and that we demand of ourselves today, were always an essential to success. If there were few laws regulating financial transactions in the Nineteenth Century, fair dealing was dictated by a man's character then just as it is now, and this restraint was an alert watchdog for men building a business to be carried on into the future.

The early Seligmans were free to seek profits in almost any direction, and they did. But like honorable men in any age, they did it honestly; they put their clients' interests before their own. Their word was their bond. They made mistakes, and paid for them. They passed on a reputation of high character, which is a most precious legacy J. & W. Seligman & Co. received from its founders, and one we are determined will never change.

We should point out that the story of J. & W. Seligman & Co. is told, for the most part, in terms of the partners of the firm, who they have been, what they did, and the people they dealt with in Government and in the business world. This is inevitable. In any organization, certain men make the decisions, they sign important documents and letters, they assume the risks, and they take the credit or blame for success or failure. The organization becomes identified with them. However, at every stage of J. & W. Seligman & Co.'s development, the partners have been backed by a highly trained, deeply loyal staff, just as we are today. The work of these men and women was, and is, a vital part of our story. Few of them are named in this book, but we are very conscious of their contribution to the firm's long and prosperous life.

Nobody, except perhaps an Alexander or a Napoleon, consciously makes history. Ordinary men do their work each day as well as they know how, and when work papers, letters, and files have served their purposes, they are generally discarded. This has been the case at J. & W. Seligman & Co. There are gaps in our story which probably no amount of research could completely fill. Too many old papers have been destroyed, too many memories have faded or passed away.

But enough of the story has been set down to establish that as the present firm of J. & W. Seligman & Co., we are the custodians of a tradition of excellence. Realization of this can be humbling; it is also the source of genuine pride. If some of that pride pervades the pages that follow, that is as it should be. Our firm has seen crises and panics, depressions and wars. It has survived them all and gone forward in periods of peace and prosperity. Our strong link with the past engenders a tolerance of the difficulties of any moment and a firm confidence that continued progress lies in the years ahead.

Francis F. Randolph. Henry C. Breck

[illegible] [illegible]

Fred E. Brown Frederick W. Page

B. W. Robertson

GUY GILLETTE

The seven partners of J. & W. Seligman & Co. manage investment funds totaling billions of dollars. Seated around the long, polished mahogany table in the Board Room, they are (clockwise from center) Francis F. Randolph, Cyril J. C. Quinn, Stayman L. Reed, Beverly W. Robertson, Frederick W. Page, Fred E. Brown, and Henry C. Breck.

ONE

What one has, one ought to use: and whatever he does he should do with all his might.

—Marcus Tullius Cicero, 106-43 B.C.

Not long ago, a tall, well-dressed man sat across a desk from Beverly W. Robertson, a partner of J. & W. Seligman & Co. in New York City, and stared at the investment advisor-broker in surprise. A prosperous manufacturer in his early sixties, he had asked the firm to handle his investment account. Robertson had turned him down.

"Don't you want new accounts?" the doubtful visitor asked. "Aren't you in the investment advisory business?"

"Yes, we certainly do and we certainly are," Robertson assured him. "We're here to help people. But, we take new clients only when we think we can do something for them. You're making plans for retirement, and you want us to advise you on your investments. The securities you own involve a lot of risk. The best advice we can give you is to cut down on your risks and build a more conservative portfolio, which can be managed with your retirement needs in mind. You don't want that advice right now, so why hire us to give it? It wouldn't be right to pay us for advice you won't consider, and we don't want to be paid for it. When you feel that we can really do something for you, we'll be glad to talk business. We'll still be here."

As Robertson strode back down the quiet corridor, after leaving his visitor at the elevators, he spent no time wondering whether he had been right or wrong. He knew—as his partners know—that the firm's one hundred years of success hadn't been built by turning away business. But neither had it been built by accepting unsound business—however profitable. The firm's reputation and record was earned after generations of providing meaningful service to clients who needed what J. & W. Seligman & Co. has had to offer.

There was a time, after J. & W. Seligman & Co. was founded on May 1, 1864, when it operated branches in San Francisco, New Orleans, London, Paris, and Frankfurt am Main, as well as in New York City where the firm's only office is today. It carried on an international banking business, underwrote Government and corporate securities of all kinds, and handled investment brokerage transactions of almost every type. And in those days, Robertson's predecessors probably would have undertaken to serve a millionaire speculator. But those days are gone. In the past twenty-five years, or so, J. & W. Seligman & Co. has become more specialized. It provides professional investment advice to carefully selected clients, manages investment funds, acts as broker for those and other customers, and performs related services.

In its dedication to advisory service and investment management, along with its brokerage func-

Beverly W. Robertson began his business career as a trainee in a New York City commercial bank. When he joined J. & W. Seligman & Co. in 1929, his first job was in the firm's syndicate department. He helped organize what has become the present Investment Advisory Service.

BOTH : GUY GILLETTE

Visitors to the twenty-first floor are greeted by Rosa N. Roth and Robert E. Parker. The reception room, which is modestly decorated in browns, golds, reds, and greens and is furnished simply in keeping with the firm's character, conveys an air of quiet friendliness. Documents related to the firm's history line the walls.

tion, the firm is unusual among member firms of the New York Stock Exchange. Others give investment advice, or manage large accounts, but few concentrate their skills and attention in this demanding field. One or another of the Seligman partners has held a seat on the Exchange for all but the first five of the firm's one hundred years of existence—since May 1, 1869. The firm still pulses with the challenge of backing its judgment with vast amounts of money in the excited atmosphere of buying and selling indigenous to Wall Street. Yet, the air of tranquility on the top three floors housing J. & W. Seligman & Co. and financial organizations it is associated with in the middle of the financial district at 65 Broadway belies its intimacy with the hubbub of the capital markets that keep America's private economy alive.

Paradoxically, as Seligman activities became more private, and its name appeared less frequently in the financial pages, its importance, measured by the scope of the firm's responsibilities and influence among investors – institutional and individual – became increasingly great. The twenty-first floor reception room, centered with a simple English dining table and hung with some of the firm's historical documents nearly as old, gives no hint of the partnership's wide-ranging interests. Yet, decisions made by the partners and men who work with them in the quiet, pine-paneled Board Room just down the corridor can affect people and institutions in places far from New York City. Investment funds watched over by these men are counted in the billions of dollars.

In addition to providing personalized investment service for its advisory clients, Seligman partners serve as Directors and officers of Tri-Continental Corporation, the Nation's largest diversified closed-end investment company, and the Broad Street Group of Mutual Funds—Broad Street Investing Corporation, National Investors Corporation, and Whitehall Fund, Inc. Combined investment assets of these four companies exceed $1,300,000,000. Their securities are owned by nearly a quarter of a million men, women, and children, and a wide variety of organizations and institutions in all fifty states and about sixty foreign countries.

Established by J. & W. Seligman & Co. in 1929, Tri-Continental is served by partners of the firm under an agreement as old as the Corporation itself.

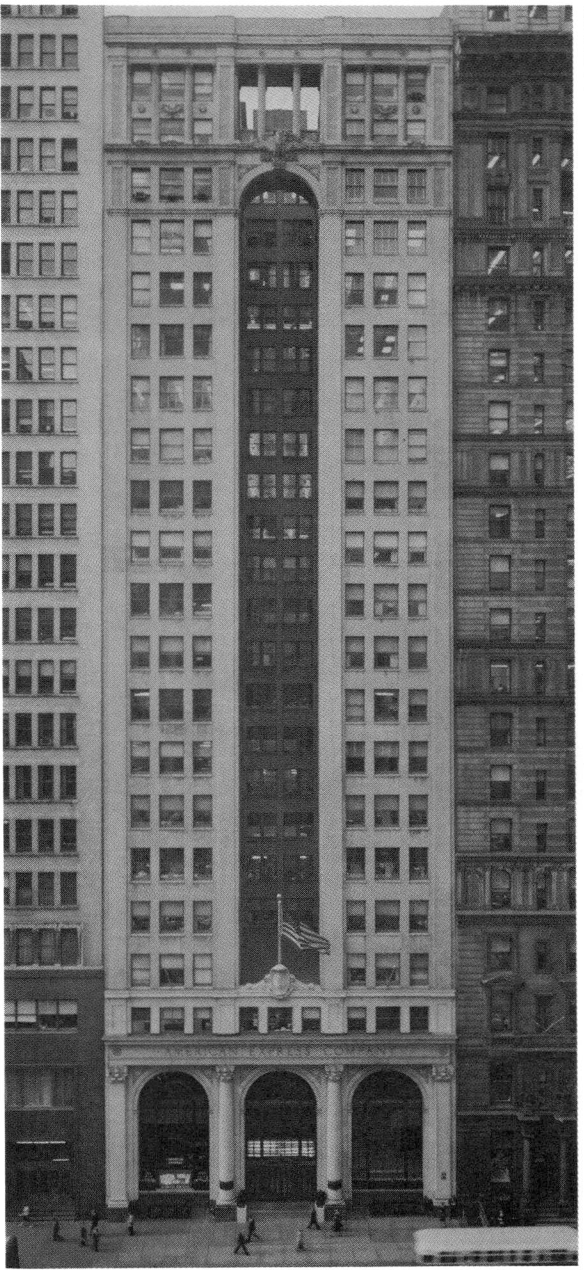
AMERICAN EXPRESS COMPANY

Since 1940, offices of J. & W. Seligman & Co. have been located on the top three floors of the twenty-one story American Express Company building at 65 Broadway—just a short walk from Wall Street. Completed in 1916, architects for the building were Renwick, Aspinwall and Tucker.

GUY GILLETTE

Francis F. Randolph, for many years the senior partner, played an important role in establishing the investment companies with which Seligman partners are now associated. He practiced law in New York and worked in Europe for the United States Treasury on reparations payments before joining the firm in 1920. His early assignments at J. & W. Seligman & Co. included general banking and new issues work along with rail and corporate reorganizations.

Broad Street Investing, oldest of the three Mutual Funds, has had Seligman partners as officers for thirty-four years; National Investors, a pioneer of the growth stock theory of investing, came into the Group in 1942, and Whitehall Fund, a balanced fund for conservative investors, was organized under the sponsorship of the firm in 1947.

Tri-Continental and the Mutual Funds of the Broad Street Group are publicly-owned investment companies. Their basic operating policies are determined by their Boards of Directors. These Boards, the majority of whose members are not associated with the Seligman firm, are elected by the stockholders of each company. Once policies have been set, the Boards rely on the officers to carry them out from day to day in the stockholders' interest. This is the business at hand in meetings held in the Board Room at 65 Broadway nearly every day.

Chairman at meetings of the investment companies' officers is Francis Fitz Randolph, senior partner, who came to the firm more than forty years ago as a young lawyer determined to become a financier. Working with him as a group to make investment decisions are his partners, soft-spoken, tenacious Cyril J. C. Quinn; Henry C. Breck, a transplanted Californian, and, a generation younger, but veterans of an average thirty years in the investment field, Fred E. Brown and Frederick W. Page. Beverly W. Robertson and Stayman L. Reed, the firm's restless managing partner, are concerned primarily with the affairs of the firm. Seligman family members are all gone— the last retired in 1937 – but the vivid memories Randolph, Breck, Quinn, and Reed have of former partners whose experience stretched back into the Nineteenth Century provide the background for a point of view which fosters the spirit, as well as the fact, of continuity with the past.

"When you go back one hundred years to the start of the firm," Francis Randolph observes, "there's only limited continuity in the kind of business done. But there is a logic in the firm's evolution, and there has been definite continuity in the way we've done business over the years."

Randolph's book-lined office overlooking New York's busy harbor seems more scholarly than commercial. The brown leather topped desk, generally heaped with papers and reports of varying urgency, mark it for a busy executive's workroom.

But the Venetian scene by Canaletto dominating one wall, fine English prints filling spaces around the ceiling-high bookcases, and an early print of Vassar College suggest active interests ranging far beyond the marketplace.

"The basic lesson we've learned from Seligman's long history," the senior partner will tell you, "is that maintaining a high character, guarding a reputation for fair dealing, and doing the best job we possibly can is sheer dollars-and-cents wisdom. These are what give a business the momentum to go on indefinitely."

"Seligman has always been devoted to giving financial service, first to the Government and then to various companies with which the firm did business over the years. And from the very beginning, it has prospered by serving individual clients. Our design today is to continue this tradition of service to institutional and individual advisory and brokerage clients, and to the investment companies."

The firm differs from many others, in Randolph's view, because "the unbroken link with the past has added to the breadth of our vision. We actively shun the quick and opportunistic in selecting an investment or in giving advice. Having gone through so many periods of ups and downs over the years unchanged as a firm tends to breed patience. Our decisions are made with the long term in mind. We are a professional firm by virtue of our education, training, and experience. Like other professionals, we have dedicated our working lives to our field and we try to do our work thoroughly. We don't risk slipping by, making haphazard moves, then hoping they'll turn out all right. We work hard for the successes we get. I think for these reasons, Seligman is universally recognized as having a high professional standing in the investment field."

The men who, with Randolph, preserve the Seligman traditions started a century ago, are as different from each other as the firm is from other houses on the Street. Typical New Yorkers in that none of them was born there, no two of the seven Seligman partners attended the same college, and only two came from the same state. The towns and cities in which they were born and raised are as widely separated as New Jersey and California, and their backgrounds and early experiences have little in common. Yet, over the years, they have evolved as close

GUY GILLETTE

Cyril J. C. Quinn went from the Army to Paris in 1919 where he worked for Herbert Hoover and his American Relief Administration during the Peace Conference, and then on to London, Warsaw, and Moscow. He joined J. & W. Seligman & Co. in 1927.

a working arrangement as is perhaps possible in any group of men.

Unlike most partnerships, in which one or two members usually are dominant, no Seligman partner exercises authority over the others or lays down a set of rules to be obeyed. Each partner participates in every decision as an independent individual and speaks his mind after bringing his personal judgment to bear on the matter at hand. Each man listens to the others and then a decision is made on the basis of the best judgment of the group. Once a decision is made, it is the firm's decision.

"Fortunately," Randolph has said, "we've been able to function for many years without emotional differences of personality or opinion. Because we have been able to work harmoniously as independent persons, I think we have profited from the aggregate of each man's individual initiative."

Each Seligman partner puts his personal reputation and private assets into the others' hands. Each is a general partner, legally able to commit all of the others or to be committed by any of the others for literally all he is worth. Yet, years of close contact has taught each of them enough of the workings of the others' minds so that they function together with mutual trust and respect.

All of Seligman's affairs are under the direct supervision of the partners working as a group, but to accomplish the varied amount of work the firm encompasses, day-to-day operation of each separate interest is assumed by individual partners. Fred E. Brown, a tall, forceful Oklahoman, is a Director, President, and Chief Executive Officer of Tri-Continental Corporation. He fills the same offices in each of the Mutual Funds of the Broad Street Group. Working closely with him, but concentrating more of his attention on investments than on administration, is Frederick W. Page, who made his reputation as one of the Nation's best-known experts in public utility finance. He is a Director and a Vice-President of the investment companies and President of Tri-Continental

GUY GILLETTE

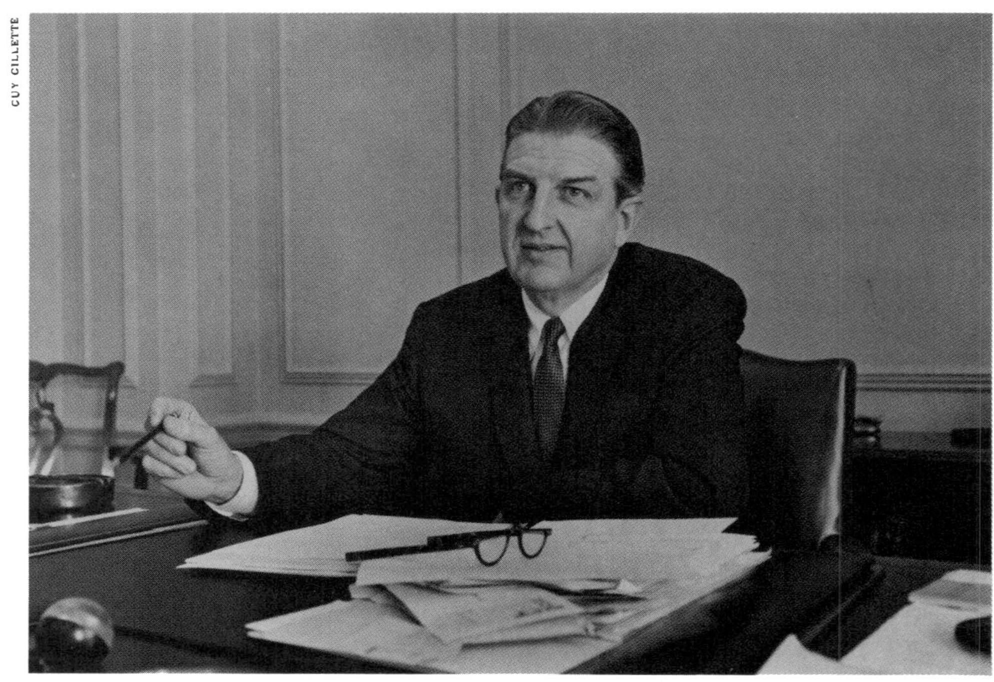

Fred E. Brown was born and raised in Oklahoma, studied finance and retailing at Harvard Business School, and joined Tri-Continental in 1936. An Army Lieutenant Colonel during World War II, he became a partner in 1955.

Financial Corporation, a wholly-owned subsidiary of the big, closed-end company.

Beverly Robertson, for whom there never seems enough hours in the working day, directs the Investment Advisory Service and administers the staff responsible for research and the countless details of this sensitive business. As managing partner, Stayman L. Reed's working day is filled with the technicalities of buying and selling securities, supervising the back office in which records are kept and securities are processed, keeping track of and conforming to legal requirements, regulations of the New York and American stock exchanges, and generally coping with the routine of "meeting the payroll" and other administrative tasks.

Randolph, Quinn, and Breck participate in all these activities and are in on all decisions. Francis Randolph serves as Chairman of the investment companies; Cyril Quinn is a Director and Vice-Chairman of Tri-Continental and a Director and Vice-President of the three Mutual Funds, and Henry Breck is a Director and Vice-President of Tri-Continental and a Vice-President of the Funds.

Tri-Continental and the three Mutual Funds of the Broad Street Group are organized in a unique manner initiated by the Seligman partners many years ago. In contrast to most investment companies, which are managed by separate concerns under contracts which usually provide essential services for fixed fees expressed as a percentage of the assets of the companies and are designed to produce a profit for their owners, the four companies operate with internal non-profit management. Officers are direct salaried employees in the same way that officers of most American corporations are salaried employees, and they are responsible to the Boards of Directors. Investment research and administrative services are provided by an organization which the four companies mutually own and operate at cost. The compensation of officers and the costs of the research and service company are shared on a no-profit basis by the four investment companies in the proportion of their assets.

This unusual arrangement has given the companies that are associated with Seligman operating expense ratios that are among the lowest in the investment company field. It has also led to the development of a highly specialized organization of more than one hundred thoroughly-trained men

GUY GILLETTE

After World War I, Henry C. Breck, a native of California, spent several years in Government service. In 1926, he said, "as I was interested in the financial world, I thought the best thing to do was to go to New York which was the center of the wheel, instead of back to San Francisco which was the perimeter." He became a partner in 1928.

Stayman L. Reed joined Seligman in 1929 after working for the American Express Company in the Orient and in Europe. He became a partner of the firm on July 1, 1942.

GUY GILLETTE

and women who provide economic and investment research and analysis and all other services required for the complex job of operating Tri-Continental and the Broad Street Group. Directing and co-ordinating this organization are among the tasks of Fred Brown and Fred Page.

Trained and experienced in investments and administration from the time he left graduate school twenty-eight years ago, Brown works in a bright, sandalwood colored office in which an Irish hunt table is reserved for group discussions and the Eighteenth Century clock on the wall helps to keep each day's activities on schedule. Wood carvings of a rampaging bull and a honey-hungry bear shaped by an Oklahoma Indian testify both to the President's Wall Street orientation and to his Southwestern heritage. But it is clearly a business office where the telephone never seems to stop ringing and the stream of department heads reporting progress or problems never seems to end.

Much of Brown's time as Chief Executive Officer of the companies inevitably is spent on matters of planning and administration—public contact. stockholder reports, correspondence, legal matters, accounting chores, employee problems—which devour the working day of all corporation officers. But amidst the maze of day-to-day detail, neither Brown, nor anyone else, is likely to forget that the chief business of the investment companies—and indeed of all activities in which the Seligman firm is engaged—is to produce investment results for people whose funds have been put to work in one way or another through the organization. For this reason, Fred Brown—as he has from the start of his career—concentrates his primary energies in the investment management and brokerage fields.

One flight down on the twentieth floor, Fred Page directs the work of the investment companies' staff from a green carpeted, comfortably furnished office at the end of a long corridor. However, his office is more accurately a committee room much of the time, for every day groups of investment men and women gather there from their offices along the corridors to develop specific recommendations for buying and selling securities.

"Our assignment," Page will explain, "is to know as much as we can about each company whose securities are held in the portfolios of the investment companies or might be considered for purchase. We maintain continual study and analysis of general business and economic conditions of a broad range of industries and of hundreds of companies to provide background and information on which the Boards of Directors can base policy, to guide investment research activities, and to develop ideas on specific investments."

"We're organized and staffed to do a complete job in a professional manner," he will tell you. "Analysts are chosen carefully and trained thoroughly over a period of time."

"Our work is original," Page likes to point out. "It is based on first-hand information gathered in face-to-face meetings with corporation executives. In a typical year, members of the staff travel roughly 200,000 miles to almost every part of North America. They make field trips to some 200 companies in about fifty industries. On an average of about ten times each working day they interview an officer of a corporation whose securities may interest us."

When analysts with an investment recommendation settle into chairs around Page's desk, they may look at ease. But despite a relaxed, patient ap-

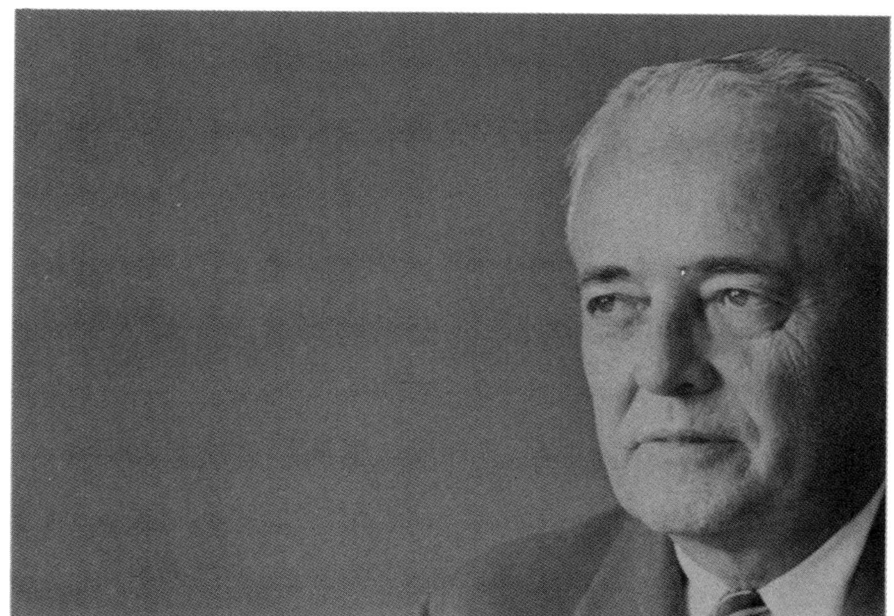

Before he joined Tri-Continental Corporation in 1933, Frederick W. Page worked for an insurance company in New York. Over the years, he has become a nationally recognized authority on public utility financing. Page has been a Seligman partner since January 1955.

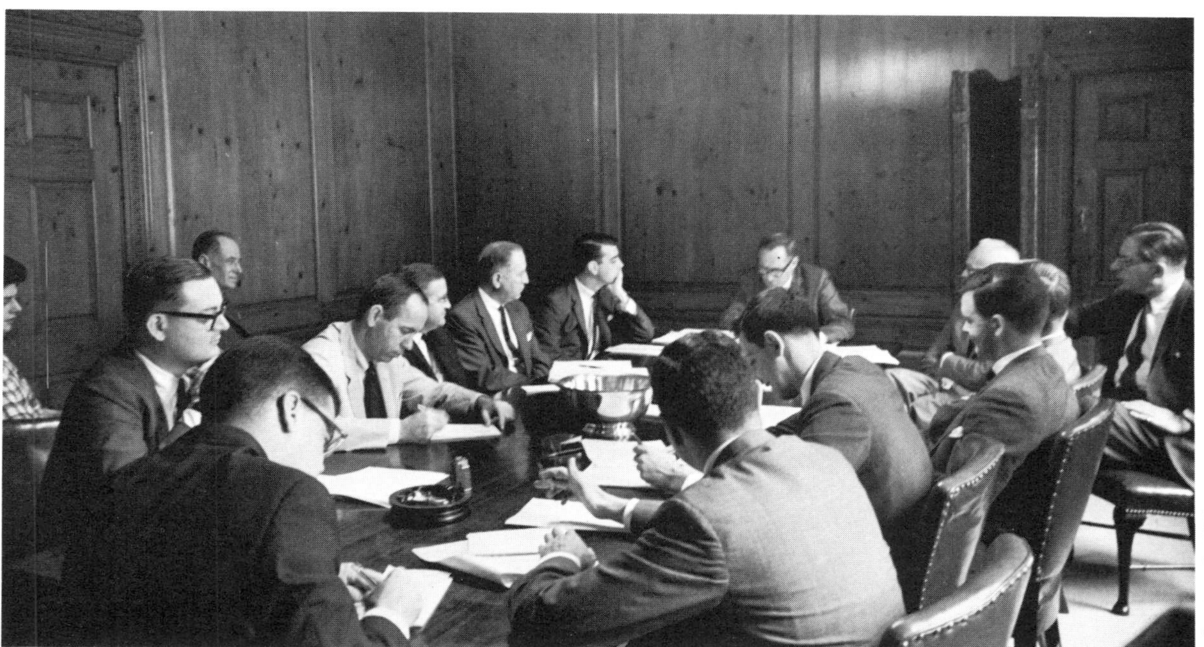

BOTH: GUY GILLETTE

Organized in depth, the Union Service research staff is expected to do a complete and imaginative job of analysis in a professional manner before recommendations to buy or sell securities for the four investment companies are proposed. Analysts (above) work under the guidance of Vice-President Stanley R. Currie (center of table, rear).

The key to J. & W. Seligman & Co.'s Investment Advisory Service is a qualified staff of account managers and analysts (above). These men, directed by Beverly W. Robertson (left), are trained to furnish the kind of service each individual, family, and institutional client wants and needs. This service is complete, thorough, and personalized.

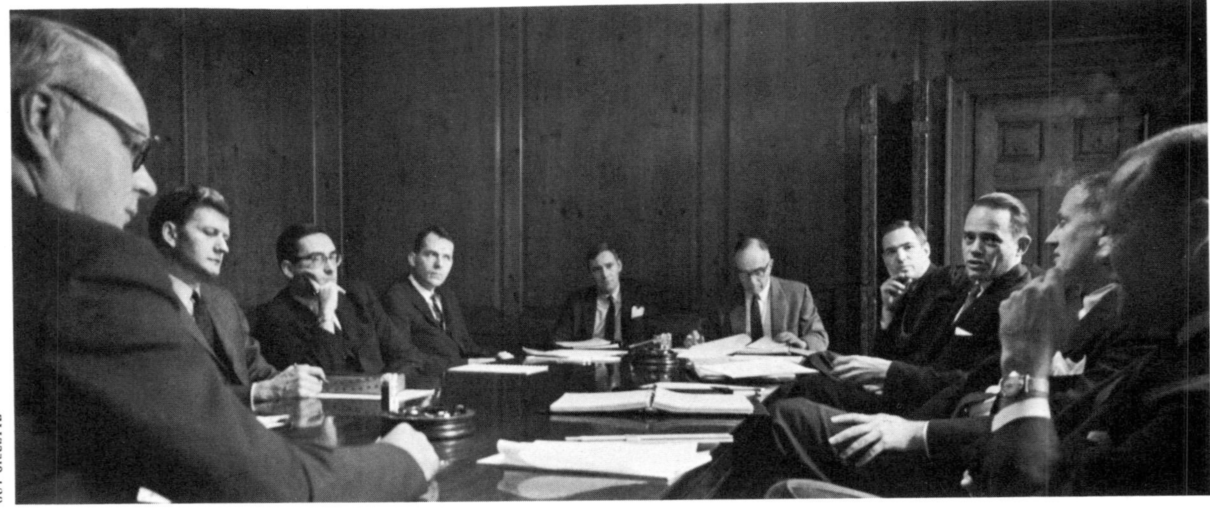

GUY GILLETTE

proach, Page, and the men who work with him, probe every recommendation for weaknesses, test it in the light of business and market conditions, and keep the analyst with the idea on his toes defending his point of view. Every analyst gets a full and careful hearing and recommendations accepted are presented for consideration and final action to the executives in the Board Room.

The assets of Tri-Continental and the Broad Street Group of Mutual Funds make up an important part of the investment funds with which J. & W. Seligman & Co. partners are concerned. Maintaining the outstanding performance records of the four companies is a demanding, full-time job for the staffs under the direction of Brown and Page.

Robertson's assignment, in close association with his partners, of managing the Investment Advisory Service is a vastly different operation. The funds in these accounts often represent the bulk of the resources of an institution, an individual, or a family group. Each must be handled on a personal, tailor-made basis, designed to meet the needs of each client, whatever they may be.

"Fundamentally," Robertson will explain, "our job as investment advisors is to study the financial position and requirements of each client and to establish and maintain on a continuing basis an investment program best suited to them. We do this for a fee based on the value of the assets in the account and the kind of account it is. Our work is like that of the investment companies in that we are concerned with securities. But the similarity ends right there."

"We take pride in being what we like to call 'the businessman friend' of the family to many of our clients. We're not, and we don't want to be, a big, impersonal machine. We choose our clients with considerable care. They choose us, I'm sure, with equal care and because we can give the kind of personal service and attention that larger advisory services may find impractical. Most of our advisory accounts are substantial in size. They have to be to make Seligman's service economic to them and profitable to us."

"There are no numbers here, no mass treatment," Robertson will tell you with pride. "Every account with which we deal is a flesh and blood person. We try to get to know each client and we try to have a close personal relationship with him or her in the same way a doctor or a lawyer tries to know his patient or client. We try to keep in regular and close touch with them, so that we can literally tailor the way a portfolio is managed to meet the specific needs of a widow, for example,

Joseph P. Mendres (left), head of the order department, and Peter W. Lange, foreign business representative, often review market conditions which could concern J. & W. Seligman & Co.'s overseas accounts. Personal contact is an important part of Lange's job, and he makes frequent trips to Europe for on-the-spot consultations with clients.

GUY GILLETTE

who must have reliable income, or an aggressive young businessman trying to make his capital grow, or a family seeking a balance between income and growth. And, we can never lose sight of the fact that we are serving people in our work, and we must always keep in mind a client's temperament and wishes, as well as his needs."

To the extent that Seligman advisory clients seek the benefits of the firm's experience and knowledge and the use of its facilities, Robertson's job is demanding but clear cut. However, personalized service, he will emphasize, often calls for far more than continuing investment advice. "After we really get to know a client, especially one which may represent the second or third generation the firm has served, it's flattering, and sometimes surprising, how often we are asked to help them with problems which are only remotely connected with investments and which may be very personal to them. We try to help whenever and however we can. When we succeed we have an added source of satisfaction and pride in our work."

Frank Leighton, long associated with the Advisory Service, can remember times when being an investment advisor has strained his knowledge far beyond his training in the investment field. Among other things, he has priced apartments, advised on comparative costs of schools, and even helped decide on how much to spend to redecorate a living room.

"This is not so strange as it seems," Robertson will tell you. "After all, people talk to their friends about the things that are uppermost on their minds, and we'd have to be impersonal indeed not to be interested and not to help whenever we can. But," the advisor-broker commented, "we don't mean to suggest that our job is cluttered with unusual chores. It's simply that our service is personal and we like it that way."

All of the Seligman partners have advisory accounts they have introduced to the firm. They often deal directly with these clients in recommending action to be taken and in making periodic reports, working with the staff of advisory account managers under Robertson's supervision. Backing up these managers are security analysts who keep up-to-date on individual investments and recommend new purchases, or possible changes, in portfolio holdings.

"Matters of basic investment policy," Robertson likes to emphasize, "are decided by all of the partners. Every client gets the full benefit of the aggregate knowledge and experience of the entire firm."

As one of the oldest members of the New York Stock Exchange, and also the American Stock Exchange, J. & W. Seligman & Co. acts as broker for advisory clients if they wish this service, for ordinary customers, for the investment companies with which it is associated, and for other institutions, buying and selling securities at regular commission rates. The firm also maintains a fully-staffed, professional income tax department directed by Raymond J. Monahan, a member of the New York bar who has been doing tax work since 1938. This department prepares Federal and state income tax returns for the partners and for many of the firm's advisory clients. Custody service is provided through which clients' securities are carefully segregated and safeguarded in deep, underground vaults fifty-six feet below the surface of Wall Street. Income is collected and paid out and such things as bond redemptions, stock dividends, and subscription rights are taken care of. Clients who come to Seligman for investment advice, of course, may take advantage of all services provided by the firm, although each is optional.

Far from being ivory tower financiers, the Seligman partners are actively involved in a wide range of business and community affairs. Collectively, they are directors or trustees of thirty-six well-known organizations, including manufacturing, shipbuilding, and insurance companies, a railroad, a savings bank, and a public utility. They sit on the boards of hospitals, a college, churches, pension funds, cultural groups, and have served on local governmental bodies. Their wide-ranging interests deepen their understanding of general business and cultural forces at work in the economy and help to sharpen their practical business judgment.

As a result of its experience and knowledge, the Seligman firm acts from time to time as a financial consultant and advisor to business organizations planning corporate acquisitions, reorganizations, or in need of impartial appraisals. Recently, Henry Breck appeared as an expert witness before the Civil Aeronautics Board in connection with a proposed merger of two major airlines. Similar consulting work has been done for many years, and each time another request comes along it is a tribute to the regard in which the firm is held among businessmen.

In describing the firm, Fred Page is apt to comment that "we are conservative. We are responsible for the productive investment of a great deal of money for many different people in all walks of life, and that's a job that has to be taken seriously and done with prudence."

To Fred Brown, Seligman is "reasonably forward looking, but certainly not an innovator. Generally speaking, we're a little slow to try new ideas. This is not because we're afraid of new ideas but rather because we have found solid success in gradual transition over the years, instead of from jumping at whatever bright new thought comes along."

The firm probably can be characterized best by some of the things that other brokerage firms do that Seligman does not. "We have few customers men," Brown will point out, "and, as typified by Peter W. Lange, who has been handling much of the firm's foreign business for thirty years, and Leon Fletcher, a former member of the New York Stock Exchange, who has a group of his own accounts, even these operate in an unusual fashion. We don't deal with the public at large. In this sense, Seligman's business is private. We discourage margin business; do no commodity business. And to enable the firm to deal at arm's length with both advi-

Younger men back those at the top to assure continuity. Walter F. Baumann, at twenty-six, the youngest analyst, studies possible investment opportunities in five industrial categories. A New York University graduate, he has acquired over five years of experience on Wall Street.

GUY GILLETTE

When the Quarter Century Club of J. & W. Seligman & Co. and associated companies held its annual luncheon meeting in the Fall of 1963, nearly one-fourth of the combined staffs attended. Members, who have known each other virtually all their working lives, gather formally each year to welcome newcomers to the group, talk old times.

GUY GILLETTE

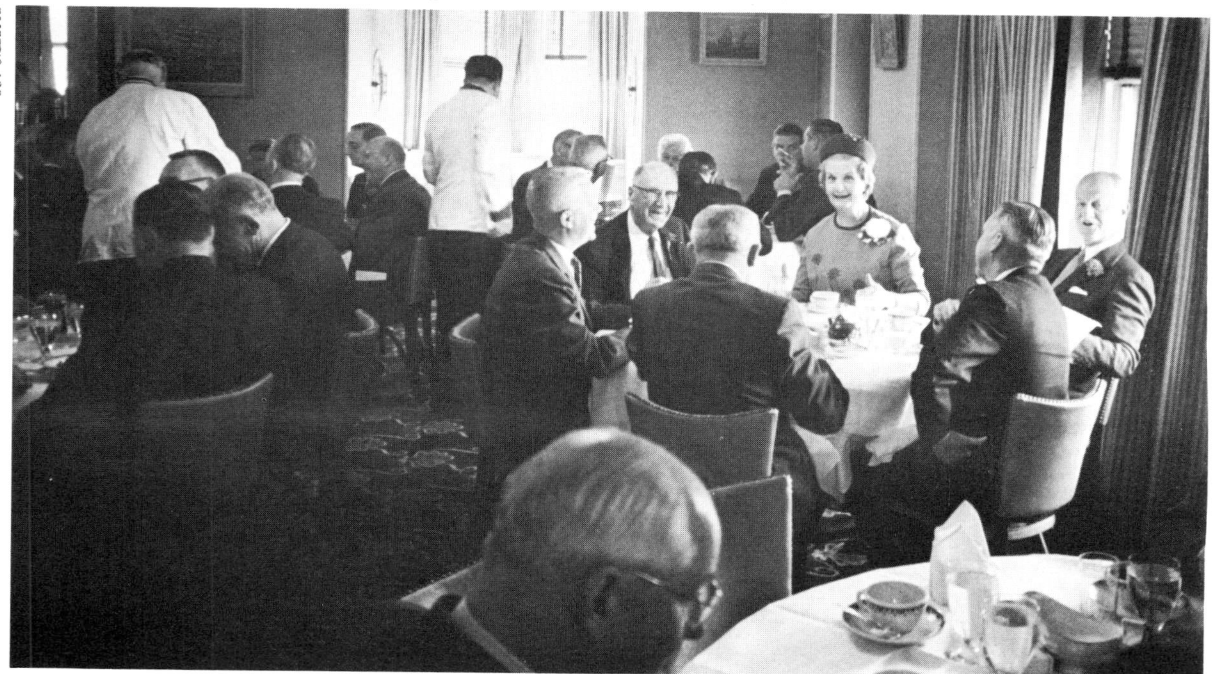

sory clients and the investment companies, we never underwrite securities or participate in selling groups, we don't maintain trading markets, and we never take a position in securities for the firm's account."

In the process of evolving from a full line banking, investment brokerage, and underwriting house into the more specialized firm it is today, Seligman has learned that it cannot be "everything to everybody." "There are things we know we don't do well," Brown will tell you, "and we don't pretend to do them. We are not a good organization for people who want to trade securities to make a quick turn in the market. This just doesn't happen to be our dish of tea. We have found that we can do reasonably well for clients who have patience, who want advice or management for the long term. But even in this respect, we don't promote our services, and we don't actively solicit accounts. We want people to want us. We let our clients speak for us, if they wish to, and we let the long-term records of the investment companies speak for themselves."

In this connection, Cyril Quinn, who has a disturbing facility for bringing self importance to earth with a silent stare, has pointed out that "in this business, you can't boast about how good your individual investment selections are over the short term. It's like a ball game. The score is in the newspapers every morning. No one can safely predict what we can do for an account. All we can promise is that we will try to do our best. We can say that good work over a reasonably long period has produced good results more often than not in the past."

Even at that, the practice of giving investment advice and managing investments is different from that of other professions. Once a patient has recovered from an illness, a doctor may be reasonably sure that fairly sensible living and a benevolent nature will keep the patient in good health, and he can turn his attention to other patients. An investment program is far more demanding. It needs continuous attention – not just when in difficulty, but all the time. The minute a security or a program is

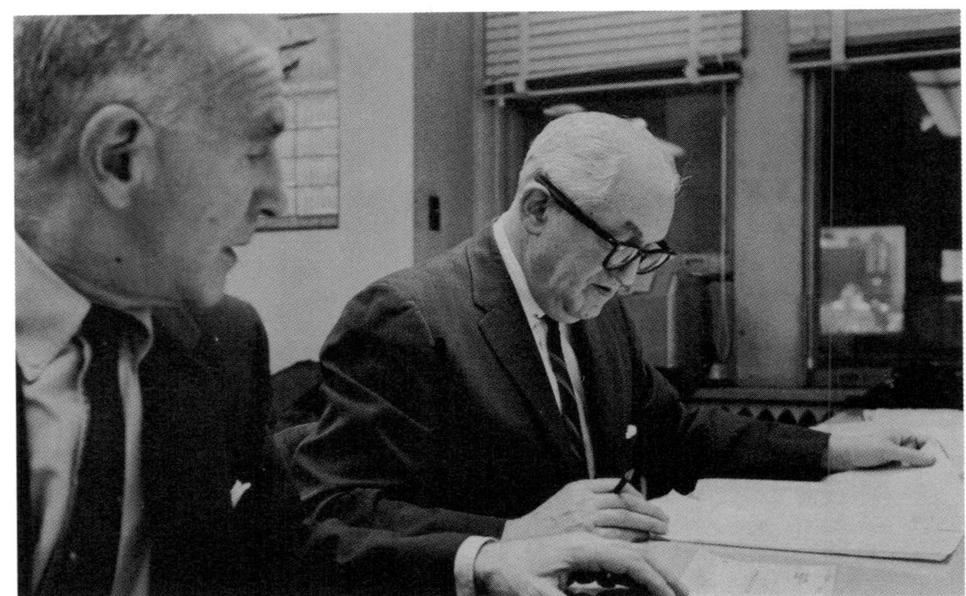

As accounting department head, Samuel Nagler is in charge of all customer and firm account records. Samuel Ripps (left) is assistant department head.

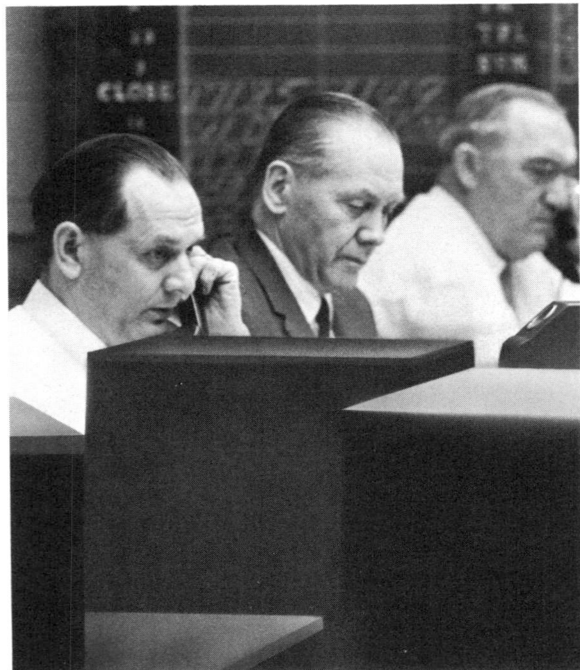

Arthur A. Weinar, John J. Welsh, and Louis B. McIntosh (from left) are securities order clerks who keep in touch with markets, execute purchases and sales, check latest stock and bond prices, supply latest market data.

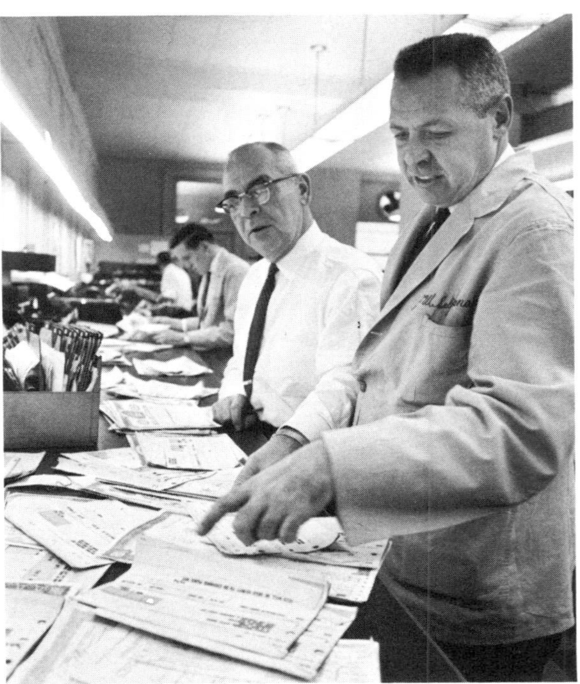

ALL: GUY GILLETTE

The cash and securities department, directed by Dominick F. Wolf, handles physical movement of securities, proxies, redemptions, coupon collections, and other brokerage functions. Edward J. Finck (front) is an assistant.

taken for granted, trouble may start. For that reason, it is essential that a firm which undertakes to advise people on their investment programs must be organized in depth to assure continuity. The men at the top must be backed with younger men who are fully trained in every phase of the firm's work, ready to take over as time goes on, and behind them must be even younger people in training to assume top level responsibility eventually.

The Quarter Century Club, an organization of partners and employees who have been with the firm or one of the associated companies for twenty-five years or more, numbers fifty-three of the 245 men and women who are potential members. All the partners and most department heads belong.

"This record of long service among employees," Stayman Reed believes, "goes a long way toward characterizing J. & W. Seligman & Co. We select employees carefully, train them well, and then expect them to perform their jobs in a thoroughly professional manner. We share profits, so that employees with a degree of seniority, and certainly those who fill key positions, are, in effect, partners in the firm, but without capital risk. This has had a great influence on the kind of people we have attracted and their loyalty to the firm."

The long service of individual employees has had another important influence, too. It has resulted in multiple skills among many of them. The firm's securities department, managed by Dominick F. Wolf, for example, is probably one of the few on Wall Street in which nearly every man can do the work of every other with equal proficiency. Samuel Nagler, who is in charge of the firm's books and customers' records, and his assistants perform functions that would be allotted to partners in many firms, and Joseph P. Mendres' securities order department has a reputation for being well-trained and efficient.

Intangibly, many years of dedication to the success of a single firm provides a sense of permanence that perhaps can come in no other way. Herbert S. Bachman, the firm's oldest employee, has been with J. & W. Seligman & Co. an incredible sixty-five years. Fred Brown likes to point out that "he came to work here fifteen years before I was born." Bachman can remember that the firm was a leading banking-brokerage house at the turn of the century when John D. Rockefeller, Sr. was a client, and Hetty Green, the storied "Witch of Wall Street" came into the office looking for a place to loan her millions at high interest. Sam Nagler and his assistant, Samuel Ripps, both of whom started their careers more than forty years ago, can remember that they were well-seasoned in the business when Frank Leighton, a twenty-eight-year veteran .ow himself, started as a runner. They sent Leighton out to deliver a package to Church & Graves at 103 Broadway and, as hundreds of new runners have, he ended up in chagrin staring at Trinity Episcopal Church and its ancient burial ground which stand as an ageless beacon in downtown New York reminding Wall Street's moneymen each day of their mortality.

J. & W. Seligman & Co. has changed in its one hundred years of life. Hundreds of men and women have carried on its obligations through their careers and trained new people to continue from where they left off. New conditions, new opportunities, and natural evolution have altered the nature of the firm's business, but its determination to serve and to go on serving long into the future is just the same today as it was in the uncertain days of the American Civil War when J. & W. Seligman & Co. began.

GUY GILLETTE

On January 16, 1899, ten days before his sixteenth birthday, Herbert S. Bachman was hired as a runner for the firm at five dollars a week. In following years, he has had positions of trust in nearly every department of the firm.

TWO

It is not the longest sword but
the longest purse that conquers.

—Daniel Defoe, 1660-1731

The Confederate guns that began the Civil War by shelling Fort Sumter at 4:30 a.m. on April 12, 1861, were able to batter the garrison into surrendering two days later by taking full advantage of the Union's inability to come to the aid of the beleagured fort. In those early April days, the Treasury of the United States wasn't in much better shape than Fort Sumter, but there was one difference and it proved to be all important. The Union was able to come to the aid of the Treasury.

Financing the War was second in importance only to the military operations themselves, and few men had more to do with the eventual success of that financing than Joseph Seligman who came to the United States from Bavaria in 1837 and eventually settled in New York City. He went abroad in the early 1860's, during his adopted country's darkest days, and helped place more than $200,000,000 worth of U. S. Government securities in the difficult European market, an accomplishment historian W. E. Dodd effusively–and erroneously–credits to one-time Treasury Secretary Robert J. Walker as a task "equal perhaps to the service of the general who stopped Lee at Gettysburg."

Joseph Seligman was the oldest of eight brothers who founded J. & W. Seligman & Co. His first job was clerk and cashier in a store at Nesquehoning, a small Pennsylvania coal mining town. He saved his money and in a year this young man, who a few years earlier had been a Greek orator at the University of Erlangen in his native land, struck out on his own as a pack peddler. In the Spring of 1839, he sent for his brothers, William and James, who also became pack peddlers and helped build the family savings until Joseph and William could open a small store. Within a few years, money was sent to bring the younger brothers — Jesse, Leopold, Abraham, Henry, and Isaac — and other members of the family to America.

During the next decade, the brothers moved from place to place, restlessly seeking greener pastures. And before settling down as merchants with an importing house and a store in New York City, and a general merchandise outlet across the continent in San Francisco, one or more of the Seligman brothers had opened and closed small stores in Pennsylvania, Alabama, Missouri, and upper New York State.

Twenty years after Joseph Seligman arrived in the United States, a virtually penniless immigrant, the eight brothers had built their joint capital into the hundreds of thousands of dollars. And in another fifteen years, their combined capital had risen into the millions.

During the 1840's and 1850's, as their resources grew steadily and the Seligman family members evolved from pack peddlers into well-to-do merchants, all the familiar attributes were evident: busi-

The Eight Seligman Brothers: 1. Joseph, 2. William, 3. Henry, 4. James, 5. Jesse, 6. Leopold, 7. Isaac, 8. Abraham.

ness acumen, great diligence, honesty, and good luck. There were, however, two-out-of-the ordinary factors working in the Seligmans' favor. The first was their system of sharing all expenses, all losses, and all profits; the second, and vastly more important, was Joseph Seligman himself.

As oldest brother, he might be expected to have the leading voice in family matters. But Joseph was more a father to his brothers than an older brother when it came to managing their affairs. Under his astute—if not always benevolent—guidance, all of the Seligman commercial enterprises prospered, particularly during the 1850's, but none more than the San Francisco store. The retailing business there became a wholesale outlet for other stores. New York was the central office. Goods shipped from the East to California around Cape Horn or via Panama were sold for gold, which was sent back to New York and sold at a premium. The mark-up on merchandise in the Far West—sometimes up to 100 per cent—was enough to make anyone believe in dreams.

Becoming a banker was relatively simple in those days and banks often evolved from a mercantile business. Most merchants engaged in at least some form of banking, and the Seligmans were no exception. They sold goods to customers on credit, loaned money, dealt in acceptances, carried deposits, paid cash to a third party on written orders, and sold gold received in payment for merchandise. During these transactions, Joseph Seligman picked up fundamentals of finance which were to stand him and his country in good stead during the Civil War.

Abraham Lincoln was elected President on November 6, 1860, but he was not inaugurated until March 4, 1861. During those four months, political storm warnings were ominous. News from the South was secession. Southern banks began to withdraw large amounts of money on deposit in the North, loans were called as the financial community began to batten down, and the Nation's economy, after recovery from the Panic of 1857, slackened. When Lincoln took office, he found that of all the Government departments, none was in worse condition than the Treasury. It was practically empty; Federal debt was increasing; Government credit was fading — fast.

The Seligmans, who understood the South because of their one-time residence there, were, nevertheless, supporters of President Lincoln and the Union cause. At the outbreak of hostilities they hastened to make positive offers of assistance to the Federal Government. It has been said one of their first wartime acts was to subscribe generously to help fit out New York's famous Seventh Regiment for active service. They also helped increase the flood of private contributions offered the Government during the first weeks of the War.

In July—after the first Battle of Bull Run—

Mathew B. Brady, famed Civil War photographer, took this picture of Lincoln and his son, Tad, in Washington. The Seligmans later advanced tuition funds for Tad's schooling when he lived in Frankfurt a/M with his mother.

BOTH: COLLECTION OF PETER QUINN

The Capitol dome was being rebuilt when Abraham Lincoln was sworn in as President on March 4, 1861. Crowds swarmed around the building early that morning waiting until after 1:30 p.m. before he received the oath of office.

Joseph went to Washington and offered the services of the Seligman firms to a Government which made no pretense of elegance and was glad to take all the help it could get. Years later when he lived in London, Isaac Seligman said, "During the Civil War, I went to Washington for a short time to assist my friend, Henry Gitterman, in his business as sutler to the Army. During my stay, I had the opportunity of attending a weekly Friday evening reception at the White House, and shook hands with President Lincoln. At that reception, I saw what would astonish a European: men appearing in their shirt sleeves! What would be thought of such an occurrence at a Court reception in London?"

Wm. Seligman & Co. in New York and J. Seligman & Co. in San Francisco received the first of many contracts for Union Army uniforms and accessories—chevrons and shoulder boards to designate rank and other insignia. The firms were well-equipped to fill these contracts, because, unlike a number of New York clothing firms which had traded with the South, the Seligmans suffered little from failure to adjust or liquidate obligations with businesses in that section prior to the War's beginning. But *The Daily Graphic* in New York reported in retrospect on February 16, 1881, the Government contracts "had to be taken at considerable risk and after other capitalists had declined them." And considerable risk there was, as a letter written by Joseph Seligman on January 24, 1862, to William L. Hodge, who apparently acted as agent for various firms in Washington, testifies:

> *Your note just received, informing me that the appropriation for the clothing of the Army is exhausted, is a startling and an alarming announcement to me, for the United States are indebted to my firm a million of dollars. Under the severe pressure of this burden we authorized you to make an arrangement for the payment of 400,000 of this sum in 3 year Treasury 7.30 Bonds, and immediately on receiving advice from you, this arrangement had been made with the Treasury I brought to Washington vouchers for the above amount, in due order and approved by Dep. Q. M. Crossman, a portion of which vouchers, I had pledged to Banks in New York for 150,000 for which sum we gave our checks payable next week. If I am un-*

able to realize this sum very promptly I see no alternative but the suspension of our house, which will drag down 20 other houses, and throw 400 operatives out of employ.

Do my dear sir, for God's sake see if you cannot make some arrangement with the Secretary, by which this dreadful catastrophe may be avoided.

This is really a question of life and death with me and I beg your earnest and prompt attention to it.

The Seligmans apparently received their money; the records show $1,437,483.61 was paid them by the Government between August 1, 1861, and July 30, 1862.

The initial surge of public support in the North which came with the declaration of war began to subside in the Summer of 1861 as the Union Army suffered a series of reverses. By Fall, the Government's financial predicament was alarming with the public showing a decided lack of confidence in the conduct of the War.

Lincoln had to get money to finance the armies, and although Congress authorized the sale of $100,000,000 worth of Government securities in foreign markets to raise funds, it proved easier to pass the bill than to sell the bonds. The credit of the United States was poorly established abroad and initial efforts to float a foreign loan met with rebuffs on all sides. English and Continental bankers were supporters of the Confederacy; in fact, the South was looking to them for its own War needs. Nevertheless, Joseph Seligman believed U. S. securities could be placed in Europe.

He went to Washington more than once in those early months of 1862, and in February, took with him a letter from A. V. Stout, President of the National Shoe & Leather Bank in New York. The letter probably gave him his first introduction to a ranking Government official. Stout wrote Secretary of the Treasury Salmon P. Chase:

Permit me to introduce to you Mr. Jos. Seligman of the firm of Wm. Seligman & Co. who visits Washington on business connected with the Government.

It is with pleasure that I endorse Mr. S. as one of our most intelligent, patriotic and responsible citizens—whose word can be relied on implicitly, and who has always given

New York's Seventh Regiment defended Washington from the Confederates early in the War. It helped to construct defenses at the city's outskirts in 1861. Lincoln's private secretaries, John G. Nicolay and John Hay, called the Regiment "the corps d'elite of the whole Union" and said its "presence" in Washington "seemed to turn the scales of fate."

COLLECTION OF THE SEVENTH REGIMENT

Fifth—It is agreed, that for and in consideration of the faithful fulfilment of the above stipulations in all their parts, the party of the first part agrees that the party of the second part shall be paid by the United States, at the Office of Army Clothing and Equipage, New York city, as follows, viz:

For each and every of the said Sergeant Majors Chevrons Thirty cents.
For each and every of the said Quarter Master Sergeants Chevrons Thirty cents

Articles of Agreement *made and entered into this Nineteenth day of August Anno Domini one thousand eight hundred and sixty one between Lt. Col. D. H. Vinton, Dep. Quarter master General, U. S. Army, of the first part, and Wm. Seligman & Co. of the city and state of New York of the second part.*

Sixth—It is further agreed and expressly conditioned, that no Member of Congress is, or shall be, admitted to any share or part of this contract or agreement, or to any benefit to arise therefrom; that it is not transferable without the consent of the proper authority; that any sale, transfer or assignment of it without such consent having been obtained, (except under a process of law,) shall and will be considered an abandonment of it, and the said party of the second part, his or their securities, be held responsible for all loss, delay or damage to the United States, which may arise from such abandonment.

Seventh. This contract is subject to the approval of the Q. Mr. General.

In Witness Whereof, The parties have hereunto set their hands and seals, in quadruplicate, the day and year first above written.

Sealed and delivered in the presence of

J. & W. SELIGMAN & CO.

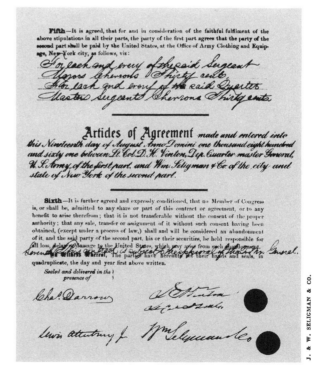

One of many contracts with the Army, Wm. Seligman & Co. undertook in August 1861 to have "manufactured and delivered" at the U. S. Depot of Army Clothing and Equipage, New York, 400 chevrons at thirty cents each—or for $120.

Congress authorized two issues of six per cent twenty-year bonds in 1861. Joseph Seligman helped sell some of them overseas, including the $1,000 coupon bond with Treasury Secretary Chase's picture on the front of it.

Joseph Seligman found the "seven-thirties" of 1861 difficult to dispose of in Europe. It was a three-year loan "with 7-3⁄10 per cent Interest payable SEMI-ANNUALLY."

his cordial support to the Government in putting down this unholy rebellion. Permit me also to say that Mr. S. as a director in this Bank has from the beginning urged, that the entire Capital of the Bank should be invested if need be, in Loans to the Government.

At first, Joseph's suggestion to sell securities in Europe was rejected, but he kept at it, supported by Assistant Treasurer of the United States John J. Cisco and the persuasive Jesse Seligman, a man who had a way with the spoken word. Permission was finally given and the Seligmans were granted the privilege of taking subscriptions abroad for 7.3 per cent three-year Treasury notes. They were to receive the same commission as other "Subscription Agents" – one-fifth of one per cent on the first $100,000 turned into the Treasury and one-eighth on all sums thereafter. This agreement did not promise much in the way of profits, but Joseph was satisfied to have been granted an opportunity to serve the Government.

Joseph Seligman withdrew from active participation in the clothing and dry goods business—which was busy with Army contracts—and went abroad in the Spring or Summer of 1862. He was not in Europe long before realizing his chosen assignment was far more difficult than anticipated. The reputation of the Seligmans was well established through their mercantile connections, but the name was not generally known otherwise. The securities Joseph managed to dispose of were virtually forced on business friends. Then, he changed tactics. He began to devote most of his efforts to selling five-twenties of 1862—bonds authorized by Congress February 25, 1862, which could be sold "at market value" for coin or Treasury notes and which were redeemable after five years and payable after twenty from date of issue, bearing six per cent interest.

Joseph decided to capitalize on two things: old family affiliations in Europe and the support of the Northern cause by the German people, who were greatly influenced by Harriet Beecher Stowe's *Uncle Tom's Cabin* and were strongly in favor of freeing the slaves. At one time, a declaration was published in New York's *Harper's Weekly* saying all Germany was so outraged at the banking firm of Emil Erlanger & Co. for having granted a loan to the "slave-driving government of the Confederacy," that firm did not dare ask for the introduction of its securities at the Frankfurt Bourse. Joseph Seligman and his brother-in-law Max Stettheimer, who worked with him, were joined by brothers Isaac and Henry in 1863. They took full advantage of such a favorable atmosphere, and concentrated their efforts in Amsterdam, Berlin, Frankfurt, and Munich.

Their success was far beyond their hopes. Not only did they dispose of substantial quantities of Government bonds and Treasury notes, but they aroused considerable sympathy for the Union cause, which was appreciated by the Government and later recognized.

In the United States, the task of financing the War by selling Government securities had been turned over to Jay Cooke, a personal friend of Secretary Chase's who had done well with an earlier bond issue and whose talents for promotion and propaganda enabled him to appeal to the emotions and patriotism of small savers: "the burthen will be light to us, and gladly born by posterity." Cooke set up an elaborate system of over 2,500 sub-agents through whom he promoted the five-twenty loan. Isaac Seligman, before he left for Europe, visited Washington and asked Secretary Chase for the same commission privileges given Cooke, but when Isaac refused to give a firm commitment for a specific amount of bonds, the Selig-

During the War, nine "great loans" were issued, and bonds were sold at the U. S. Sub-Treasury in downtown New York. "The war bonds . . . were bought," the New York Herald *said, "because it was patriotic to lend to the government in its time of need . . . Inhabitants of the remotest town were given the opportunity to buy them."*

The Soldier in Our Civil War . . .

Jay Cooke, Private Banker

Jay Cooke, of Philadelphia, is given credit for being to the Union during the Civil War what another Philadelphian, Robert Morris, was during the Revolution — the most important financier to the U. S. Government.

A Civil War Centennial project of the American Jewish Archives, the poster shows Abraham (right) and Henry Seligman (center) at the Frankfurt Bourse; is partly captioned, "Jewish Financiers Sell Bonds to Save the Union–1862." It is symbolic, for Abraham and Henry were not in Europe. Joseph was and sold bonds with Max Stettheimer until 1863 when Isaac and Henry joined them. In 1862, Abraham and Henry were in San Francisco.

COURTESY, AMERICAN JEWISH ARCHIVES, CINCINNATI, OHIO

Wall Street, in New York, was quiet on a Sunday in 1864 – the same year J. & W. Seligman & Co. was established – when an unknown photographer stood on the Sub-Treasury steps and pointed his camera east toward the colonnaded Custom House. He undoubtedly did not have any intention of capturing for posterity the Street's narrowest building, Lilliputian No. 25½, three stories tall, (at far right), with its bold sign, SODA AND CONGRESS WATERS.

MUSEUM OF THE CITY OF NEW YORK

mans had to remain content as one of Cooke's subagents. By January 11, 1864, they had placed nearly $125,000,000 of the five-twenties overseas.

Before Joseph returned to New York early in 1864, and had definitely decided to open a banking house, he wrote on March 10: "Respecting bro. James plan now of quitting Imprtg & going entirely into Banking . . . we are not yet fitted for a strictly legitimate Bankg Business, unconnected with Importing or manufacturing. If as bro. James says 15 to 25% can be made in a National Bk it would be folly to do anything else unless indeed there should be danger of gold going up & U. S. securities declining." He had been considering this idea for some time; profits realized on the sale of gold shipped East grew; the firms already participated in merchant banking on a small scale, and his experiences in Europe proved the merit of such a move. Old World bankers and financiers seemed impressed with the Seligmans' abilities. They had a number of invaluable contacts and had acquired considerable prestige. The brothers also had influential friends in Washington; they were well known in Republican Party political circles; Government officials respected their advice in financial matters.

Support the Seligmans accorded the Union from the War's outset helped them in more ways than one. In helping the Government raise money and clothe its Army, they also increased the fortune which was the keystone of the family's subsequent banking activities.

When the brothers finally decided to form a banking house, they also decided that, for the time being, the old merchandising firms would continue in business. Once the necessary details were worked out, all that remained was the formal announcement which changed the pack peddlers-turned-merchants into international bankers. On May 1, 1864, the firm of J. & W. Seligman & Co., Bankers, was established at 59 Exchange Place, New York City. May 1 was on Sunday that year.

THREE

There is a tide in the affairs of men which,
taken at the flood, leads on to fortune.

—William Shakespeare, 1564-1616

The international banking and investment firm the Seligman brothers founded May 1, 1864, was the product of their experiences and background in the United States and in Europe. They were quick to profit from the boundless opportunities proffered by American's dynamic, young economy. But their success was not unique for the times.

J. & W. Seligman & Co. was one of several noted investment banking houses formed in the latter half of the Nineteenth Century whose founders were from German Jewish families. "This group" of families, Cleveland Amory, the chronicler of society, noted in 1960, "has, in fact, been dubbed by Jews as well as Christians the 'Jewish Grand Dukes.' Stern in regard to aristocratic standards and values and with a strong aversion to publicity, they are rarely written about—which is exactly what they prefer." They established themselves economically in the United States in one of two ways. A very few immigrated with enough capital or expertise to make an immediate mark on the American economic scene. Most arrived with scant resources and were forced to begin at the very bottom in the new world.

At the end of the century, members of both groups had coalesced into a financial elite which existed within, but often remained distinctly outside, the larger society of New York City. The place these families made in the financial world is important, since the story of their success is a vital segment of America's economic history.

There was a tremendous flow of emigrants from Europe to the U. S. for two decades beginning in 1830 and Germans were the preponderant national group to emigrate during this period. This often is attributed to dreams of freedom engendered by the political unheavals both before and after the Revolution of 1848; actually, a prime factor was a yearning for economic opportunity as well as for freedom.

German Jews in their own country were locked in a vise-like grip of economic limitations on one hand, and repressive legislation on the other. As peddlers, storekeepers, moneylenders, and retailers, they suffered from disruption of the peasant economy and at the same time were wrapped in a straitjacket of regulations because of their religion. Hope lay in emigrating to the new world.

Immigrants of the mid-Nineteenth Century were seldom wealthy. Families saved to send one of their number in hopes he would do well enough to send for the rest eventually. Joseph Seligman, born November 22, 1819, oldest of eight boys and three girls, was typical in this respect. When he set out from Baiersdorf, a village of some 2,000 in Bavaria, he reportedly had only $100—sewn into the lining of his pants. In other respects, he was unusual. He had attended the University of Erlangen near Bai-

Joseph Seligman, whose first name's initial gave the "J" to J. & W. Seligman & Co.—"W" is for William, a brother —immigrated to the United States in 1837 from Bavaria.

COLLECTION OF GEOFFREY T. HELLMAN

COURTESY, 2. BURGERMEISTER, BAIERSDORF

The birthplace of the Seligman brothers, on Judengasse in Baiersdorf, West Germany, still exists. It is now the residence of an electrician. A savings bank is next door.

ersdorf and acquired a liberal arts education. He had achieved high honors, and learned to speak English, Greek, and French, along with the German and Hebrew he already knew.

If Joseph thought his future lay in America, convincing his father, David, was something else. The elder Seligman wanted his serious-minded son to join him in the wool weaving trade. His mother sided with Joseph. Fanny Seligman's profits from the small notions shop she operated had helped finance the boy's college attendance and she wanted him to rise above the station in life which the Bavarian government and society imposed on him. Leaving the homeland seemed the only way.

Joseph Seligman, aged seventeen, began his journey in July 1837, with a group of townsfolk, eighteen in all, who had decided to try life across the Atlantic Ocean. The group left Baiersdorf for Bremen in two wagons. The trip took seventeen days and they camped along the road at night. At Bremen, Joseph bought passage for forty dollars, boarded the schooner *Telegraph,* and with eighty-two others, sailed steerage for forty-two days. He landed in New York on Monday morning, September 24, and left to join Lewis Seligman, a cousin, who had written glowingly about life in America. His destination was the little town of Mauch Chunk (now Jim Thorpe), Pennsylvania.

Once in the United States, the average immigrant's capital dwindled steadily, but a great number of German arrivals had sufficient means to find a way to one of many scattered regions of the country (unlike later generations of immigrants whose poverty kept them concentrated in the port of New York). When a new home had been reached, the next step was to find work.

Passing through New York, Joseph may not have noticed the distress the Panic of 1837 had spawned, but he was lucky to have cousin Lewis Seligman waiting in Mauch Chunk. Lewis Seligman undoubtedly introduced him to Asa Packer. Barely in his thirties, Packer was already Mauch Chunk's leading businessman. He had established a yard for the construction of canal boats which hauled coal from the local mines, and by 1842 he was a member of the Pennsylvania House of Representatives. Before his life was over, he served as County Judge and U. S. Congressman, built the Lehigh Valley Railroad, and founded Lehigh University in Bethlehem, Pennsylvania, with a $1,000,000 grant in 1865.

Asa Packer hired Joseph Seligman as a clerk and cashier. He was soon Packer's private secretary for $400 a year. He learned vernacular English, carefully observed American ways, and lived frugally. His goal was to go into business for himself and after only one year, he was ready.

Packer protested when his young secretary resigned; offered to raise his salary to $500 a year if he would stay. But Joseph's mind was made up. His capital was small—barely $200. Nevertheless, he bought some merchandise, packed it carefully, threw it over his shoulder, and went to work as a peddler. By Spring of 1839, Joseph had saved $500. He wrote his parents and urged them to send William and James, the next oldest brothers, to join him. Along with passage money for the brothers, he enclosed $100 to repay his mother the sum she had given him when he left Baiersdorf.

Of his trip to America, James Seligman recalled on his eighty-eighth birthday, "Two wagon loads of peasants again left the little village, my brother William and myself among them. I was then fifteen years old. We each had $40 from our mother sewed up in a bag which was tied around our waists under our clothes . . . When we reached Bremen we at once boarded the sailing vessel that was to take us to the New World. The ship carried 400 passengers...large cots were placed close together, and seven of us slept in one cot...In the stormy weather we were crowded together in utter darkness for two and three days. It makes me sick to think of it, and the less said about it the better."

For the next ten months, while Joseph and William peddled their wares and steadily increased their capital, James worked as an apprentice to two different carpenters. "My first job," he recounted, "was shingling the roof of a shed in a cemetery, where I had to work long after nightfall—not a very pleasant task for a fifteen-year-old boy. Perhaps this is why I took a dislike to the trade. After six months my employer failed and I went to work for another carpenter upon the same terms. When this man also went to the wall after four months I decided to quit the business and went back to Mauch Chunk," and demanded to be taken into the "firm."

Whatever his failings as a carpenter, the young man soon proved to be a wonder at peddling. After his return, James later said, "My brother Joseph then went to Bethlehem and expended $300 for jewelry—rings, bracelets, and watches—some gold-plated, others German silver. With these goods as a loan and the $40 given me by my mother which I had carefully saved, I went to work peddling, and on the first day sold more than $100 worth of goods. I kept at the occupation and went through Pennsylvania . . . with good success." With the profits he reaped, added to those of his brothers, the Seligmans were able to open a small merchandise store in Lancaster.

Asa Packer, painted from life by De Witt C. Boutelle, was Joseph Seligman's first employer. Packer became a Democratic Congressman; he later founded Lehigh University.

LEHIGH UNIVERSITY

James then talked his brothers into letting him take a peddling tour through the South. With part of his share of the family funds, he purchased a cart and horse and a heterogeneous collection of merchandise, and near the end of 1840 started on a trip which was to have a far-reaching effect upon

COLLECTION OF GEOFFREY T. HELLMAN

At eighty-eight, James Seligman remembered arriving in New York sick with smallpox. The third of eleven children, he attended school in Bavaria until eleven when, he says, "my parents thought I was old enough to learn a trade, and I was sent to Flow, about one hundred miles from home, to learn the weaver's trade from my uncle."

the brothers' future. Returning to Lancaster in the Summer of 1841, after touring much of the southeastern part of the country, he showed his thunderstruck brothers a profit of—James remembered—$1,000 "which was more than either of my two brothers had earned and influenced them to go South with me." But there were four brothers now. Jesse Seligman had arrived while James was on tour.

Jesse was at the *Gymnasium* studying to enter the University of Erlangen when William and James came to the United States, he recalled in New York on October 1, 1891:

After receiving glowing letters from my brothers in America, I asked permission of my parents to go to the new country also. They assented, and on May 1, 1841, I started for Bremen, and after reaching there I learned that the vessel that was to carry me across was a small ship bearing the name Johan Georgic. *When on board, I inquired for my cabin . . . I found it was also to be occupied by three other passengers . . . The bed, while not a bed of roses, consisted of a soft wooden board, with a blanket to cover the occupant while he enjoyed his peaceful slumbers.*

The menu . . . was made out daily and consisted one day of pork, beans and a cup of water; the next day, of beans, pork and a cup of water, and the following day of a cup of water, pork and beans; and so on throughout the voyage, which occupied forty days and forty nights, from shore to shore.

On the last day of that voyage . . . on the 4th of July . . . when I awoke I beheld Staten Island in all its beauty. My first thought was to offer a fervent prayer to the Almighty God for having brought me over safely to what I then regarded as Paradise itself, and my second thought was to swear allegiance to the government of the United States.

After remaining in this city for two weeks . . . I had just sufficient money left to take me to Lancaster . . . where . . . I remained . . . a few weeks, during which time I learned the English language to some extent, and, at the same time, mastered the science of smoking penny cigars.

Jesse disagreed about the profit James brought back from his selling trip through the South, and said it was "about $800"– not $1,000 – but "we concluded to take the advice of this purse-proud Nabob–that we would better our condition by removing to that section of the country."

The brothers pooled their resources. They had $5,000 in merchandise fully paid for, a small amount of cash for emergencies, and an infinite capacity for hard work. In the late Fall of 1841, Jesse remembered:

> *The four of us came on to New York and took passage in a schooner, which took six weeks to make the trip to Mobile...*
>
> *On our arrival . . . we immediately sought out a boarding-house; and as we had been nearly starved on our voyage, I need not assure you that our appetites were whetted to do justice to our provender when we reached the dining-room . . . When we retired for the night, we were honored by a serenade . . . with which our ears were not at all familiar.*
>
> *We soon discovered that this beautiful concerto came from a swarm of mosquitoes... Notwithstanding their musical turn of mind, they were out for blood, so to speak.*

Since limited capital prohibited opening a business in Mobile, Jesse said they "thought it advisable to go to some interior town, and Selma was selected as the place where we should pitch our tents." They opened a small store, and leaving Joseph in charge, made a "tour of inspection of the surrounding country, to be absent four weeks, at the expiration of which time we were all to meet in Selma again, and compare notes."

A banquet Jesse's friends gave him at Delmonico's many years later was an opportunity to reminisce, and he did: "The traveling salesmen of that period did not enjoy the luxuries that men of that vocation now expect, and as it was not customary to have a porter to carry your grip or parcel, we were obliged to perform that task ourselves. We were so much encouraged by the result of our first trip that we concluded to make another for four weeks, and we found that our supply of merchandise was diminishing very rapidly."

James made a trip to New York City in 1842 where he met other members of the family–Leopold, Abraham, Isaac, Babet, Rosalie, and Sarah–who had come over at the brothers' behest. Their mother had died, and in 1843, their father

"In his business life," The Daily Graphic *commented, Jesse Seligman "is cool, circumspect and conservative. No extraneous influences are allowed to sway his judgment... and his word, once given, is as good as a bond."*

Harper's Weekly

ALABAMA DEPARTMENT OF ARCHIVES AND HISTORY

Greene County courthouse, in Eutaw, Alabama, was probably the most important building in the Southern town when the Seligmans operated a store there in the 1840's. Eventually, they had three dry goods stores in Alabama.

managed to make himself unique in the annals of the family by failing in business. He left Baiersdorf with his son, Henry, and came to New York. As time went by, Henry joined his brothers and they established stores northwesterly from Selma in the towns of Greensboro, Eutaw, and Clinton, Alabama.

The Seligmans did more than operate dry goods stores in the South. In a small way, they participated in politics. Neither Jesse nor Henry could vote, but they were enthusiastic supporters of Henry Clay, the Whig Presidential contender for 1844. Barbecues and music were "indispensable adjuncts" to a Presidential campaign in those days, the *Rochester* (New York) *Herald* noted many years later, and when the candidate visited Eutaw, Jesse Seligman "attended a barbecue as a Henry Clay musician" and volunteered his services on the flute "to accompany the best violinist in the neighborhood." Henry Seligman, according to the February 26, 1909, issue of *The American Hebrew,* "entertained an affection and esteem bordering on adoration" for Clay and "wept" when he was defeated.

In 1846, a year after their father died, James went North to found J. (for Joseph) Seligman and Brothers, Merchants, and to attend the September wedding of his sister, Babet, to Max Stettheimer. The new firm was located at 5 William Street in New York City–later numbered 1 William Street where, in 1906, J. & W. Seligman & Co. started to build its own building.

The Seligmans kept their Alabama stores, and, Jesse claimed, "continued to be prosperous until the year 1848, when we thought that we might better our condition by coming North. Joseph Seligman and William left early in the Spring, and brother Henry . . . and myself remained to wind up the business." A year later, J. Seligman and Brothers, *Merchants,* became J. Seligman and Brothers, *Importers,* at 46 Pine Street.

Max Stettheimer and William Seligman went to St. Louis in 1848 and formed Stettheimer &

Avocations, A Magazine of Hobbies and Leisure

Joseph, William, James, and Jesse Seligman spent six weeks traveling from New York to Mobile, Alabama, by schooner in the Fall of 1841. This picture, by W. J. Bennett, shows the city opposite the marsh in 1842.

THE CHASE MANHATTAN BANK MONEY MUSEUM

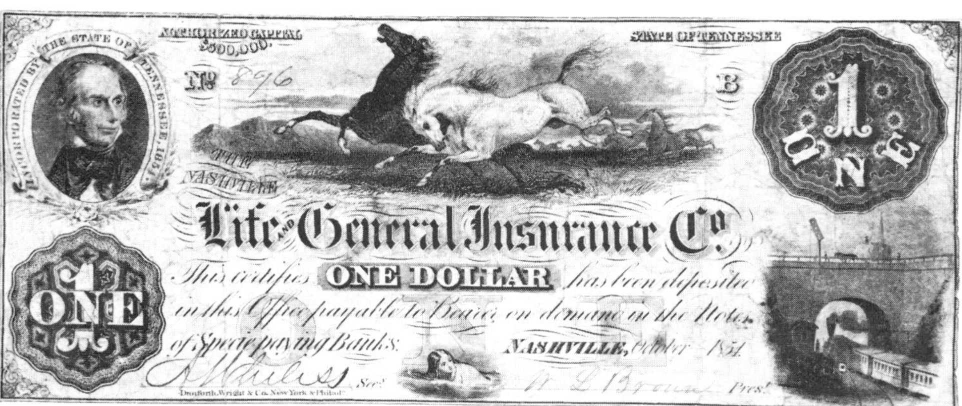

Three years after his death, Henry Clay was shown on a state bank-note in Tennessee. In 1844 he was the Whig Presidential candidate and visited Eutaw. Jesse and Henry Seligman were ardent supporters.

J. & W. SELIGMAN & CO.

J. Seligman and Brothers, Merchants, was named for Joseph but established by James on New York's William Street, 1846. A year earlier, architect Robert Kerr drew "FROM NATURE AND ON STONE" the frenzied activity on nearby Broad Street. Three young boys (front center) seem far more interested in learning the art of lighting and smoking penny cigars than studying the Custom House's Greek Revival architecture at the head of Broad on Wall Street. Businessmen, too, show very little concern for the building—or boys.

The earliest known advertisements of any Seligman business first appeared in the Watertown *(New York)* Jeffersonian *October 19, 1849 (top two). On December 10, readers were tempted by velvet trimmings and more shawls.*

COURTESY, DAVID F. LANE

BY ALVIN HUNT. **Watertown Jeffersonian.** TERMS.

TWELFTH YEAR. WATERTOWN N. Y. FRIDAY MORNING, OCTOBER 19, 1849. NO. 39.

SHAWLS! SHAWLS!!

200 ALL WOOL LONG SHAWLS of the Richest Colors and Latest Styles, just arrived, and will be sold at prices which cannot fail to suit all purchasers. Brocha, Cashmere, and Silk Shawls we offer for sale now at lower prices than ever heard of. J. & H. SELIGMAN, at the N. Y. City Dry Goods Store. October, 19, 1849. 39

LINENS.

THE largest stock of Irish Linens, Table Cloths, Toweling, Napkins, &c., ever seen in this place, just received at SELIGMANS' No. 4, Woodruff's Block. Oct. 19, 1849.

200 Pieces of Velvet Trimmings, all colors, and a large assortment of Belt Ribbons, just received at J. & H. SELIGMAN'S, Dec. 10, 1849. 47

A Fresh supply of *BROCHA & WOOL LONG SHAWLS*, just opening, at the New York City Dry Goods Store, No. 4 Woodruff's Block. 47

Ulysses S. Grant, His Life and Character

A young lieutenant—his name: Ulysses S. Grant—liked horses, riding, and racing. He met Jesse and Henry Seligman while at the New York City Dry Goods Store and when he was billeted at Madison Barracks.

Bros., importers of dry goods, at the corner of Locust & First Streets. *The St. Louis Directory* three years later shows no entry for the company, but lists a W. Seligman & Co. at 166 North Main Street. Abraham Seligman had, by then, joined William in St. Louis as a clerk, and Max Stettheimer, in the meantime, returned to New York. He joined J. Seligman & Brothers, Importers, which had changed its name to Seligman & Stettheimer, Dry Goods Importers, after Max's father, Jacob Stettheimer, had been admitted into the partnership in 1850.

These were busy, formative years. When Jesse and Henry returned to New York from Alabama, in the Summer of 1848, they "started a business in the beautiful town of Watertown, Jefferson County," and, said Jesse, "with the assistance of the ladies, always partial to me, we soon increased our business." That Fall, Joseph and James went to Europe and in Munich, Joseph married his cousin, Babet Steinhart. He also sought out and paid his father's creditors.

The firm of J. & H. Seligman opened the New York City Dry Goods Store on Public Square in "the business heart" of Watertown, New York. One day that Winter of 1848-1849, a five-foot eight-inch unmilitary-looking First Lieutenant of the Fourth Infantry, "his face short and squarish . . . set off by a . . . close-cropped beard which he soon shaved off . . . unruly, sandy-brown hair," rode horseback over the eleven miles of dirt road from Madison Barracks in Sackets Harbor on the edge of Lake Ontario to Watertown. He was Ulysses Simpson Grant and he visited the New York City Dry Goods Store to buy "a bit of finery for his bride of a few months." "On our acquaintance, Jesse Seligman recalled, "we immediately became friends."

"One of the most disastrous fires Watertown ever had," according to newsman David F. Lane, "broke out May 13, 1849." The *Watertown Jeffersonian,* the town's weekly, reported five days later in an on-the-scene, eye-witness account that the "GREAT CONFLAGRATION!" which "burnt" 100 buildings and put "Watertown in Ruins!" also destroyed "J. & H. Seligman, Dry Goods, loss $6,500. Insured $4,500." In the same issue, plans to rebuild were announced; a week later, "plans were going forward;" by June 15, foundation walls were started; by August 3, the Seligmans' store was rebuilt and open again at No. 4 Woodruff's Block.

Jesse Seligman recalled that "in 1850, when the 'gold fever' broke out in California," the store was left "in the hands of my brother Henry, so that I might venture out there to ascertain whether we could not still further improve our condition." Henry Seligman saw a great deal of Lieutenant Grant who was stationed at Madison Barracks for the second time in 1851. In off-duty hours, the Lieutenant played checkers, whist, and poker with Watertown merchants. He chewed tobacco and smoked cigars, but his famed taste for whisky wasn't apparent while he was stationed in upstate New York. In fact, Lieutenant Grant, it is said, "was instrumental in forming Rising Sun Division No. 210" of the Sons of Temperance Lodges "in Sackets Harbor, becoming its presiding officer and marching in temperance parades."

The Fourth Infantry left Madison Barracks June 18, 1852, when it was ordered to the Pacific Coast. By coincidence, Henry Seligman closed the New York City Dry Goods Store that year and went to California.

Four and one-half years earlier, James Wilson Marshall, building a sawmill by American Creek, near Coloma, California, had looked closely at the millrace and found flakes of gold. The news spread slowly but by year end, it had been "confirmed" in the East. The Gold Rush began.

Jesse Seligman, with Leopold, traveled by ship via Panama to San Francisco, with a staggering load of $20,000 worth of merchandise. It took more money than the brothers really could afford, but, Jesse argued, the goods would be worth five, six, or seven times their cost in California.

The journey to the West Coast turned out to be back-breaking, unhealthy, and long. The tropical landscape of Panama was beautiful to look at but uncomfortable to travel through and getting across the Isthmus was hard. The Panama Railroad, then being built, wouldn't be finished until 1855. From its terminus, passengers—who invari-

COURTESY, DAVID F. LANE

Dr. John D. Huntington's woodcut shows the New York City Dry Goods Store at No. 4 Woodruff's Block (right). It reads: "Dry Goods, J. & H. Seligman." The building, now called Hotel Woodruff, has changed little in 115 years; the original Seligman store area is still in use—by a modern dry goods store.

A rare daguerreotype of San Francisco by Albert S. Southworth, dated 1850-1851, confirms what Jesse Seligman said: "Very high winds prevailed at times . . . there was a scarcity of water . . . the houses were frame structures (...a few...of iron)." And he "saw...great danger of a conflagration."

THE METROPOLITAN MUSEUM OF ART, GIFT OF I. N. PHELPS STOKES, EDWARD S. HAWES, ALICE MARY HAWES, MARION AUGUSTA HAWES, 1937

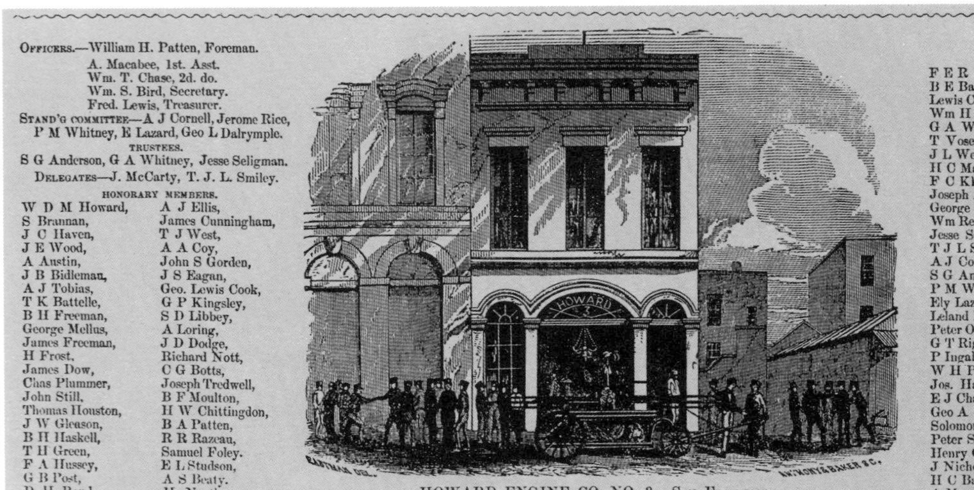

OFFICERS.—William H. Patten, Foreman.
A. Macabee, 1st. Asst.
Wm. T. Chase, 2d. do.
Wm. S. Bird, Secretary.
Fred. Lewis, Treasurer.
STAND'G COMMITTEE—A J Cornell, Jerome Rice, P M Whitney, E Lazard, Geo L Dalrymple.

TRUSTEES.

S G Anderson, G A Whitney, Jesse Seligman.

DELEGATES—J. McCarty, T. J. L. Smiley.

HONORARY MEMBERS.

W D M Howard, S Brannan, J C Haven, J E Wood, A Austin, J B Bidleman, A J Tobias, T K Battelle, B H Freeman, George Mellus, James Freeman, H Frost, James Dow, Chas Plummer, John Still, Thomas Houston, J W Gleason, B H Haskell, T H Green, F A Hussey, G B Post, D. H. Rand, A J Ellis, James Cunningham, T J West, A A Coy, John S Gorden, J S Eagan, Geo. Lewis Cook, G P Kingsley, S D Libbey, A Loring, J D Dodge, Richard Nott, C G Botts, Joseph Tredwell, B F Moulton, H W Chittingdon, B A Patten, R R Razeau, Samuel Foley. E L Studson, A S Beaty. H. North,

HOWARD ENGINE CO. NO. 3,—SAN FRANCISCO.

ACTIVE MEMBERS.

F E R Whitney, B E Babcock, Lewis Cohen, Wm H Bazin, G A Whitney, T Vose, J L Wells, H C Mallory, F C Kline, Joseph Aikin, George Laidley, Wm Revere, Jesse Seligman, T J L Smiley, A J Cornell, S G Anderson, P M Whitney, Ely Lazard, Leland Lincoln, Peter Ostrander, G T Rigsby, P Ingalls, W H Patten, Jos. Hartshorn, E J Chase, Geo A Buxton, Solomon Isaacs, Peter Smith, Henry Osborn, J Nicholson H C Barnes, A Manning, B Barnett, Benj. Schloss, Frank Mailott, Lewis Reinstine, Jerome Rice, A Friedlander, C Guliver, A Macabe, Wm H Stephens, J Gavitt, S M Locke, W H Thorne, Samuel Buckley, I E Wolfe, George L. Dalymple, W T Chase, W S Bird, George Davis, S McIntire, Chas Smith, S L Jacobs, Fred. Lewis, C A Johnson, M W Murray, J A McCree, S W Kipp, H Eaton, J B Bellows, Antonia De Le Marra. B. Gardner, Samuel Wainright, J Bound.

Golden Era Illustrated, COURTESY, WELLS FARGO BANK

On the night of the fire, Jesse Seligman joined Howard Engine Company No. 3. The three-story frame firehouse located "on southerly side of California street, near Sansome," was featured in Golden Era Illustrated, *July 1854. Jesse was one of three trustees and also an active fire fighter.*

ably seemed to wear bright red shirts—traveled by boat to Gorgona, not far past the middle of the Isthmus. "Here I found," Jesse reported later, "there were not mules enough to carry all of my wares to Panama in time to enable me to reach the steamer, so I was obliged to wait for two weeks, when I boarded the *Northerner,*" a wooden side-wheeler.

The *Northerner* was warped alongside its dock at San Francisco in the Fall of 1850 "near Sansome and California Streets, the bay reaching as far as that in those days." The Seligmans were among 37,000 wealth seekers who landed during the year in a town that just two years earlier had a population of only 800. But, the brothers were two of the few who did not surrender to the temptation of looking for gold. They "searched for a store . . . and the only one that there was the slightest prospect of securing was on Commercial Street." There, J. Seligman & Co., General Importers, was founded. Before the end of the year, Jesse's optimistic predictions had been justified. About half the stock was sold at an almost unbelievable markup—cheap tin cups and pans sold for five dollars; whisky and wine was twenty to thirty dollars a quart, and a five dollar blanket often retailed for forty. Coins smaller than half-dollars weren't accepted by tradesmen. Urgent letters for more goods were dispatched to Joseph in New York.

San Francisco had already gone through four disastrous fires, so when a substantial brick structure—one of the city's few—was built early the following year, Jesse leased space. The new location was next to the Tehama House—"kept by a Captain Jones"—at the corner of California and Sansome Streets. "After being there a short time," declared Jesse, "a fire broke out on the 3rd of May on what was then known as the 'Plaza.' I at once went there to assist some friends in removing their merchandise, but soon found that it had gained such headway that it would probably sweep the entire city."

The fire had started shortly after eleven p.m. —probably the work of an incendiary. Within hours, the business section was in flames. Hollow spaces under the planked streets served as blowpipes to spread the fire, and the planks carried the flames from block to block. "I immediately returned to my own building," Jesse recalled, "and found that the Tehama House . . . was guarded by a number of . . . waiters, who were covering the roof with wet blankets, and who also stood in readiness with buckets of water. I at once explained to Captain Jones that if my house were to take fire, nothing could save his hotel from destruction, as it was built of wood, and I suggested that he transfer a number of his men to my roof . . . He acted upon my suggestion; and it was well that he did so, for the Customhouse, on the corner of Montgomery and California Streets, took fire and swept everything before it, with the exception of the building that I occupied and Captain Jones's hotel."

Howard Engine Company No. 3, assigned to fight the fire in the district where the Seligmans' store was located, "did me great service . . . and I joined the company that night, serving and running with the machine for several years . . . Of all the dealers in merchandise, I was the only one whose house was saved, and as I had many articles that were needed at that time, I soon disposed of much of my stock, though I made no attempt to increase or reduce my prices."

Murder in San Francisco at this time, for some reason, was not considered so serious a crime as theft, and shooting on sight was common. According to Jesse Seligman, one day when he was ploughing along a muddy street, a bullet whizzed past his head. He wheeled around, drew his own pistol, and prepared to fight it out. Less than fifty yards

CALIFORNIA HISTORICAL SOCIETY, SAN FRANCISCO

Historian Lucius Beebe says dinner at the Tehama House in the 1850's was "gay and fashionable. There might be charades, guessing games, blindman's buff, chess, checkers, cards, singing, dancing, and . . . acting . . . after supper.

A Committee of Vigilance was organized in June 1851 to establish law and order in San Francisco. It disbanded; was recalled in 1856. The headquarters, in 1856, was called Fort Gunnybags. Jesse Seligman was a Vigilante.

THE SOCIETY OF CALIFORNIA PIONEERS

Harper's Weekly

Then called the "Revulsion," Panic in 1857 was blamed on extravagant women, betting, Bank of England expansion, tariff restraints, war in Crimea, credit system, New York bank contractions, California gold, railroads.

away a stranger gripped a smoking gun. When he saw Jesse, the man walked toward him, doffed his hat and said, "I mistook you for another man."

"The affairs of the city became so disorganized," Jesse declared, "that it was unsafe for anyone to walk in the streets without being well armed, for there was no telling at what moment one would be attacked by thieves, thugs and desperate characters that had overrun the city. It was, therefore, found necessary to organize a Vigilance Committee to suppress this lawlessness and rid the town of bad characters. I became a member of the committee, and remained so until perfect order was restored."

Once organized, the Committee of Vigilance went to work. Their first prisoner was John Jenkins, alias Simpson or Simpton, who was caught after entering G. W. Virgin's office the evening of June 10, 1851, and stealing a safe. The Vigilantes took him to their headquarters and tried him for his life. The verdict came at midnight: guilty. Jenkins was heard to plead, "Shoot me like a man, don't hang me like a dog." Nevertheless, he was hanged two hours later from a projecting beam of a building in the Plaza for all to see that the Committee meant business. When a coroner's jury later named nine Vigilantes responsible for the hanging, 183 citizens–Jesse Seligman among them–signed a resolution attesting to their joint responsibility for the execution. Public opinion supported them and no prosecutions resulted.

The Committee tried ninety-one cases (forty-one discharged, fifteen handed over to authorities, fourteen ordered to leave California, fourteen deported, four hanged, one whipped, and two undesignated) and disbanded. It was called together again in 1856, and again Jesse was one of the members.

Between committees, Jesse left San Francisco for New York and Europe, where "during my stay in Munich, I became engaged" to Henriette Hellman, sister of Max and Theodore who were later associated with the Seligmans.

Jesse's Watertown friend, First Lieutenant Ulysses S. Grant, was on the way to Fort Vancouver, Oregon Territory, when he landed in San Francisco "early in September" of 1852, the same year *Parker's San Francisco Directory* carried an advertisement for "J. SELIGMAN & CO. Importers and wholesale dealers in European and American fancy and staple dry goods, boots and shoes, hides, clothing, cigars, etc. Cor. California and Sansome Streets, Smiths New Buildings, San Francisco."

While the San Francisco store was helping to increase the Seligmans' worth, the youngest brother, Isaac, attended Free Academy, now a part of the College of the City of New York. "I graduated," he said, "in 1853 . . . I did not really pass the entrance examination . . . but the Faculty took compassion on me, and allowed me to enter." Invited to join Seligman & Stettheimer, which had moved to a new location at 40 Beaver Street in 1852, Isaac declined and opened his own shop, as an embroidery merchant, at 24 Cedar Street. However, Isaac did travel abroad in 1855 "to make purchases for the New York business" in exchange for gold, which was sent to New York from San Francisco, and then shipped to London to pay for imported goods.

Despite his prominence in business, municipal, and social affairs, Jesse Seligman left San Francisco in 1857, "arriving in New York in the fall . . . during the great panic." Henry, Leopold, and Abraham Seligman were left in charge of the West Coast business.

The Seligmans went through the Panic of 1857 unhurt. With foresight, they had liquidated all except prime securities and stored their hard money in strong boxes before the Panic hit. Joseph and James, with Jacob Stettheimer, sister Babet's father-in-law, ran Seligman & Stettheimer on Vesey Street. Wm. Seligman & Co., moved from St. Louis, was next door, and Jesse was a participating partner. Henry was a silent partner. All, except Isaac, shared the profits of each firm. Finally, in 1860, he abandoned the lace business and joined Seligman & Stettheimer. For the first time, all the brothers were in business together.

The country was once more prosperous. There were bumper crops in cotton, wheat, and corn; anthracite coal and pig iron production were at their highest; business was excellent. It was an impressive time. But it was also, says historian Roy F. Nichols, a time when "pride, politics, patience, prudence, pique, petulance, and plotting had all been mixed up in a highly complex emotional melange." And although "nobody planned it that way," it all exploded when the first Confederate shell fell on Fort Sumter.

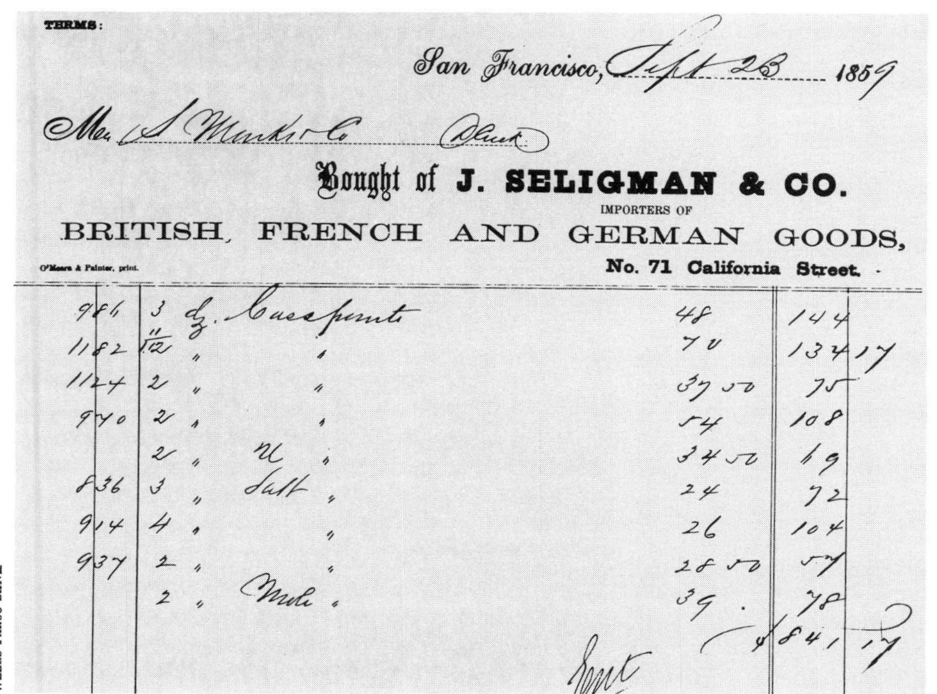

TERMS:

San Francisco, Sept 23 1859

Mess. S. Marks & Co

Bought of J. SELIGMAN & CO.

IMPORTERS OF

BRITISH, FRENCH AND GERMAN GOODS,

No. 71 California Street.

O'Meara & Painter, print.

981	3	dz. Cass pants	48	144
1182	1 11/12	" "	70	134 17
1124	2	" "	37 50	75
940	2	" "	54	108
	2	" M "	34 50	69
836	3	" Salt "	24	72
914	4	" "	26	104
937	2	" "	28 50	57
	2	" Mole "	39	78
				$841 17

Sent

WELLS FARGO BANK

J. Seligman & Co.–"J" for Jesse – continued to prosper as the Fifties neared their end. Probably not typical, but indicative, is an invoice of September 23, 1859, for $841.17.

FOUR

Peace will come soon and come to stay, and so come as to be worth keeping in all future time. It will then have been proved that among free men there can be no successful appeal from the ballot to the bullet.

—*Abraham Lincoln,* 1809-1865

"War is declared," *Harper's Weekly* proclaimed on April 27, 1861. "The die is now cast, and men must take their sides, and hold to them." The adjoining column displaying a patriotism which plainly ignored the fighting man in the ranks and not a little optimism, announced, "Any officer in either service can obtain the *Weekly* gratuitously for six months by sending his address to this office."

As Federal failure followed failure, the War became deadly serious. It was not until the end of 1862 that the tide of eventual defeat turned toward the Confederacy. On January 1, 1863, Lincoln issued the proclamation he had promised the previous September: abolition of slavery within the bounds of the territory controlled by the Confederacy.

Joseph Seligman, then in Europe, wrote his brothers in New York: "I am truly sorry to learn the reverse which Burnside has suffered near Fredericksburg, this will throw us back another year at least . . . Max who was with us this week also sees the difficulty of starting in any safe sort of business in Europe . . . Still, I do not feel like importing goods. Had we succeeded at Fdksbg & gone to Richmond I would have advised you to draw for every dollar as the hope of a large cotton export would have run exchange down before long but things have changed now & we shall have no cotton to export for a long time probably . . . How we are going to emerge out of this war God only knows. My wife in connection with some friends is preparing lint for our poor wounded men." The next week he commented, "The political news have lately been so discouraging that I have given up all speculating on that point . . . I hope Br. Abrm has safely reached N. Y."

Joseph's concern for his brother, known to be traveling from California to New York via Panama, was prompted by word that the Confederate man-of-war *Alabama* was in the Caribbean, where in December its crew had boarded the Northern ship *Ariel* which plied between New York and Panama. The Rebel raiders allowed the *Ariel* and its passengers to sail on their way unharmed, but no one could guess what might happen the next time. Abraham Seligman reached New York safely, but Joseph didn't know it when he wrote on January 13, "The attack of the Alabama on the Ariel was really news to me . . . Next month I expect to get letters from you respecting the safety of the Pacific steamers and if luckily the Alabama should have been caught by that time I hope to be able to go to London and make some advantageous Insurance terms." On January 23, Joseph said, "I am glad to learn . . . the safe arrival of bro Ab in your midst, for which I am truly thankful, especially as he had a narrow escape from falling into the hands of the Alab[a]."

Joseph Seligman was worried that his brother, Abraham, would be made prisoner of the Confederates on his way to New York, via Panama, from San Francisco sometime in late 1862 or early 1863. He came close, because on December 7, the Confederate cruiser Alabama *captured the steamship* Ariel, *southbound from New York to Aspinwall (now Colón), Panama, with a Marine batallion and 500 women and children. The* Ariel *was soon released.*

Frank Leslie's Illustrated Newspaper,

COURTESY, THE MARINER'S MUSEUM, NEWPORT NEWS, VA.

At this point in the War, many people yearned for peace at any price, even though it might mean sanctioning the Confederate States of America, but not Joseph. "I am sorry to see bro. Wm. reconcile himself to the idea of a disruption of the Union," he wrote. "It strikes me that the country would be unfit to live in after that, in fact I do not see the least chance of peace unless thro' a reconstruction of the Union."

On February 2, Joseph's letter from Mainz reflected his continued concern. "Our want of success at Richmond and Vicksburgh with the daily expenditure of 2 millions have of course had much to do to elate our enemies both North and South, while the Emancip. Proclamation has discouraged many people who had hopes of the South soon coming back to the Union. As I have so often said, the wealth of the country is being decimated and people are rich in imagination only. Calif. is the only exception up to this time. Query, how long will it last even there." Earlier, William had informed Joseph "the Cal. capital has swelled to $900,000," confirming that business was, indeed, good on the West Coast.

The general conduct of the War and the failures of the Union in battle continued to disturb Joseph Seligman thousands of miles across the Atlantic, and his brothers' attitude also worried him. "Your letters seem as cool as a cucumber," he wrote on April 30, "the American self-reliance and ultra sanguine feeling undoubtedly affects you as everybody on the other side of the water—I cannot persuade myself that God has entirely forsaken our country, but believe she is destined to submit to unspeakable trials for a series of years."

James Seligman, on the other hand, was enough encouraged by Union progress to write Joseph it would be a good idea for the brothers to invest $100,000 in Government securities. Joseph turned thumbs down: "Do not be afraid," he responded, "that the Government will want no more money after the 1 June—Even if the South should have been whipped so badly as to offer to make peace, the Gov't will need hundreds if not thousands of millions yet, to pay for claims of all description and for the purpose of emancipating the Negro."

When Confederate General Robert Edward Lee was defeated at Gettysburg, he retreated to Virginia; Major General George Gordon Meade, Union commander, was not able to follow up the victory. Although the battle marked a turning point in the War, Lincoln needed still more men, and his call for draftees set off some of the bloodiest riots in the Nation's history. Accounts of both the Union's success at Gettysburg and the vicious rioting reached Joseph at about the same time. On July 29, 1863, he wrote his brothers, "The news of Union victories have made me feel happy, as also

During his European stay, when he was about forty-two years old, Joseph Seligman took time from his task of placing Federal securities and had his portrait painted.

COLLECTION OF GEOFFREY T. HELLMAN

the retreat of Lee across the Potomac . . . by telegram I am shocked to see the riot and bloodshed which the Rebel sympathisers in N. Y. have brought about to prevent the draft—I shudder at the thought of what you and the whole North would have suffered at the hands of the Democrats if Mead had lost instead of gained the late battles of the 2 and 3d . . . Altho' I know the character of the party and people opposed to our present Government and the country I have yet confidence enough in the wisdom and patriotism of the masses to hope of an early putting down of all 'copperheads'—You complain that Halleck keeps the movements of our armies secret. What else ought he to do with so many Copperheads in our midst?" In a postscript, he commented, "I am just now in possession of yours of the 14th and find that the riot of the 13th was truly a most lamentable affair, and have no doubt but what the leading Democrats were the wirepullers. Bro. Wm's description also of the wealthy ladies at the North wearing Rebel cockades, etc. etc. is heart sickening and I am almost tempted to resell the U. S. Stock which I bought and keep my hands clear of the present degenerated American race."

On the first day of September, Joseph Seligman, his mind back on business, conjectured that, "If the next election should prove as we all hope, Republican, I would then be in favor of investing capital in manufacturing as in that case the tariff would hardly be lowered during nearly 5 years. Should the country however vote Democratic then we shall have a reduced tariff again, and Importers would fare better than manufacturers. The coming year will tell the tale, in the meantime things may shape themselves sooner to admit of our importing reasonable quantities of goods, but large importations will be attended with a great risk until gold has gone to par again."

Lincoln faced re-election in 1864; there were many who thought he was unable to win the War; others wanted him to compromise with the Confederacy and end hostilities. Members of his own Party were often as vociferous against him as his Democratic opposition and some of them proposed Grant to replace him. Though Joseph Seligman knew Ulysses S. Grant, he favored Lincoln's re-election, and said in no uncertain terms, December 30, 1863: "I see the d - - d Herald nominates Grant. This is probably done to cause a split between Lincoln and Grant."

While Joseph hoped to see Lincoln back in the White House for another four years, he was also busy planning the postwar future for himself and his brothers. "Should we conclude to go into Banking," he declared early in 1864, "my presence in Europe during this summer and winter may be necessary to put things into train for Banking business . . . Should on the other hand we conclude to go into N. Y. Banking (National Banks) then I think I shall consider it prudent to return as soon as possible, in order to open something of that kind."

The day J. & W. Seligman & Co. was founded, Grant was preparing the Army of the Potomac for the campaign which ended the Civil War. Both started in the first week of May. The Seligmans continued placing Government securities. Seligman & Stettheimer and Wm. Seligman & Co. were doing well in the mercantile business and moved into larger quarters on New York City's Church Street.

Salmon P. Chase, often at odds with the President and ever threatening to resign as Treasury Secretary, quit for the fifth time on June 29, 1864,

"I know him . . . If he is not killed or disabled in battle, he will suppress the rebellion in the West within a year, if I am any judge of men," Jesse Seligman said in 1862, about two years before Ulysses S. Grant, by then a Lieutenant General, posed for Mathew B. Brady.

COURTESY, ANSCO HISTORICAL COLLECTION

William Pitt Fessenden (below) was named Treasury Secretary by Lincoln after Salmon Portland Chase resigned. First a Whig and later a Republican, Fessenden served capably. Under his Secretaryship, the Government was able to raise funds required to prosecute the Civil War.

COLLECTION OF PETER QUINN

Harper's Weekly

"Let us be thankful for the victories gained," Joseph Seligman wrote after he learned of General Robert E. Lee's defeat at Gettysburg and other Union successes. Lee surrendered to Grant. April 9, 1865, in Virginia.

COURTESY, G. L. BARNES, LONDON

Seligman Brothers was established in the Fall of 1864. Isaac, the resident partner, knew his way around London and must have walked or ridden over the area called Gracechurch Street as it was, looking north, circa 1865.

COLLECTION OF GEOFFREY T. HELLMAN

Youngest of the eight brothers, Isaac Seligman had a reputation for barbed invective when business did not go as he wished. He helped establish the firm's London branch and, later, The Anglo-Californian Bank, Limited.

and Lincoln accepted the resignation. Albert Bushnell Hart, a biographer of Chase, claims he "was taken by surprise that the President had not put the resignation through the usual course of remonstrance, argument, and recall; and his anger and disappointment are too frankly recorded in his own diary: 'There I found a letter from the President, accepting my resignation . . . on the ground of the difference between us indicating a degree of embarrassment in our official relations which could not be continued or sustained consistently with the public service. I had found a good deal of embarrassment from him; but what he had found from me I could not imagine.'" From Lincoln's viewpoint, it seems Chase had politicked too hard for too long to obtain the Presidential nomination for himself.

Three months before Chase left office, he had authorized a $200,000,000 bond issue, "TO BE REDEEMED IN COIN," the Government advertised in *Harper's Weekly,* April 23, 1864, "at any period, *not less than ten nor more than forty years* from their date, and until their redemption FIVE PER CENT. INTEREST WILL BE PAID." The issue—commonly called "ten-forties"—all but failed, primarily because the five per cent interest rate was too low. The Seligmans did place some of the bonds abroad, but the loan brought the Treasury only $73,000,000.

William P. Fessenden of Maine took over as Secretary of the Treasury July 5. While he had been Chairman of the Senate Finance Committee, Fessenden had taken a leading role in framing measures concerning revenue and appropriations and, as an Eastern seaboard lawyer, did not bring into office a hostile suspicion of banking interests. Fortunately, the appointment was generally well accepted, for the Secretary needed all the support he could get. At the close of the Government's fiscal year on June 30, 1864, the cash balance in the Treasury gave Secretary Fessenden the total sum of $18,842,558.71 to pay the expenses of the Government—which included the $2,000,000 and more it cost per day to finance the Civil War. The Treasury was almost empty.

Fessenden acted quickly. "Late in July," Jay Cooke's biographer, Henrietta M. Larson, writes, "$200,000,000 of three-year notes, bearing interest of 7.3 per cent in currency, were offered. . . The loan went slowly and as the autumn passed it became evident that the sales would be far behind the government's needs even though the credit of the government was improving considerably. To meet the growing deficit, an issue of $40,000,000 in five-twenties was also offered." Joseph Seligman formed a group of German bankers in New York and prepared to bid for $50,000,000 of the 7.3 per cent three-year notes. The Secretary rejected the offer because the amount raised was to be turned into a fund for the Treasury to draw upon as required, rather than paid immediately in specie. The Government's *Report on Finances for the Year 1864* noted the group "was not able to furnish the assistance required upon terms which, under existing conditions of law, the Secretary felt authorized to accept . . . notwithstanding a professed and, as the Secretary was convinced, a real desire to aid the government."

After his rebuff from Secretary Fessenden, Joseph, with Isaac Seligman, sailed to England to establish the first overseas branch of the New York firm. Isaac was young — not quite thirty — but qualified to head the London branch. He was intelligent and he knew his way through Europe. The clothing contracts with the Government obtained "through brother Joseph's great popularity in Washington," Isaac declared, "enabled the importing firm to increase its capital, which the banking firm, when it started business, found very useful. With the additional funds thus obtained, the importing branch was able to increase its volume of business, and I was soon sent to Europe to buy goods." In 1926, when he was ninety-one and more than three score years after the event, he recalled, "I established in London [at 3, Angel Court], in co-operation with my eldest brother, Joseph, the firm of Seligman Brothers" in the Fall of 1864. "I began by engaging two boys as clerks, one of whom was soon removed by his father because there was so little for him to do."

While Isaac's young clerk's father was deciding the boy had no future with Seligman Brothers, Joseph traveled to Frankfurt to meet with Max Stettheimer and Henry Seligman, who had left San Francisco after an outstanding career. Later in 1864, the three established Seligman & Stettheimer, Frankfurt a/M. Henry, as manager of the branch, became prominent in the German city, but he maintained his United States citizenship, as did all of the Seligman brothers, except Isaac, who became a British subject in 1897. While the banking branches were being organized, Joseph, James, and Jesse were resident partners in New York City; Abraham and Leopold continued at J. Seligman & Co. in San Francisco, and William divided his time between importing and banking in New York.

William took an active part in politics, too, and campaigned for Lincoln's re-election. According to *The New-York Times,* September 28, 1864, "The first of a series of grand mass meetings in the City of New York to aid the cause of union and liberty" through the election of President Lincoln was held at Cooper Institute. Stand Number One was assigned to the German portion of the meeting, numbering about 3,000 people. William Seligman was chosen as chairman and made a most impassioned plea for the re-election of Lincoln for the preservation of the Union.

When Joseph returned to New York from the Continent later that year, many of his friends and business associates warned about the inevitable postwar inflation and thought the Seligmans fool-

COLLECTION OF PETER QUINN

Crowds waited in front of City Hall in New York to pay their final respects to Abraham Lincoln, shot days before by an assassin. Joseph Seligman was a member of the Memorial Committee that was formed to escort the body.

hardy to enter banking as a primary business. But seldom pessimists, they continued their plans, even though a contemporary reportedly observed, "because the Seligmans acquired wealth by selling dry goods, they thought they were fitted to be bankers."

The end of the Civil War was predictable once Grant resolved, in May 1864, "to Fight it out on this Line, if it takes all Summer." And when Lee surrendered on April 9, 1865, it was, for practical purposes, over.

But before he could turn from the horror of civil war to binding up the Nation's wounds, Abraham Lincoln of Illinois was shot on Good Friday, April 14. He died the next day. Joseph Seligman was a member of the Memorial Committee which escorted the body to the Governor's Room at New York's City Hall, where the martyr lay in state on April 24. Andrew Johnson was the new President.

Peace meant different things to different people after Grant's bloody campaign of attrition that ended the War. To the South it brought carpetbaggers and years of economic stagnation. In the North it spurred frenzied industrial and commercial growth on a mammoth scale and, eventually, brought reorganization of Government finances. Washington's fiscal problem was three-fold: it called for refunding the National debt into a more rational form, revision of the tax system to carry the debt, and the restoration of a dependable standard of value by the resumption of specie payments. Refunding the debt was the first order of business.

Hugh McCulloch, former Indiana banker and Comptroller of the Currency, had been named Secretary of the Treasury March 7, 1865, as Lincoln began his second term. Unlike his predecessors, his background easily made him the most qualified of the three Secretaries with whom the Seligmans had thus far had contact, and he remained in office until Andrew Johnson's term expired. Throughout McCulloch's tenure, J. & W. Seligman & Co. was in constant communication with him and kept him informed of matters in which he and they were interested. A letter from the firm's old copybook, dated April 1, 1867, suggests the nature of this activity. "We received a private telegram from our London house," the letter reads, "advising that our Bonds have this day declined . . . owing to *fears of political complications on the Continent* . . . We called on Mr. Van Dyck with the dispatch, but as he had suddenly been called away owing to the dangerous state of Mrs. Van D.'s health, we thought it proper to address you this letter, as it may possibly be of service to the government." H. H. Van Dyck was Assistant Treasurer of the United States in New York.

The Seligmans' interest in governmental fiscal affairs took time, but it was not their sole activity. The firm continued to receive substantial gold shipments sent from San Francisco to New York or

COLLECTION OF GEOFFREY T. HELLMAN

At twenty-eight, in 1872, Theodore Hellman had his picture taken in New York. Starting at two dollars weekly in one of the Seligman stores, he soon earned $3,500 a year. He became the New Orleans branch manager in 1868.

London; purchased and re-sold bills of exchange; extended commercial credits and issued letters of credit on good security, and it had begun to make stock exchange transactions on a very moderate scale. New York's *The Commercial and Financial Chronicle* in July 1866 commented that, "Foreign bankers were buyers of old 5/20s for shipment by Wednesday's steamer and have bought still more largely for export tomorrow. Perhaps it may be a safe estimate to judge the amount sent to Europe this week at 2,500,000 to 4,000,000, a considerable portion of which has been sent by the Seligmans to the Continent."

Looking forward at the War's end, Joseph Seligman realized the South offered good opportunities for banking – especially discounting of cotton exchange bills – and it would need vast supplies for Reconstruction. He decided to establish a branch of J. & W. Seligman & Co. in New Orleans that Fall, and Max Hellman, Jesse's brother-in-law, was placed in charge of Seligman, Hellman & Co. One of the first Northern firms to open in New Orleans after the War, it began business at 33 Carondelet Street.

The branch prospered. On February 27, 1867, Joseph wrote Max Hellman: "We are getting the name of having the choicest Southern bills, which tells to our advantage." In March: "We would say that, with the exception of Brown and you, *we have reason to know* that every other banker *has lost money* this season in purchasing bills in New Orleans." But the firm also made errors: "We received yesterday," Joseph wrote New Orleans on February 25, 1868, "some 23 large bars, which you state to be gold and which the U. S. Assay Office returns to us as being *pure brass*. Had they been gold they would have been worth about 1/4 million dollars to judge by the weight. We are glad you made no advance on them, but we had to pay freight to New York and also $5.00 to the U. S. Assay Office for their trouble." And then the mild remonstrance: "Please be more careful in the future."

Jesse Seligman's younger brother-in-law, Theodore Hellman, had joined Seligman, Hellman & Co. in January 1868. His first job after coming to the United States from Munich was that of errand boy in one of the Seligman dry goods firms – at two dollars per week. At seventeen, in 1861,

The Seligmans worked well with Hugh McCulloch, Treasury Secretary under Presidents Lincoln and Johnson and later Chester Alan Arthur. Associated with Jay Cooke, he also was a Director of The Anglo-Californian Bank.

COLLECTION OF PETER QUINN

SELIGMAN & CIE

Max Hellman, who didn't resemble his brother, Theodore, said, in June 1868: "I am off on the Russia, and shall have very little time to go to Germany, as I want to go to work at once in Paris." Both had come from Munich.

The Rue des Colonnes was a colorful street in Paris in 1865 and William Seligman, who laid the groundwork for the Paris branch, probably passed through it frequently. Seligman Frères & Cie was opened for business in 1868. The street—and buildings—exist today and are close to the Paris Stock Exchange.

he was a chief bookkeeper at a salary of $3,500 per year. At twenty-four, he was a partner in Seligman, Hellman & Co. Max Hellman had returned to New York preparatory to moving to Paris.

Wm. Seligman & Co. was liquidated in October 1866 and William visited Paris. On his return to New York and the next Spring, J. & W. Seligman & Co. decided to expand its international activities by opening Seligman Frères & Cie in the French capital with William as resident partner. At the last minute Joseph insisted William needed Max Hellman as a counterbalance. This resulted in a prolonged intrafamily squabble but the Paris branch finally opened at 46 Rue de Lafayette on October 1, 1868 – with William *and* Max Hellman in charge. The following day, the New York office shipped Seligman Frères & Cie 38,000 Mexican silver dollars.

While a new venture was begun in France, an old one, Seligman & Stettheimer, New York, was being liquidated and the brothers' apparently unsatisfactory relationship with Jacob Stettheimer was ended.

The West Coast branch, J. Seligman & Co., still had Leopold and Abraham Seligman in nominal charge, but with Joseph supervising from New York City. The company was slowly developing into a banking house, although the resident partners were having some trouble developing into bankers. Abraham and Leopold tried, but they just weren't adept at banking. During 1867, Joseph tried to teach them the rudiments of the calling by mail. Apparently there was some hope for one of the two, probably Leopold, and on May 29, Joseph strove mightily to hammer some basic precepts into their heads.

"You are, of course, green yet in the banking business, as we were a few years ago, and it is only through extraordinary caution and knowledge, trusting no one, except we knew from our own knowledge that he was safe beyond all doubt, that we got along without making heavy losses . . . The main thing in a banker is safety, with ability to reach his money at a moment's call."

"The subject of taking deposits is rather a risky one, inasmuch as depositors can (and will in times of panics) call for all their deposits, which is enough to break any but the very strongest banks. You will at first not take any deposits on call from anyone . . . Never lend money without a security, which you can sell at any time . . . Never endorse or go security for a living man."

He could not have made it more simple, but the rueful tone of a letter sent Abraham nineteen days later indicates the partners in San Francisco had not grasped the idea:

I am afraid, dear Abe, you are not smart enough for the California bankers and brokers, for whenever gold goes up you appear to get stuck with currency and whenever it goes down you "cannot get much." You must be wide awake and if you don't get correct quotations daily from here we will telegraph you daily or whenever a change directs.

By the Summer of 1867, the decision to close out the merchandise portion of J. Seligman & Co. in San Francisco was made with regret. From a business viewpoint, however, the store tied up a large amount of capital that could be put to a more profitable use. It had been the family's most prosperous enterprise, but on August 19, an agreement was made to sell out its stock of goods to Albert Levi, who was Henry Seligman's brother-in-law, and a man named K. B. Elfeld.

Joseph hadn't given up on making Leopold a banker. "After collecting up, we may probably get Brother Leopold to take hold of some other branch of our banking business." Several days later, he hoped "Brother Abe will join Brother Leopold in endeavoring to collect up all that is due us, getting everything which cannot be collected in good shape, but expect you to grant no unnecessary indulgence, so that we do not lose much interest, as we already lose enough on selling the stock, which costs us 110¢, at 90¢, which on $500,000 worth of goods is alone a loss of $100,000. Therefore, I trust there will be no interest lost on debts and every-

Leopold Seligman enjoyed art, and may have preferred painting or drawing to banking, yet he never gave up. After leaving San Francisco, he went to London and became resident partner with Isaac at Seligman Brothers.

COLLECTION OF GEOFFREY T. HELLMAN

thing collected up close."

J. Seligman & Co., "importers of British, French and German Goods," became a banking house on October 1, 1867—despite the resident partners' shortcomings.

Until the day of his death, there was only one leader in the numerous Seligman firms: Joseph. He issued instructions, laid down restrictions, apportioned funds, made major decisions, and allotted roles. His seven brothers were expected to follow the leader, and they usually did, although not always. There were frequent differences of opinion; bitter disputes.

The Seligmans were a proud family and one of their proudest attributes was their integrity. One Julius Hart reportedly circulated a false rumor about J. & W. Seligman & Co. On April 17, 1867, Joseph sent Hart the following letter, and the next day received an apology:

Mr. Ridgely, a customer of ours informs us that you have made a statement to him that

Abraham Seligman, with Leopold, operated the store in San Francisco which was developing into a banking house. Later, he worked with Henry in Frankfurt; proposed the firm establish branches in St. Petersburg and Vienna.

we had 50,000 Pounds protested Exchge returned to us. The above statement being entirely untrue, may still have a tendency to injure us, and we therefore ask you to retract all and every assertion of that kind made, previous to our handing the case to our lawyers.

Joseph Seligman's dominant characteristic was perhaps his cautiousness in most business ventures, which he excused with, "I may be mistaken, but I prefer to err on the safe side." He was generous. Writing to Henry Cohn, San Francisco, on October 23, 1869, Joseph said:

> *Your letter of the 14th addressed to Mr. Jesse Seligman, asks us to release Mr. Sternberg from his guarantee to repay us the $15,000 cash advanced you two years ago and to take Mr. Lerlebach for $13,000 instead, keeping besides Lerlebach's note, the 300 shares water stock, and you add that Brother Abe has encouraged you to address us and promised to speak a good word for you, which he actually has done and which is natural, for whoever knew of a Seligman who was not charitable and kind and served his neighbors, especially those who have been unfortunate.*

The request was granted. But Joseph's generosity had its practical limits. On March 19, 1870, he wrote Guiterman Bros., Amsterdam:

> *During your difficulties we have abstained from addressing you on the subject of the cash loaned you, which silence on our part you no doubt appreciated.*
>
> *But after this long delay we deem it not indelicate to remind you that we are still in the land of the living, and that periodical remittances even if in small amounts would now be very acceptable and we are sure on reflection you will agree.*

Edwin Robert Anderson Seligman, the famous economist and son of Joseph who was named after the defender of Fort Sumter, has said, "My father was the most tolerant of men, but he was also very intolerant of anything not quite up to the standard—sometimes being a little unfair to stupid people."

Although they left something to be desired as bankers, Leopold and Abraham found some success in exporting wool and wheat from San Francisco, just as Seligman, Hellman & Co. shipped cotton. The Californians also held up their end by shipping gold to the East. It was used by the New Yorkers in an extensive arbitrage business in greenbacks and gold, made possible by constant fluctuations in the price of the metal.

General F. E. Spinner, the Treasurer of the United States with a signature so elaborate that Lincoln thought it could never be counterfeited, entered into an agreement with the Seligmans in April 1866. He directed D. W. Cheesman, Assistant Treasurer at San Francisco, to accept currency deposits from J. Seligman & Co. This arrangement, which saved the Government the expense of sending greenbacks to California and allowed J. Seligman & Co. to obtain Treasury drafts in San Francisco, worked satisfactorily until the following February when Cheesman, apparently reacting to criticism of the Seligman arrangement, refused to take further deposits from the company. Joseph Seligman went to Washington and saw Treasurer Spinner who told him that Cheesman customarily received one-quarter of one per cent premium on currency transfer orders on New York, and this permitted him to decline the Seligman deposits at par. On March 2, 1867, Joseph wrote agreeing to pay the premium and Spinner wrote Cheesman, three weeks later:

Seligman & Co. did the Government good services at a time when it was much needed. –They placed with you to my credit at par, taking their pay at New York in like funds on receipt of your certificates of such deposit, an amount reaching nearly two million dollars.–It would have cost the government a round little Sum to have transported this amount from here to you; and then it would eventually have been necessary for the government to have it brought back at another bill of Express.–If other parties were willing to have performed this Service, they failed to make it known.–

Now, while it was not intended, and is not now intended, that Messrs Seligman & Co. should have a Monopoly of this business, yet it is right that they should have a preference when they will pay you the current rates be that par or a premium–

The department has two objects in mind; first, to facilitate its own transactions between the Atlantic and the Pacific Coast; and Second, to keep the rate of Exchange as near par between the two as may be.

This is the best money arrangement that can be made both for the Government and the people of both Sections; and I think no one, Save perhaps interested brokers, who wish to buy Exchange at a discount, and Sell at a premium, will have reason to Complain of our arrangement.

In the era of transition following the Civil War, one important development from the Seligmans' point of view was the laying of the first successful Atlantic cable by Cyrus W. Field in July 1866. When it opened, their first message was addressed to Field; the second, reading, "California gold arrived will add hundred bonds after that hold up exchange unsalable – Josef." was sent to Seligman Brothers, London.

The cable vastly improved communications with Europe but the service was unpredictable at first. Employees for the cable company were suspected

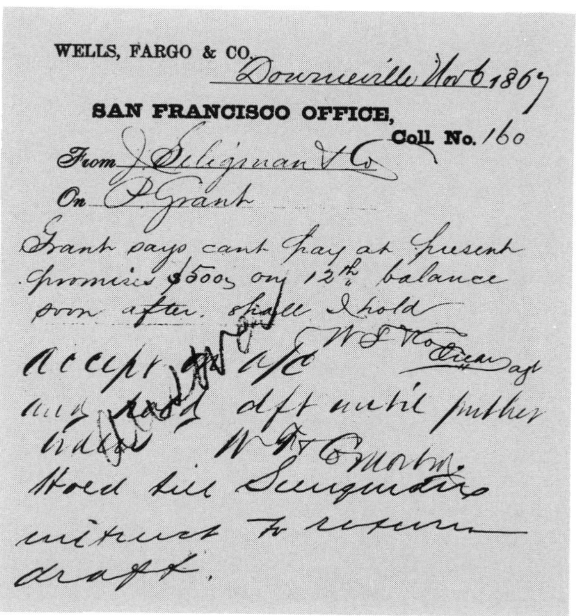
WELLS, FARGO & CO. Downieville Nov 6 1867

SAN FRANCISCO OFFICE, Coll. No. 160

From J. Seligman & Co

On P. Grant

Grant says cant pay at present promises $500 on 12th balance soon after. shall I hold

Hold till Seligman instruct to return draft.

WELLS FARGO BANK

P. Grant, J. Seligman & Co. advised Wells, Fargo & Co. in 1867, "says cant pay at present promises $500 on 12th balance soon after, shall I hold." At the bottom is a notation: "Hold till Seligman instruct to return draft."

of being open to bribery and the messages of the most generous were thought to be given priority. J. & W. Seligman & Co. had its troubles and Joseph wrote Field, May 11, 1867:

> *We beg to submit the following facts, showing plainly that there is a serious irregularity in the forwarding, receipt or delivery of our cable dispatches and would ask you to investigate and remove the cause or causes of these detentions, which have resulted in serious disadvantages to us:*
>
> *1–Dispatch dated London Thursday morning (9th May) reached us at 10 p.m. on the 10th May;*
>
> *2–Dispatch dated London Thursday afternoon (9th May) reached us at midnight on the 10th May;*
>
> *3–Dispatch dated London Thursday evening reached us on the afternoon of the 10th at 1:48 p.m. Bad enough, but not quite as bad as the two previous dispatches.*
>
> *4–Our Frankfort dispatch of six and a half of last evening, which we ought to have had last evening was received at 11:36 this morning.*
>
> *For your guidance in ferreting out the delinquent, we beg to say that we have reason to know that dispatches sent from London at the time ours were forwarded have been received by other bankers twelve and eighteen hours in advance of ours.*

While Joseph complained about the Anglo-American Telegraph Company service, Isaac was having his worries in England. "The chief business in the arbitrage of stocks and exchanges was transacted between New York and London and, being alone, I had a great load on my young shoulders," Isaac recalled many years later. "I remember being so excited by these daily transactions, involving so great a mental stress in sending and receiving telegrams every few minutes, that I got into a nervous condition; so much so that I had to give up walking home of an evening along the Thames Embankment for fear of taking a sudden plunge into the river, thus ending my career."

Isaac turned out to be made of sterner stuff than he imagined at the time. Within a few years, "when my brother Leopold came to London, and my two nephews . . . and my son Charles, entered the business," he took Joseph's advice to let the younger men assume some of the responsibilities, and "the stress and strain upon me became less." In reality, Isaac thrived on excitement and had outlived all of his brothers when he died in 1928 at ninety-three.

LIBRARY OF CONGRESS

SIGNATURE, COLLECTION OF GEOFFREY T. HELLMAN

U. S. Treasurer F. E. Spinner—called "Father Spinner" by Lincoln—said "Seligman & Co. did the Government good services." His signature was elaborate and illegible.

FIVE

As one hande washeth another, and both of them the face, so one brother ought to support another, and all of them to procure the honour of their house.

—*Stefano Guazzo, 1530-1593*

The 650 delegates to the Fourth Republican National Convention, assembled in Chicago May 21, 1868, chose Ulysses S. Grant as their Presidential candidate on the first ballot. "Amid prolonged cheers," says *The History of the Republican Party,* "a full-length picture of the general, painted on canvas, was lowered at the rear of the platform, and a white dove was liberated to fly about the hall."

"Peace and universal prosperity—its sequence—with economy of administration," Grant promised in his acceptance letter, "will lighten the burden of taxation, while it constantly reduces the national debt. Let us have peace."

The Seligmans, as might be expected, favored Grant and, on July 14, Henry Seligman predicted from Germany to Elihu B. Washburne, who was to become Secretary of State, that "Grant will walk over and beat" the Democratic candidate, Horatio Seymour of New York. Abraham Seligman worked for the General's election in California while Joseph, James, and Jesse supported him in New York. On Thursday morning, March 4, 1869, Joseph Seligman stood behind his friend, the President-elect, as the oath of office was administered. In the evening he attended the Inaugural Ball.

Secretary of the Treasury Hugh McCulloch left at the end of Andrew Johnson's term, and Grant first named Alexander T. Stewart, a prosperous New York merchant, to the Treasury post. The Senate turned Stewart down. Years later, Joseph Seligman's son, Isaac Newton, revealed in a candid interview for the *Portland Oregonian* that "General Grant was my father's personal friend and asked him to be Secretary of the Treasury after A. T. Stewart's confirmation had failed in the Senate. But the bank needed him, and his brothers begged him to let politics and public office alone."

Even though none of the Seligmans ever became part of Grant's official family, they made their influence felt when George S. Boutwell of Massachusetts was confirmed as Secretary of the Treasury. Moreover, the firm quickly offered its banking services to the new Administration. Seven days after Grant took office, Joseph Seligman wrote Secretary of State Washburne the firm's overseas branches "would be glad to act as Disbursing agents for our Government (for Diplomatic and other disbursements) at a lower rate of commission than Andrew Johnson's Agents have hitherto done, and believing that both President Grant and you would be glad to be served by friends and especially when it can be done at a savings to the Treasury, I would respectfully bespeak your kind intervention."

Within a few days, J. & W. Seligman & Co. was appointed "Financial Agents of the Government, as far as transmission of funds to foreign countries is concerned." In acknowledgment on March 17, the firm wrote the Secretary that, "We are obliged, and shall endeavor to give satisfaction to the Government." This was the beginning of a type of Government service which the Seligmans continued to perform off and on for many years.

Secretary Washburne was a friend, but he also knew from personal experience that the Seligmans' business was founded on mutual trust in which a client's word was sufficient guarantee of performance. While a Congressman from Illinois, he had done business with the Seligmans and the firm had explained to him that, "We shall be very happy to purchase in Frankfurt 200,000 U. S. Bonds for you, and would say that there is no necessity for you to send any Bonds as margin, as we require none from you."

Early in Grant's Administration, Joseph Seligman, at the President's request, devoted much of his time to helping Secretary of the Treasury Boutwell form a policy for stabilizing United States currency and refunding the public debt. Boutwell and Joseph agreed there could be no effective resumption of specie payments until confidence had been restored, and the high rate of interest – six per cent –being paid on Government bonds was widely felt to reflect unfavorably on the Nation's credit. When Boutwell gave his official report in December 1869, he presented a formula for refunding that he and Joseph Seligman had devised. But the Secretary insisted, over protests, that new bonds should be issued at four and one-half per cent interest. Joseph felt that Boutwell was trying to force the interest rate too low, too soon, and to buttress his argument he asked his brother Henry to find out how German bankers might react to the plan. In a letter to Boutwell on February 18, 1870, Joseph gave Henry's findings, couched in all the polite terms of protocol.

COLLECTION OF GEOFFREY T. HELLMAN

Henry Seligman, head of the Frankfurt branch, was described as being short, rather stout, genial, and kindly. Until his death, The American Hebrew *stated, "He religiously subscribed for the New York* Daily Tribune."

> *We take pleasure in informing you that our house in Frankfurt, Messrs. Seligman & Stettheimer, have consulted nearly all the leading bankers and capitalists in that part of Germany and the almost unanimous opinion is that our 62s can be readily converted into a 5% Bond, and the later issues at a lower rate hereafter. The Credit of the U. S. is gradually but surely assuming its deserved rank in the estimation of capitalists and we congratulate you upon the success of your policy.*

Joseph Seligman had enough confidence in Henry's report to press his views on members of Congress, many of whom believed that even five per cent was too low, and felt that a rate as low as four and one-half per cent even for future issues was an absurdity. Boutwell thought Joseph's "interference" with Congress unwarranted, and a coolness began between the two men which would turn into open enmity before much longer.

Yet, Congress makes the laws. The Acts of July 14, 1870, and January 20, 1871, authorized the sale of various issues of bonds totaling $1,500,000,000 at rates varying from five down to three and one-half per cent and payable in from ten to forty years. This legislation, supplemented with subsequent acts, shaped the character of the public debt for the next twenty-five years.

The Seligmans were confident that in return for their help in working out the refunding formula they would be offered a prominent part in underwriting the $200,000,000 issue of five per cent bonds Boutwell planned for 1871, and they weren't alone in their expectation. Other firms quickly began to send J. & W. Seligman & Co. feelers for a share in the issue.

It soon became clear, however, that Boutwell planned to give the Seligmans as little part in the sale of the loan as possible and this worried William Seligman who was staying in Frankfurt. He shared his feelings on March 1, 1871, in a letter to Washburne.

> *Last evening I was shocked and stunned, by a telegram . . . saying Mr. Boutwell has appointed as agents in Europe for the conversion of U. S. Bonds* [*several firms excluding the Seligmans*]*...Thus, we, contrary to our confident belief . . . are under the circumstances existing, slighted by our govt . . . We do not know, what has caused us this neglect and injustice, whether it is personal aversion against us on the part of Mr. Boutwell or lack of confidence or whether it is the work of intrigue and selfishness on the part of competitors.*

Finally, Boutwell announced he would "offer the loan to everybody," and although displeased by the decision, J. & W. Seligman & Co. determined to cooperate with the Treasury, even when other leading banking houses decided not to participate in the loan. Joseph told his brothers, however, that "the whole business is doomed to failure, unless more intelligence is infused into it."

Joseph was right; the bonds sold so poorly that Boutwell agreed to let Jay Cooke & Co. form a banking syndicate to dispose of the unsold balance. Two selling groups were formed; one in New York,

COLLECTION OF GEOFFREY T. HELLMAN

In Paris, William Seligman, a connoisseur of fine food and rare wines, was a prominent member of the Bourse, a founder and vice-president of the American Chamber of Commerce, and resident partner at Seligman Frères & Cie.

COURTESY, ANSCO HISTORICAL COLLECTION

A Democrat-turned-Republican, George Sewall Boutwell was the first Internal Revenue Commissioner. Later, as Grant's Treasury head, he worked to stabilize currency; refund the debt. By 1900, he was once more a Democrat.

In 1865, the New York Stock Exchange erected a building (center) at 8-16 Broad Street. The firm became a member four years later. This remained the Exchange's home until 1901. The telephone was only about a year old; the incandescent lamp not yet invented when this photo, circa 1877, was taken.

MUSEUM OF THE CITY OF NEW YORK

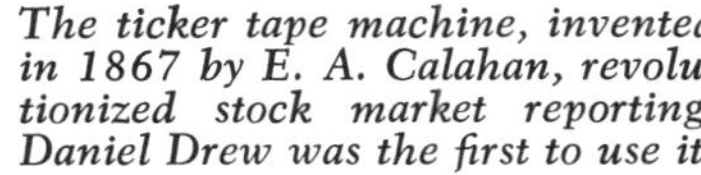

The ticker tape machine, invented in 1867 by E. A. Calahan, revolutionized stock market reporting. Daniel Drew was the first to use it.

The New York Stock Exchange

the other in London, and Seligman branches participated in both. The issue was then oversubscribed, and led President Grant to declare that it "had established American credit abroad."

J. & W. Seligman & Co.'s difficulties with the Secretary of the Treasury undoubtedly irritated the firm's partners, but their reputation continued to grow. As early as 1870, Matthew Hale Smith was writing about the firm in *Twenty Years Among the Bulls and Bears of Wall Street* as "one of the largest houses on the street . . . The senior member of the firm . . . is a self-made man . . . Six years ago he gathered his brothers together, and founded the house now so well known . . . Distinguished for integrity, industry and perseverance, the business of the house increased till it became established in all the great centres of trade in the world . . . Affable, courteous and polite, the members of this firm are among the most popular in the street . . . On the breaking out of the war, Mr. Joseph Selegman [*sic*] visited Europe and did more, probably, than any man, in inspiring confidence of capitalists in the ability of the government to meet its liabilities . . . The head of the house in New York is a social prince, and distributes to his friends an elegant and generous hospitality."

However princely Joseph may have been in his private life, the Seligman firm had prospered regally in the six short years of its existence as a bank. To handle a growing brokerage volume, James Seligman had been admitted to membership on the New York Stock Exchange as one of 173 members of the Government Bond Department – upon payment of $1,000 on May 1, 1869. This was the beginning of the firm's continuous membership in the Nation's most important financial market place. In New Orleans, during the early 1870's, Seligman, Hellman & Co. maintained a growing business in cotton bills, exchange, and shipments of Mexican silver dollars, even though Theodore Hellman's management didn't always please Isaac Seligman. Theodore had been Joseph's son-in-law for exactly eleven months on April 7, 1873, but Isaac didn't care and gave both a piece of his mind:

The earliest known advertisement of J. & W. Seligman & Co. was published in Appletons' Hand-Book of American Travel *in the year 1870.*

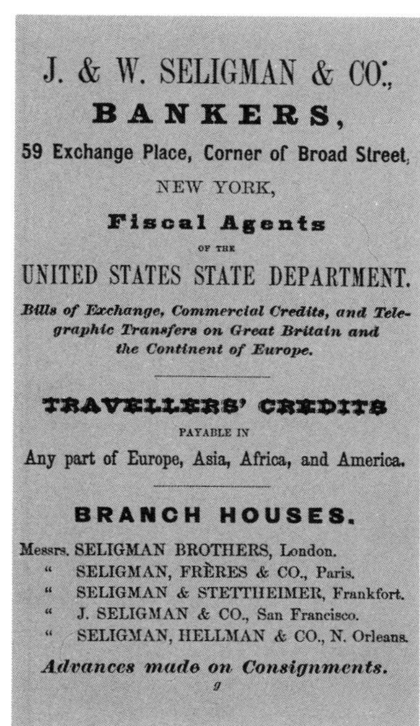

J. & W. SELIGMAN & CO.

CONSOLIDATED EDISON COMPANY OF NEW YORK, INC.

Gas lighting was popular in New York, 1876, and an Ornamental Gas Light (Standard) Post stood in the center of 26th Street and Fifth Avenue, near the Statue of Liberty's hand-torch (right) which was displayed as a fund raising measure.

I dare say the difficulty at [*New Orleans*] *to obtain proper bills are very great, but the difficulties here to get rid of them and after having got rid of them are still greater . . . If Theodore cannot send us only* A 1 bills, *you must find some other occupation for him.*

Three years after Joseph hoped that "we may probably get Brother Leopold to take hold of some other branch of our banking business," Leopold was transferred from San Francisco to London as resident partner with Isaac. There his growing grasp of the business was shown in a letter he wrote to Joseph in August 1872. Half-apologizing for a transaction which gave little profit to the firm, he noted wisely, "A nimble sixpence is better than a slow shilling." Leopold continued to work at banking, but he seemed to prefer painting at which he was reasonably talented.

Six thousand miles away in California, Abraham now headed the West Coast branch with Ignatz Steinhart, who, prior to joining J. Seligman & Co., had been a merchant in San Francisco. He also was Joseph's brother-in-law. In 1871, Joseph's son, David, went West to start a two-year training period in banking. Paris and Frankfurt were primarily occupied with foreign exchange and arbitrage transactions, but also were building reputations as issuing houses. Railroad and municipal bond issues were popular and J. & W. Seligman & Co. often marketed large amounts of such securities both in New York and abroad. After the Franco-Prussian War, the Paris branch sponsored an issue of City of Baltimore securities. That same month, January 1872, Frankfurt participated in a Hungarian loan. Joseph, at this time, was "working night and day"–unsuccessfully–to obtain an issue of Jersey City securities for Paris and Frankfurt.

The Seligman brothers continued their original arrangement for sharing risks and profits, and Isaac was responsible for a job which he considered "unique." For many years, Isaac said, "the eight brothers acted as members of one firm, and, what rarely occurs, no account of private incomes or expenditure was kept, and the profits were

Joseph Seligman believed Mrs. Lincoln should be given a Government pension, and sent President Grant a letter she had written. He thought if Grant would recommend aid for the widow, a pending pension bill would pass.

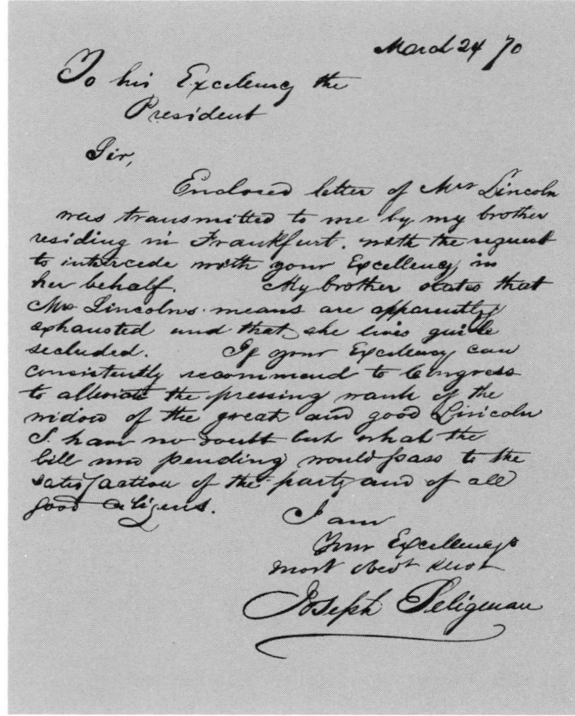

March 24 70

To his Excellency the President

Sir,

Enclosed letter of Mrs Lincoln was transmitted to me by my brother residing in Frankfurt, with the request to intercede with your Excellency in her behalf. My brother states that Mrs. Lincolns means are apparently exhausted and that she lives quite secluded. If your Excellency can consistently recommend to Congress to alleviate the pressing wants of the widow of the great and good Lincoln I have no doubt but what the bill now pending would pass to the satisfaction of the party and of all good citizens.

I am
Your Excellency's
most obedt servt
Joseph Seligman

J. & W. SELIGMAN & CO.

The times when Mary Todd Lincoln bought 300 pairs of gloves in four months ended when her husband died. After much debate, Congress voted a pension to the widow. This photo, copyright 1865, is probably by Brady.

LIBRARY OF CONGRESS

equally divided. At a later date, the profit of the united firms was divided into three portions, the three eldest brothers taking a larger share than the two next eldest, and these again a larger share than the three youngest brothers, but still there was no debit of private expenses charged to anyone. Each trusted the other to spend just what was necessary to maintain his family in comfortable circumstances. After some years, as the family increased through marriage and the growth of children, each individual brother was debited for his family expenses. The private ledger was kept by me in London, and I sent an annual balance sheet, recording the credit and debit sides to New York, Paris and Frankfurt. Private speculation was never allowed, or, rather, never indulged in."

Seligman Brothers, London, made its debut as an issuing house on January 10, 1872, when, in conjunction with Paris and Frankfurt, the branch offered $4,000,000 City of Washington, D. C., bonds over its own name. Isaac was angered when London received an allotment which he considered inequitable. "This place," he wrote from London, "is the great place for our future loans and if the damned jackasses in Frankfort could only be brought to see this it would be of great benefit to us in the future."

Despite his complaints, Isaac later told Joseph that the Washington loan "opened the ice for us . . . I have treated myself to a new house . . . costing . . . about £22,000." Later, he even admitted his inexperience: "I was nervous lest the issue might be a failure, so . . . I placed the greater part among some Greek firms, who were at that period among the foremost mercantile houses in London. I let them have the bonds at 2% under the issue price. When the issue was made, the applications were so numerous that I was compelled to buy back from

On May 16, 1870, Henry Seligman wrote Missouri's Senator, Carl Schurz, from Frankfurt urging a pension for Mrs. Lincoln. Schurz, who had a reputation for personal integrity, had campaigned for Lincoln in 1858 and 1860.

BOTH : LIBRARY OF CONGRESS

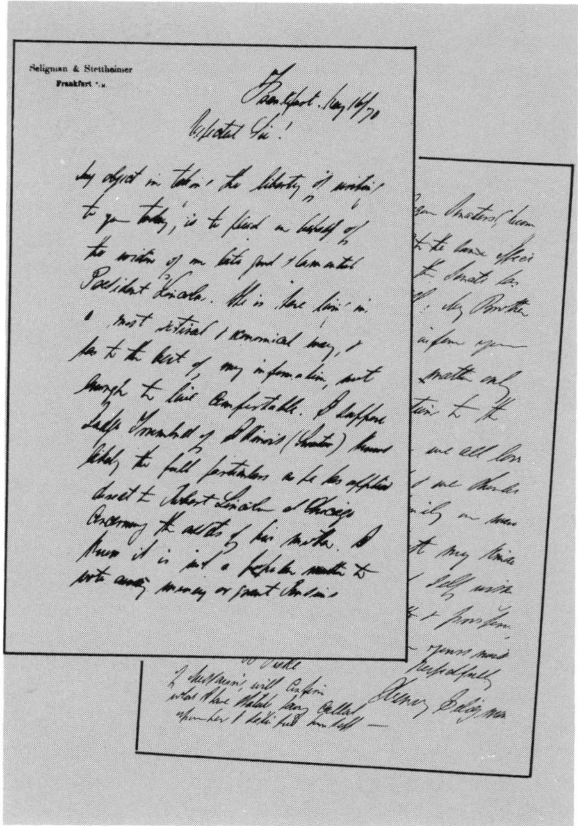

Seligman & Stettheimer
Frankfurt a/M

these parties the bonds I had placed with them, paying them 2% profit."

In New York, J. & W. Seligman & Co. was developing into an issuing house for corporate securities. One of the first issues was the New York Mutual Gas Light Company, "which was destined to light a naptha torch which should illumine and for a time bewilder the gas industry of New York," Frederick L. Collins reported in *History of the Consolidated Gas Company.* "It received its franchises in 1868 at which time the . . . value of stock outstanding stood at $450,000," Daniel P. Parker of New York's Consolidated Edison Company said. Prospects apparently were not viewed with over-enthusiasm, since, according to Collins, shares "were sometimes traded for drinks at the corner saloon!" "Two years later," says Parker, "a group of prominent men, including the Cornelius Vanderbilts (father and son) and Joseph Seligman, became interested in the company . . . value of the stock soared to $5,000,000; the price per share rising to $100. Its introduction of naptha process in 1871, and its laying of 24 inch gas mains the year following, made New York Mutual Gas Light Company the second largest producer and distributor of gas by 1876—sending out more than a million cubic feet of gas per day." "Among its ten thousand customers," Collins claims, "were the biggest consumers in town—A. T. Stewart's Broadway store, the new and old post offices, the Western Union Telegraph Company, the Union League Club and the Grand Central."

The Seligmans had reached the top. But they remembered their own humble beginnings. Joseph became active in New York charities. He served as first president of what became The Hebrew Orphan Asylum of the City of New York; Jesse Seligman later served as Vice-President and President until

1894. Joseph also helped to found New York's Mount Sinai Hospital and gave funds to establish Ethical Culture Society kindergarten schools. Henry Seligman helped to run the San Francisco Jewish Orphan Asylum and when he went to Frankfurt, he headed a number of benevolent societies. In the early 1900's Henry contributed to a children's nursery in Baiersdorf, his home town, and the grateful villagers made him an honorary citizen and placed a plaque on the Seligmans' birthplace. In 1929, the London Seligmans donated additional money to the nursery and the street on which it is located was renamed Seligmannstrasse. During the early days of the Third Reich, the street was known as Adolf-Hitler-Strasse. Earlier this year, the Second Bürgermeister of Baiersdorf said it was "again renamed Seligmannstrasse in 1945."

Henry's concern for the less fortunate, and his strong ties with the United States, were reflected in his efforts to help Mary Todd Lincoln, the President's widow, who was living in seclusion in Frankfurt with her son, Tad, in 1870. Despite her husband's estate of some $110,000, Mrs. Lincoln convinced herself she was poor, printed an appeal for aid in the New York newspaper, *The World,* and sold some of her personal effects at auction before sailing for Europe. Senator Charles Sumner of Massachusetts introduced a bill in Congress to authorize a pension for her. When Henry Seligman visited Mrs. Lincoln in Frankfurt he was touched by her circumstances and advanced money for her living expenses and schooling for Tad. Henry told his New York partners what he had done and J. & W. Seligman & Co. wrote to Robert Lincoln in an attempt to collect the tuition money advanced to his mother. There is no record he responded.

On March 24, 1870, Joseph Seligman wrote to President Grant urging the pension bill be approved and he enclosed a letter Mrs. Lincoln herself had written Grant.

Henry Seligman must have thought the pension was unlikely to be authorized when he wrote a six-page letter to Senator Carl Schurz of Missouri on May 16 urging Congressional approval of the bill. "My object in taking the liberty of writing to you today," Henry declared, "is to plead on behalf of the widow of our late good & lamented President Lincoln. She is here living in a most retired & economical way, & has to the best of my information, not enough to live comfortable . . . Why had you dear sir seen her as I have done last New Year living in a small street in the third floor in 2 dirty rooms with hardly if any furniture, all alone, grieved & nearly heart broken, you would have said with me can it be possible that the wife of our great man lives in such a way, & is our Nation not indebted to him who gave up his life for the sake of freedom, that our great & rich country cannot show at least its gratitude towards his sacred name by some small testimonial in giving to his family a comfortable Home . . . My brother Joseph in New York can inform you that we all urge this matter only on account of our devotion to the Name of Lincoln whom we all love & respected so much, & we should not like to see his family in want for anything."

During the Chicago Fire, about 100,000 fled their homes. The mayor issued a proclamation entrusting "the preservation of the good order and peace of the city" to the Army, under the command of Lieutenant General Sheridan.

COURTESY, CHICAGO HISTORICAL SOCIETY

PROCLAMATION!

The preservation of the good order and peace of the city is hereby entrusted to Lieut. General P. H. Sheridan, U. S. Army.

The Police will act in conjunction with the Lieut. General in the preservation of the peace and quiet of the city, and the Superintendent of Police will consult with him to that end.

The intent hereof being to preserve the peace of the city, without interfering with the functions of the City Government.

Given under my hand this 11th day of October, 1871.

R. B. MASON, Mayor.

The center of Chicago burned and thousands of buildings were destroyed. A stereoscope view, popular after the event, showed the burned area, looking south on Wabash Avenue through the "Hole in the Wall." About 300 died.

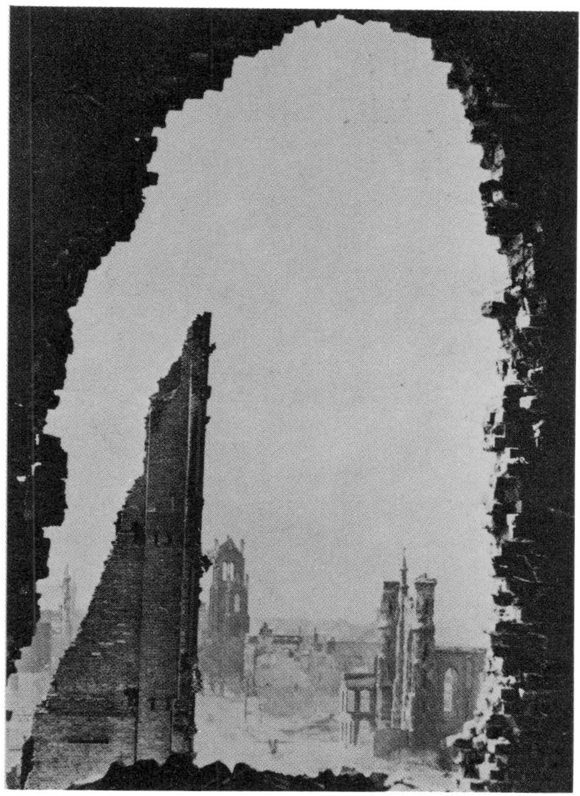

LIBRARY OF CONGRESS

Finally, the Senate, voting 28 to 20, passed a pension bill on July 14, allowing Mrs. Lincoln $3,000 a year, after Senator Sumner had agreed to reduce the amount from $5,000.

Another opportunity for charitable work came when, according to legend, a cow belonging to Mrs. Catherine O'Leary kicked over a lantern in a barn at 558 DeKoven Street on Sunday, October 8, 1871, and started the great Chicago fire. Rainfall finally killed the fire after nearly four days in which 17,450 buildings were burned, property worth $196,000,000 was destroyed, and some 300 died. Contributions for the aid of the people of Chicago came from all over the world and relief funds were subscribed by the citizens of Frankfurt—Henry Seligman among them—and conveyed to Chicago's Mayor, R. B. Mason, by J. & W. Seligman & Co.

A month after the fire, the firm wrote "To his Honor, the Mayor of the City of Chicago . . . We now hold at your disposal said $12,500 Bonds, or their proceeds in either gold or currency, if the latter with the premium added. Good people irrespective of nationality and creed come to your relief and we are glad to be the medium of their efforts." In total, the bonds, accrued interest, and later contributions from Frankfurt, gave the people of Chicago $18,275.

While the Seligmans were helping unfortunate persons, people elsewhere were helping themselves to the public's money. New York City was in the grip of William Marcy Tweed, Grand Sachem of Tammany Hall, a one-time social club which controlled the local Democratic Party. By 1871, Tweed and his followers had plundered millions from the City and made elections a farce. "When the desperate condition of municipal affairs which grew out of the corruption and misgovernment of a band of villainous politicians called for energetic action of leading citizens," according to the *Encyclopaedia of Contemporary Biography of New York,* "Mr. [Joseph] Seligman had a place on the famous 'Committee of Seventy' which remedied this deplorable state of affairs."

But corruption was not peculiar to New York. President Grant's "naive trust in almost anybody who professed to be his friend," the Republican Party *History* contends, "attracted grafters and spoilsmen, who misled him on patronage and on policies. This complacence, combined with his overzealous enforcement of reconstruction measures in the South, resulted in a revolt by 'liberal Republicans' who early in 1872 nominated Horace Greeley" for President.

Joseph Seligman's response to local and national conditions was a call for reform in New York City and State and continuing support for Grant. On October 4, J. & W. Seligman & Co. joined fifty-nine other firms in petitioning for Grant's return to the White House. At a Cooper Institute rally on October 18, *The New York Times* reported, presiding officer Joseph Seligman told the crowd:

> *That General Grant has made mistakes we do not deny; that among 60,000 office holders, some unworthy and objectionable parties had been appointed he sees himself, and is continually correcting. But that Grant tries*

LIBRARY OF CONGRESS

THE ANGLO-CALIFORNIAN BANK

LIMITED.

Successors to J. Seligman & Co.

LONDON OFFICE.............3 ANGEL COURT

SAN FRANCISCO OFFICE,

No. 412 California Street.

Authorized Capital Stock......$6,000,000
Subscribed Capital Stock...... 3,000,000
Paid in Capital Stock.......... 1,500,000
Remainder subject to call.

Directors in London ;
HON. HUGH McCULLOCH, REUBEN D. SASSOON,
WILLIAM F. SCHOLFIELD. ISAAC SELIGMAN.
JULIUS LINGTON.

Managers in San Francisco :
RICHARD G. SNEATH, IGNATZ STEINHART.

THE BANK IS NOW PREPARED TO open accounts, receive deposits, make collections, buy and sell Exchange and issue letters of Credit available throughout the World, and to loan money on proper securities

The Stock of this Bank being held by leading Bankers and Capitalists of Europe and America, the Bank will have superior facilities in the negociation of State, Municipal and other securities abroad.

R. G. SNEATH,
IGN. STEINHART, } Managers.

1y2

NOTICE.

MESSRS. J. SELIGMAN & CO., HAVING transferred their Banking Business and good will to the Anglo-Californian Bank, limited, would request all persons indebted to them to settle their accounts with MR. IGNATZ STEINHART (412 California street), who is authorized to sign in liquidation.

J. SELIGMAN & CO.

San Francisco, July 21, 1873. j2

J. Seligman & Co. became The Anglo-Californian Bank, Limited in July 1873. An advertisement in the San Francisco newspaper, Daily Alta California, *announced formation of the new bank and the liquidation of J. Seligman & Co. at the same time. The London office of the bank was at 3 Angel Court, same address as Seligman Brothers. Isaac was one of the bank's London directors.*

to do his duty toward his country honestly and conscientiously, everyone who knows him well must concede, and I have known him well a number of years. . .

He has maintained peace within and without our borders; has paid off nearly $400,000,000 of our national debt, and reduced taxes upward of $300,000,000.

Still the people's hero, Grant won easily. Reform swept New York State, however, and General John A. Dix became Governor while William F. Havemeyer moved into the Mayor's office. In return for his support, the new Mayor appointed Joseph Seligman a member of the Board of Education, a post he held until 1875. In 1876, when Joseph was urged to run for the mayoralty himself, he refused.

Joseph Seligman took his obligations as a citizen with great seriousness, but he had a business to run, and his mind was at least equally occupied during Grant's second Presidential campaign and the months that followed with plans to launch The Anglo-Californian Bank, Limited, a publicly-owned commercial bank the Seligmans formed as successor to J. Seligman & Co. in San Francisco.

In mid-1872, Abraham Seligman had traveled to Europe from California, presumably to discuss the creation of the new bank, although Isaac, who handled almost all of the details in London, thought very little of his brother's help. He commented that Abraham had come to London "probably because he has nothing better to do." Despite his outspoken impatience, Isaac was able to write on January 27, 1873, that "we are commencing to take active steps in the new Bank... matter and hope before long to make good reports of our progress."

Within three months Isaac had all but completed the job. The Board of Directors, including former Secretary of the Treasury Hugh McCulloch, who then was affiliated with Jay Cooke, McCulloch & Co., London, and Isaac himself, had been formed. A public offering of the stock provided the necessary £400,000 capital, and, most important to the Seligmans perhaps, J. & W. Seligman & Co. was officially designated the Anglo-Californian's New York agent, even though the firm had subscribed to only £10,000 of the new bank's stock.

Both before and after The Anglo-Californian Bank took over from J. Seligman & Co. and began operations on July 2, 1873, Isaac was as fussy as a mother hen in getting his brothers to leave no detail unsettled. Before the bank opened he wrote a series of insistent letters hoping that "you will find some A 1 man . . to become head manager." And when it was decided that David Seligman, Joseph's son, and Ignatz Steinhart, his brother-in-law, would co-manage the enterprise, with Abraham continuing as partner in residence, Isaac lectured them at length on their duties as bankers. "I need not call to your attention," he reminded them, "to the great moral responsibility you now have . . . With God's help our reputation will be enhanced by the Success of your management of the Bank; while should you mismanage affairs, you may rely upon it that our good name would suffer immensely, and nothing would be so deplorable as to suffer in reputation."

Isaac went on to instruct them in "sending *weekly* summaries" of transactions, "intelligible reports," and cautioned them to be "exceedingly careful not to incur any bad debts, not to lock up your money in any unnegotiable security, and not . . . to lend money to prominent politicians with the prospect of having to wait years before you can get it back." To emphasize his concern about young David's and Steinhart's abilities he wrote to New York and asked Joseph to impress upon them "to have a good corresponding clerk who can write a faultless business letter . . . for I should be ashamed to let the Directors read such rigamaroles as dear David writes, and such ungrammatical English as Ignatz sends at present."

Just before The Anglo-Californian Bank opened, Joseph Seligman arrived in San Francisco to see for himself that everything was in order, a move which Isaac had "scarcely anticipated." The London partner was even less prepared to have Joseph remove his son, David, as co-manager and replace him with Richard G. Sneath, of whom no one in London had ever heard. Isaac was surprised but wrote Joseph that "there is not the slightest objection to the appointment . . . only the Board had better wait until form letters of resignation from David arrive, and some statement is received from you as to the gentleman intended to replace him . . . you must bear in mind that things here are done . . . systematically, and not . . . reckless and slopshop."

The stock market had been uneasy while the

Harper's Weekly

Three kinds of men described the Panic of 1873, (top, l to r): LOST; THE PAYING TELLER; GAINED. *Jay Cooke & Co. suspended on September 18 (center). To keep abreast of latest events, men kept* AROUND THE STOCK INDICATOR.

new bank was getting under way. Several firms failed, prices declined sharply, then rallied for a time, and by September 19, 1873, Joseph Seligman was writing to London, "We have quite a panic in Wall Street and numerous failures, and the end is not yet. Jay Cooke & Co. suspended yesterday noon . . . Let us thank God that we have made no losses."

Three days later, Joseph declared, "The numerous failures among Bankers and Brokers brought on such a fearful panic on Saturday, that . . . a number of us telegraphed the President & Secty Treasy to come on immediately. I spent with a number of Bank Presidents . . . Jesse included nearly all day Sunday with the President."

It appeared that banks were in desperate need of cash, but all that President Grant would agree to do was to instruct the Treasury to buy as many Government bonds as were offered, up to a limit of $44,000,000, an amount held in a special reserve account. "We wanted more," Joseph said, "but the President would not agree to deposit his currency with the Natl Bank as it was clearly illegal." Later the same day, Joseph telegraphed, "The situation is much improved, Grants plan appears to have had the proper effect."

About this time, Joseph took the opportunity to speak to Grant "asking him to appoint" Seligman Brothers "to the Navy agency whenever he thinks it proper to remove McCullough [*sic*]. He told me that he had already considered it and would speak to the Secy of Navy. The latter is here today, sent for me, and told me he does not wish to remove McCullough yet tho' he may do so in a few weeks or months, that he is anxious to sustain McCullough's Credit at least until all the Navy's Drafts running on McCullough had been paid."

Although Government efforts to pour money into the banks seemed to mitigate the Panic at first, the effect was only momentary, and by September 23 Joseph confessed to Isaac, "Things look decidedly blue this evening, most of the Banks decline to pay out Greenbacks or currency today and the Chicago Banks are reported suspended." To make it even worse, William Seligman, who had felt "vexed and nervous about the large amount of investments" held by the New York branch of the firm, threatened to quit the

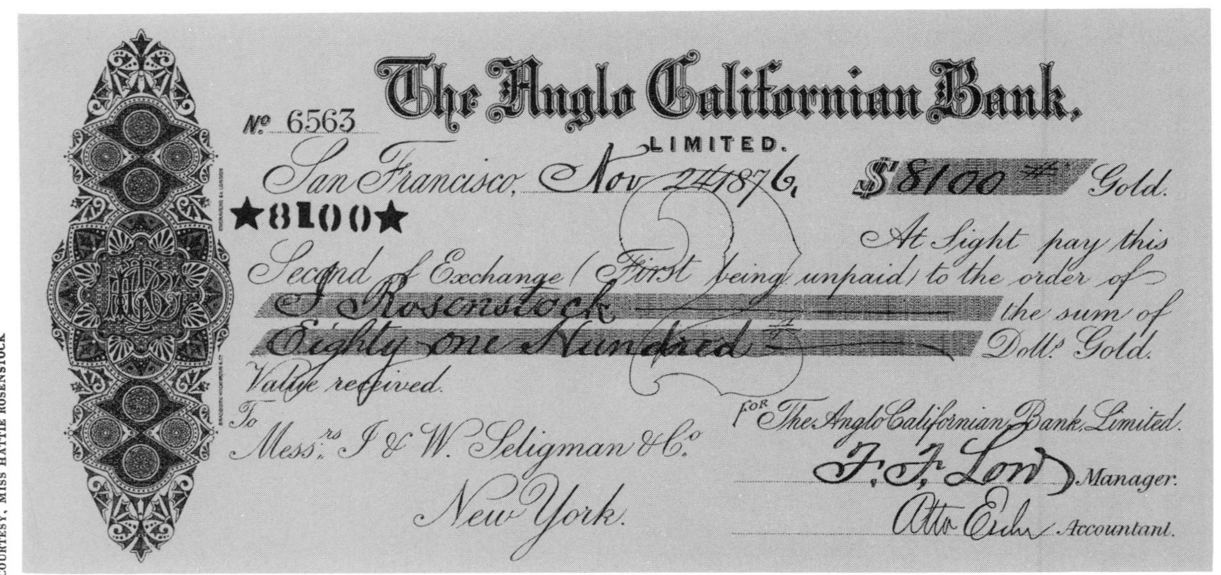
The Anglo Californian Bank.
LIMITED.
No 6563
San Francisco, Nov 24 1876. $8100 Gold.
★8100★
At Sight pay this Second of Exchange (First being unpaid) to the order of J. Rosenstock the sum of Eighty one Hundred Doll.s Gold.
Value received.
To Mess.rs J & W. Seligman & Co. New York.
For The Anglo Californian Bank, Limited.
F. F. Low Manager.
Accountant.

COURTESY, MISS HATTIE ROSENSTOCK

In the past, money transfers were handled by bills of exchange. Two were issued, a first and second, and each was sent by a different route since loss was not uncommon. The first presented was valid. F. F. Low, former California Governor and Minister to China, was co-manager of The Anglo-Californian when he wrote and signed a "Second of Exchange" for $8,100.

partnership. Joseph was angered when Isaac tended to sympathize with William. He told him sharply that:

While I shall invite that selfish Bro. Wm. to carry out his threat and leave the concern on the 1st of Jan'y my self respect will impel me to tender the same invitation to you Bro. Isaac if you continue to vex us and bother us for an error in judgment . . . Now I shall not have time to write Bro. Wm. Please inform him that he is mistaken when he expects that we will buy him out and give him our obligations for his share. We shall do no such thing, but want him to come here in Jan'y and take his 1/8th share of assets, consisting of railroad bonds and shares, mining shares, property bad and good debts, and attend personally to collecting them and my word for it, he will find himself in better health than by eating heavy dinners, drinking heavy wines, writing heavy letters to us, and doing nothing else.

No sooner had Joseph put down rebellion from one direction than it rose from another. Steinhart wrote to complain about his co-manager of The Anglo-Californian Bank and when Joseph got a chance to reply on September 27, he told his brother-in-law, "Your letter . . . coming as it does in the midst of an unprecedented panic gives me such a pain . . . you must try to get along."

Writing to Isaac January 6, 1874, Joseph explained that the co-managers had "differences of opinion and different views as to the details of the business . . . our friend Sneath imagines there is a prejudice in the American mind against foreigners or Israelites (which we are sure there ought not to be and *is not* among intelligent Americans)."

Then Richard Sneath resigned and Joseph told him "Your letter . . . has shocked and grieved me greatly . . . after your promise to give the Bank a trial for twelve months, you suddenly ask the acceptance of your resignation, ostensibly for the reason that you disapprove of a co-manager . . . You are now pleased to say that the Bank would have more friends among the Americans but for their foolish *prejudices* against *the religion of the Bank* . . . Don't you think Mr. Sneath, that you err in this respect and do injustice to the mercantile community of San Francisco?"

Being unwilling to place total blame on either of the men, Joseph wrote in equally strong terms to Steinhart, but his efforts to make the co-managers patch up their differences failed. Abraham Seligman, who had moved into the Frankfurt branch after Max Stettheimer died in 1873, journeyed to San Francisco and hired Frederick F. Low, a former Governor of California, as Sneath's successor. Low held the post until 1891. During this period, Henry Seligman, Jesse's son, was an errand boy and apprentice in The Anglo-Californian Bank for five years before returning to New York in 1880 to work at J. & W. Seligman & Co.

The Seligmans relinquished control of the bank in 1888 when most of their stock was purchased by Lazard Frères & Co. Through a series of mergers the old Anglo-Californian is a part of what became Crocker-Citizens National Bank in San Francisco on November 1, 1963. J. & W. Seligman & Co. sold its remaining shares in the bank in 1912, ending what had started as a trip via Panama to the gold fields sixty-two years before.

CROCKER-CITIZENS NATIONAL BANK

Ignatz Steinhart, Joseph Seligman's brother-in-law, was co-manager of The Anglo-Californian Bank at the time it opened. He resented that Richard G. Sneath, also a co-manager, had his name first in the list of management.

CROCKER-CITIZENS NATIONAL BANK

The Anglo-Californian Bank, Limited opened for business in 1873 at 412 California Street in San Francisco. By 1876, according to the San Francisco City Directory, quarters for the Bank were at 422 California (above).

BOTH: CALIFORNIA STATE LIBRARY

Richard G. Sneath (above) was as headstrong as Ignatz Steinhart, and Joseph wrote Isaac Seligman in 1874: "Last summer we discovered that he had an exalted opinion of himself... Steinhart had also the same trait of character."

Sneath quit the Bank in February 1874, and Abraham Seligman returned to San Francisco to replace him. He chose Frederick F. Low as co-manager and described him as "a perfect gentleman, intelligent, upright and urbane."

SIX

They come, they stay, they make their mark,
writing big or little on their times . . .

—*Allen Drury, 1918–*

When Joseph Seligman sent Isaac in London "a detailed statement of our status in New York and San Francisco as per January 1, 1874," the relaxed tone of his letter reflected the end of the Panic of 1873. "We have all of us made mistakes," he wrote to William soothingly, "and the result has been one year's labor without pay. I am quite satisfied, provided we profit by the lessons."

With a touch of self-congratulation, he reflected, "Think of having gone through the various crises since 1857, and especially the recent without borrowing a dollar from any bank and always having fair balances in cash, both here and in Europe."

Within a few weeks, however, continuing pressures of business brought the partners back to their usual, outspoken way of dealing with each other. During late 1873, Theodore Hellman, manager of Seligman, Hellman & Co. in New Orleans, had turned in exceptionally good profits, "making from $40 to $50,000 net." But early the next year he advanced funds to a cotton shipper without getting proper security, and lost $23,500 on the deal. "Dear Theodore," Joseph declared sharply, "be spared similar mistakes in the future, as I would rather lose double the amount than to be published as a dupe."

While the brothers took turns scolding each other, each of them continued to work hard for the good of the firm. Seligman Brothers had been relieved as the State Department's overseas fiscal agent in the summer of 1871, and Jay Cooke, McCulloch & Co., in London, had been made agent for the U. S. Navy, an account the Seligmans wanted. When Cooke's firm failed, Navy Secretary George M. Robeson had authorized a temporary transfer of funds to Isaac's branch of the firm, and Joseph had commented, "I don't care a great deal for it except as a stepping stone upwards toward the Navy Agency and that I will probably get yet provided I find that I want to have anything more to do with the Government."

Despite his seeming diffidence Joseph was writing to President Grant at about the same time offering "our services . . . in buying any drafts of your various departments in London . . . The members of our London house, who are all citizens of the United States, would be but too glad to be of service to the Government." After performing the duties involved in the office for almost a year, Seligman Brothers was appointed temporary Fiscal Agents for the Navy Department at London and the appointment was later made permanent.

The Navy Agency was of modest profit but an important source of prestige for the firm. A letter written to Secretary of the Navy Richard W. Thompson in 1878 indicates that the volume of official payments was substantial at times. "We have a dispatch from London," Joseph reported to

Ulysses S. Grant and Navy Secretary George M. Robeson, on May 26, 1876, signed the document appointing Seligman Brothers as Fiscal Agents of the U. S. Navy. The London branch held the position until April 1885; again from early in 1889 until April 1893, and also from April 1897, when McKinley was President, until July 1, 1913.

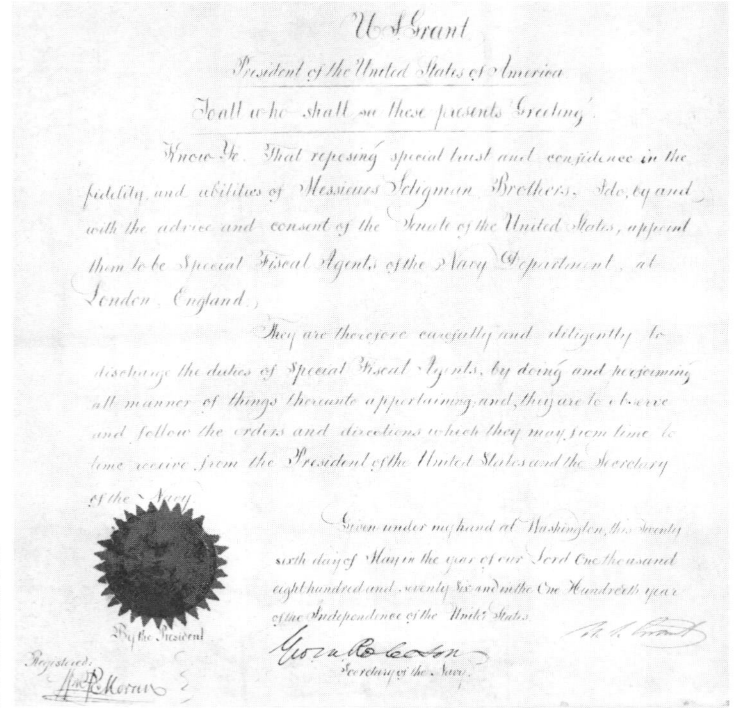

U. S. Grant

President of the United States of America

To all who shall see these presents Greeting:

Know Ye, That reposing special trust and confidence in the fidelity and abilities of Messieurs Seligman Brothers, I do, by and with the advice and consent of the Senate of the United States, appoint them to be Special Fiscal Agents of the Navy Department, at London, England.

They are therefore carefully and diligently to discharge the duties of Special Fiscal Agents, by doing and performing all manner of things thereunto appertaining; and they are to observe and follow the orders and directions which they may from time to time receive from the President of the United States and the Secretary of the Navy.

Given under my hand at Washington, this twenty sixth day of May in the year of our Lord One thousand eight hundred and seventy six and in the One Hundredth year of the Independence of the United States.

U. S. Grant

By the President

Geo. M. Robeson

Secretary of the Navy.

Registered:

J. & W. SELIGMAN & CO.

Richard W. Thompson, said Jesse Seligman, was "a great statesman and lawyer." Navy Secretary during the Administration of President Hayes, Thompson later was chairman of the American Panama Canal committee.

LIBRARY OF CONGRESS

Washington, "advising that Drafts aggregating . . . nearly $400,000, were paid by the Navy Agents during this month . . . which shows that the Captains and Paymasters of the Navy have discovered that you are a rich Secretary." An official connection with the Government was also helpful in the business of selling United States bonds in Europe, in which the Seligmans were once more about to become involved.

Like most bankers of every age, Joseph Seligman was a firm advocate of sound money in which the people could have confidence and which would hold its purchasing power over the long term. He had long been disturbed by the Treasury's failure to remove from circulation depreciated greenbacks – notes first issued during the Civil War which were not backed by gold. When William A. Richardson, Boutwell's successor in the Treasury, issued more greenbacks, Joseph criticized the move with all his force. He commented sarcastically on the "statesmanship, the far-reaching sagacity of our inflationary friends in Congress, who boast that they are practical men. They know, as everyone knows, that when a man fails it is for want of money and that plenty of money always gets him out of his troubles. Ergo! Just so it must be with a great nation. Would you make its finances flourish? . . . Create greenbacks! . . . You have only to set a press in motion. Since money is what business needs, let us make money so that business can flourish! Why should the country languish when money, the great regenerator of its commerce and trade, can so easily be created!"

At Tarrytown, New York, on the last day of February 1874, Henry Seligman, visiting from Frankfurt, made a speech in support of Joseph's point of view. He criticized "legislative meddling by Congress and violations of the principles of a stable national currency. What our people desire of money at the present moment is . . . a certain stability of value."

Although President Grant's view coincided with that of the Seligmans – "I am not," he said, "a believer in any artificial method of making paper money equal to coin" – his veto of the bill creating more greenbacks "came quite unaware and unexpectedly upon the community," Joseph wrote Isaac April 24. He added, with some satisfaction, "We heard of it about an hour before anyone else in the Street."

Soon after Grant's veto, Richardson left the Cabinet and Joseph Seligman was introduced to his successor, Benjamin H. Bristow of Kentucky, by General Horace Porter, the President's military secretary. After talking with the new Secretary about plans for refunding more of the National debt, Joseph told his brothers, "He would be happy to negotiate his 5% bonds through us." Earlier, the Seligmans had expressed an interest in the bonds. Joseph was advised by the Treasury Secretary "that the Government will favorably consider the claims of our house to be one of the syndicate" which would take charge of the issue. He questioned how to get into the group, and decided it would be better to form his own in competition with such firms as London's N. M. Rothschild & Sons, a branch of the most powerful private bank in the world.

"As soon as I have finally obtained the loan with a satisfactory option," Joseph told Isaac June 9, "it will be time to consider the propriety of giving Rothschild a participation, which, although not popular with the American people, may be prudent for us." Isaac formed a syndicate of bankers in London, Paris, Amsterdam, Frankfurt, Brussels, and Berlin, while Joseph prepared to make a firm bid for $25,000,000 of the new bonds.

Then Secretary Bristow began to hedge. "I return this morning from Washington," Joseph reported on June 10, "without having completed the loan, although I am encouraged to believe we shall obtain it shortly after the adjournment of Congress . . . The Secretary feels that jealous bankers will stimulate Congressmen to pass a bill sending a congressional committee to Europe to negotiate, or some such inimical move. I frankly expressed to him my disappointment in not obtaining the loan with a reasonably long option . . . But he was firm and so was the President, to whom both the Secretary and I repaired for his opinion." Characteristically, Joseph added, "I have great hopes of succeeding, although nothing is certain in this world."

Before the general public was aware that Grant had named Benjamin H. Bristow as his Secretary of the Treasury, Joseph Seligman wrote to William in Paris on May 26, 1874: "I know the man by reputation, but not personally."

LIBRARY OF CONGRESS

By July 3, Bristow still hesitated, and Joseph commented:

> *It now appears the Secretary, being very timid and afraid of criticism . . . especially as he has been assured by competitors that without a stronger combination the Seligmans will not be likely to make a success of it . . . Now the President and Mr. Bristow appear both anxious that we and the Rothschild group should work together, as they both say no one could beat that great combination . . . I fear that the haughty and proud Rothschilds would not consent to let us come in as their peers and I should not consent to join on any other terms.*

President Grant's cottage at Long Branch, New Jersey, was near Joseph Seligman's summer home. The house, according to Harper's Weekly, *stood "directly on the Bluff, some distance beyond the most western line of hotels, and commands a fine view of the ocean on one side, and of the village and landscape on the other." The house was described as "a very tasteful . . . elegant bit of summer architecture."*

Joseph's fears were well-founded. The Rothschilds, accustomed to dominating any deal in which they participated, were not at all anxious to allow the Seligmans a position of importance. The powerful bankers agreed to let the Seligmans have a quarter interest in the issue, but would give them no voice in managing the sale and no place in the advertising. Joseph was willing to concede to the Rothschilds the entire management of the issue, provided that the firm was given a three-eighths interest and the Seligman name was included in the advertisements in "New York and either Paris or Frankfurt." When the Rothschilds refused, he advised Isaac:

> *If next week . . . the Rothschilds have not acceded to such terms as you and Paris can honorably accept, I will telegraph you to advise your associates to renew my authority, but in addition to put up 2%, which, if I can bid for $40,000,000 to $50,000,000 firm, will make it hot for Rothschild, as I cannot conceive that Bristow will ignore us and give the loan to Rothschild even if they outbid us . . . as we can be of use to the Administration and Rothschild cannot.*

Joseph's strategy worked. A compromise allowed the Seligmans to sign a joint bid for the loan and Joseph, pleased but still wary, told Isaac, "We have at last advanced so far as to be able to join in a bid with Rothschild . . . which is, after all, a feather in our cap, and although our participation of 28% is small, I am contented."

But when Joseph went to Washington with the syndicate's bid for the bonds, he found that Bristow had changed his mind again. He would not agree to a twelve-month option. Finally, after minor modifications and a Presidential conference at Grant's summer home at Long Branch, New Jersey, Bristow accepted the bid. Joseph reported to his partner in London:

> *It is dangerous to eat cherries with big people, especially politicians, afraid of criticizing newspapers and of jealous competing bankers, and I trust that the Rothschilds can be induced to accept Bristow's compromise . . . with the option . . . I am aware that it is an unbusinesslike option, but these politicians do not understand business and do not care a penny whether we take it or not. Bristow practically told us he would prefer that we should reject*

Baron Lionel de Rothschild was not only an outstanding financier, he also became the first Jew to sit in the English Parliament. The multibillionaire, once he was seated, is recorded as having made not a single speech.

After his term as President expired, Grant made a triumphant world tour. In London, and Frankfurt, too, he was wined and dined by the Seligmans. And while in Paris, he had his photograph taken by Théodore Humblot.

it. But it would give our enemies a chance to crow over us if we lose it altogether.

Two days later, on July 27, he declared to Isaac, "Our connection with Rothschild will do us an immense deal of good both here and abroad and maybe lead to more transactions." Then he added with the obvious pleasure: "Morgan—J. P. of Drexel, Morgan—is very bitter in his jealous expression about our getting the loan.

In view of the Seligmans' newly established relationship with Baron Lionel de Rothschild, head of the family's London bank, Joseph explained to Isaac that "having now broken the ice, I wish you to cultivate this connection." To help, he wrote three pages to his London partner, suggesting that he "let the Baron read them," and saying in part:

Please say to the Baron that we feel highly honored in participating with his great house in negotiating the 5% U. S. bonds; that we never concealed the fact from the President and the Secretary that the House of Rothschild (properly successful in all they undertake) would be certain to make a good market for the U. S. 5's and while we were quite satisfied in leaving the sole management in London to the Messrs. Rothschild, we believe that on consideration the Baron will agree with us that our cooperation and joint management in New York will be of considerable advantage to the syndicate.

Whether the Baron ever saw Joseph's letter is not known, but Isaac saw the Baron more than once in the years that followed and the two banking houses worked together on several more underwritings of U. S. bonds. When Lot M. Morrill of Maine became Secretary of the Treasury in 1876, additional refunding was undertaken, and "through the great influence which my brother Joseph, as well as brother Jesse, had with the United States Government," Isaac said, "we were enabled . . . to issue in London, in conjunction with Rothschilds and Morgans, a $300,000,000 United States 4½% loan." In the next Administration, "On July 12, 1877," he added, "we issued a 4% loan together with the Rothschilds, Morgans and Morton Rose."

Long after J. & W. Seligman & Co. had been accepted as a leading international banker in its own right, Isaac's reminiscences suggested that dealing with Baron Rothschild in person was

"We wish everybody to understand," Puck *magazine commented sarcastically, "that we wouldn't do or say anything to hurt the feelings of [Treasury Secretary] John Sherman—not for twenty-seven cents and a piece of pie."*

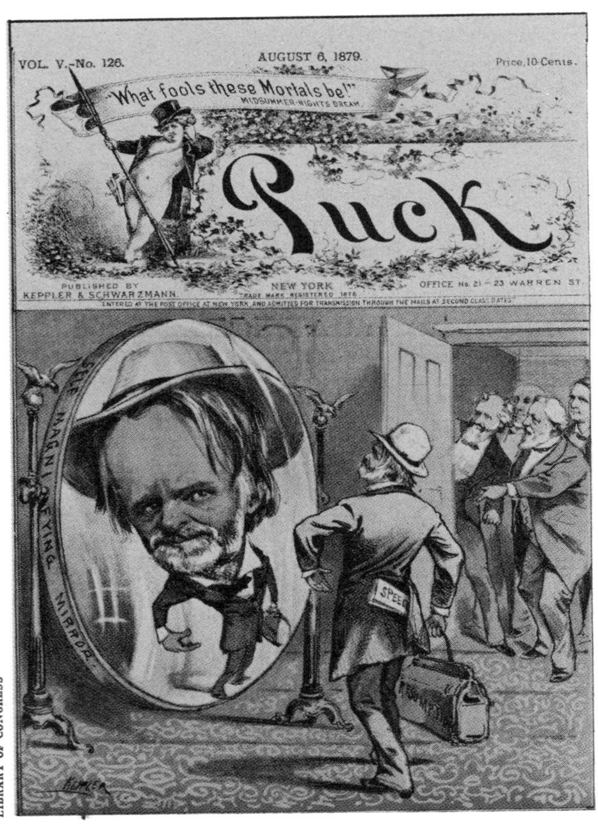

LIBRARY OF CONGRESS

probably not so formidable an assignment as it had seemed when the firm was trying to "break the ice," nor were bankers in those days completely without humor. Isaac recalled that "one day, when the first United States loan was being handled by the old Baron Rothschild, I had occasion to call on him at his house—it being Saturday, and the Rothschild office closed—to communicate to him the contents of a telegram received from our New York firm. The Baron was sitting at a table strewn with documents. He said, 'I am a better Jew than you; you go to business on Saturdays; I do not; my office is closed.' "

"I replied, 'I think you do more business in this little room on Saturdays than I do during the whole week in my office.' "

Although letters and documents which have survived tend to suggest that Joseph Seligman as head of the firm was invariably all business, there was a warm, human side to his character which his brothers must have appreciated as a counterbalance to the incessant lectures on banking matters they were subject to from New York. He could scold William for his high living, for example, but Joseph was obviously pleased with the acceptance William had gained in Parisian society. On December 19, 1877, Joseph wrote to Richard C. McCormick, United States Commissioner General, to ask him:

> *In filling the offices for Commissioners in Paris, please do not omit to appoint Mr. William Seligman, of course as Honorary Commissioner, without pay . . . as brother William is at the head of a large American banking house in Paris and entertains all nice Americans, he is well fitted for the office.*

William got the appointment and helped to negotiate reciprocal trade treaties with France.

Nor was Joseph above giving parties himself. When Grant left the White House, Joseph and Jesse held a dinner at Delmonico's for the former President and "forty or fifty" guests. "General Grant was then fully relieved from all public cares," Judge Noah Davis later recalled, "and felt that the honors shown him on that occasion were the tribute of pure and disinterested esteem and affection . . . He gave a warm expression of his esteem for the Seligmans and for their services to the country and himself." Later when Grant toured the world, other Seligman brothers entertained him in London and in Frankfurt.

It would be easy to imagine that the Seligmans' influence in Washington was primarily a result of the brothers' long-time friendship with Ulysses S. Grant. However, Rutherford Birchard Hayes and his temperance-minded wife, Lucy, had scarcely settled into the White House when newly appointed Secretary of the Treasury John Sherman, former Senator from Ohio, asked Joseph Seligman, Levi P. Morton, August Belmont, and several other bankers to come to Washington to "advise him on what he considered a very important matter."

According to Edwin R. A. Seligman, Joseph's son, the Secretary told the group "you are considered to be the greatest banking experts in this country. I need your assistance. I want each of you to go into a separate room and work out a plan for refunding the balance of the Government war debt and resuming specie payments."

Each banker submitted his recommendations. A week later, Sherman sent for Joseph Seligman and told him that his plan was "by all odds the clearest and most practical and that it would be adopted." The plan called for building up a gold reserve of approximately 40% of the greenbacks outstanding through the sale of bonds for coin. At the same time, Joseph suggested that additional bonds be issued to refund older issues still outstanding. There was to be no contraction of paper money, which was to be redeemed for gold as presented and paid out again to meet Treasury requirements.

Joseph Seligman realized the Treasury might run into difficulty in selling additional bonds, but he had great respect for Sherman's skill in finance, and he was convinced that once the country realized the Secretary was in earnest, public confidence would be restored and the plan would succeed. It did, and on December 17, 1878, paper currency was quoted at par for the first time since 1861.

After working with Secretary Sherman on the Nation's tangled finances, Joseph Seligman and his family decided to take a vacation at the Grand Union Hotel in Saratoga Springs, New York, as they often had in the past. On instructions from Judge Henry Hilton, who ran the hotel as part of the Alexander T. Stewart estate, the Seligman party was refused accommodations. The Judge had decided that Christians did not like the company of Jews.

Although Joseph reportedly "treated the whole matter of his repulse lightly," it was the first well-publicized case of anti-Semitism in America, and the issue became front-page news. When Hilton hinted in a letter to *The New York Times* that the Seligmans had little respect from their banking associates, officials of August Belmont & Co., Drexel, Morgan & Co., Morton Bliss & Co., and The First National Bank responded in print that "Judge Hilton is under a misapprehension as to the relations of the Messrs. Seligman and their associates, which always have been, and are, of the most satisfactory character."

Lucy Hayes probably knew what a Cold Handle Sad Iron was for. But Rutherford, her husband who happened to be President, probably didn't. And then, it's likely that neither knew they had given this testimonial for an ad.

Harper's Weekly

JOHNSON WILSON & CO., NEW YORK, 1894 (FROM: N.Y. PUBLIC LIBRARY PICTURE COLLECTION)

Henry Ward Beecher was shocked to learn Joseph Seligman had been refused accommodations at the Grand Union Hotel. This first widely-publicized case of anti-Semitism in the U. S. prompted a famous Beecher sermon.

COURTESY, MRS. WALTER A. BRITTEN

The Grand Union Hotel, Saratoga Springs, New York, was once the world's largest. It occupied seven acres, had 834 rooms, 1,474 doors, 1,891 windows, twelve miles of carpeting, and one mile of marble tiling. It was demolished on its 150th Anniversary in 1952.

Harper's Weekly

A protest meeting against Judge Hilton's decision to allow only gentiles at the Grand Union Hotel was canceled when William Cullen Bryant, the famed poet-editor, said opinion on the controversy already had been "heard from the mouths of everybody in public places."

A mass protest meeting was called, but canceled at Joseph's request after William Cullen Bryant, the poet, commented the matter was already "heard from the mouths of everybody in public places," and Henry Ward Beecher, the most noted preacher of his day, made the Saratoga Springs incident the subject of his famous "Jew and Gentile" sermon on June 24, 1877:

> *I have the pleasure of the acquaintance of the gentleman whose name has been the occasion of so much excitement–Mr. Seligman. I have summered with his family for several years . . . and I have learned to love and respect them . . . When I heard of the unnecessary offense that has been cast upon Mr. Seligman, I felt that no other person could have been singled out that would have brought home to me the injustice more sensibly than he.*

During the controversy, irate shoppers boycotted A. T. Stewart's Broadway department store –which Judge Hilton also managed–contributing to its failure. It was later acquired by John Wanamaker, the merchant.

About eighteen months later Joseph Seligman, with his wife and their son, George Washington, visited the Theodore Hellmans in New Orleans after spending much of the winter in Jacksonville, Florida. Joseph, aged sixty and troubled with a heart ailment, ate dinner in an upstairs bedroom the evening of Sunday, April 25, 1880, called out to the maid for brandy, drank it, and died.

SEVEN

To improve the golden moment of opportunity, and catch the good that is within our reach, is the great art of life.

—Samuel Johnson, 1709-1784

Monday, April 26, 1880, the day after Joseph Seligman died, the office of J. & W. Seligman & Co. at 59 Exchange Place was closed. Jesse Seligman, the *New York Herald* reported the next day, became "head of the banking firm."

Among letters of condolence received by the firm, Secretary of the Navy Richard W. Thompson's was typical in its praise of Joseph:

> *Not alone in the house with which he has been so long associated will this void be felt, but its influence will extend through a large circle of business acquaintances who, during his life, so readily recognized his firm integrity in the pursuit of what he believed to be right and just. In my official capacity as Secretary of the Navy, I have had especial opportunities to understand and appreciate his character.*

Horatio Alger, Jr., the noted author, had tutored Joseph's children for a dozen years. Some believe that part of the inspiration for his remarkably successful "rags to riches" books for boys came from Joseph's real life experiences. Alger maintained that had Joseph "devoted his energies to any one of the so-called learned professions, he could hardly have failed of achieving distinction. His remarkable judgment . . . fitting him perhaps in a special degree for the judicial office." It must have pleased Alger to learn that Joseph willed a bequest to The Newsboys' Lodging House, an establishment where the writer spent a good deal of his time seeking local color and ideas for his books.

Isaac Newton Seligman, Joseph's son who had come to New York after being trained in New Orleans in "a back room where I worked over books for $10 a week," and his brother, David Joseph Seligman, were admitted to the firm shortly after their father's death. Jesse's son, Henry, returned from San Francisco to work in the New York office, and James' son, Jefferson, fresh from studying medicine in Germany, began his business career with Seligman, Hellman & Co. in New Orleans under the tutelage of Theodore Hellman.

The New Orleans branch manager was an unusual man. His directorates ranged from the Louisiana National Bank to the Jockey Club, and he was Honorary Commander of the Fourth Battery of the Louisiana Field Artillery known as "Hellman's Guards." According to his son, George S. Hellman the art critic, he was very superstitious and believed in dreams. George Hellman claimed his father, in a dream, "had seen two numbers recur and recur. It was the time of the great California Lottery. So the next morning . . . he bought the two numbers . . . They cost twenty dollars apiece." He sold one ticket to a friend. "It won the fifteen thousand dollar prize. The number Theodore retained—154077—won the greatest prize of all—a hundred thousand dollars." When Seligman, Hellman & Co.

Horatio Alger, Jr., said Isaac Newton Seligman, "was a tutor in my father's family for a dozen years. He wrote some of his books in our house." Alger was extremely nearsighted; at times mistook an apple for a billiard ball.

Munsey's Magazine

J. & W. SELIGMAN & CO.

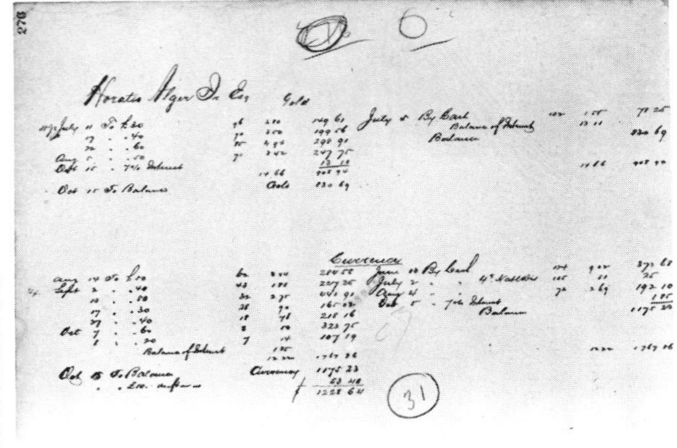

Page 276 *of* Monthly Statements, No. 2., J. & W. S. & Co. *is conclusive proof that in 1873, Horatio Alger, Jr., the noted childrens' author, maintained his account at the firm. Alger, whose creative ability was insignificant, really believed the poor boy had an opportunity to grow up, marry the rich man's daughter, and get rich himself. In effect, although he wrote about 120 books, he rewrote the same story 119 times. A Harvard graduate, he became a minister in the Unitarian Church; then a famous writer.*

was closed for good in 1881, Theodore moved to New York, and Jefferson Seligman became a cashier at J. & W. Seligman & Co.

As a businessman, in the words of *The Daily Graphic,* Jesse Seligman was "cool, circumspect and conservative . . . He carefully weighs all his opinions before expressing them, and his word, once given, is as good as his bond." The new head of the firm was "simple almost to austerity."

Records of the New York Telephone Company show that J. & W. Seligman & Co. was first listed in the telephone directory in 1881 and the office could be reached by asking Central for "New 777." It even may be that Jesse first learned through the newly installed instrument of the shooting of President James Abram Garfield.

Less than three months after his inauguration, while walking through the Baltimore & Potomac depot in the Capital, Garfield was shot by Charles J. Guiteau, a disgruntled office seeker. To make him more comfortable, the President was taken to a cottage at Elberon, New Jersey, not far from Jesse Seligman's summer home at Long Branch. Postmaster General Thomas L. Lane later recalled, Jesse Seligman "with that thoughtful consideration and tenderness which distinguished the man . . . showed the official family of the dying President, courtesies and kindness . . . which can never be forgotten." Chester Alan Arthur was sworn in as President on September 19, 1881.

During the year, J. & W. Seligman & Co. moved temporarily from 59 Exchange Place because the building it occupied was to be torn down in an early instance of the rebuilding of the financial district which never seems to end. In place of the old structure rose the Mills Building, praised by a contemporary as "the Wall Street architectural wonder of its day . . . surrounded by rat-traps of only three or four stories." The firm was at 94 Broadway for a short time, then returned to its old address—probably in 1882—and to new second floor offices.

About this time, eighteen-year-old Albert Strauss was hired as an office boy for five dollars a week. Four years later his twenty-one-year-old brother, Frederick, came to work as a correspondence clerk at four times the pay. Jesse Seligman may have been aware of their employment, but he was involved in a far more important matter started in 1879 when Ferdinand Marie de Lesseps, the seventy-five-year-

The oldest son of Joseph Seligman, David Joseph had been trained in California; was admitted as a partner circa 1880. He died unexpectedly, barely forty-seven years old, following an appendicitis operation in 1897.

COURTESY, MRS. RHODA S. PRUD'HOMME

The Daily Graphic

An anonymous contemporary, quoted in The Daily Graphic, *said, "I regard Jesse Seligman [shown seated in his private office] as among the ablest financiers of Wall street and America...he has made a business of success."*

old French engineer who completed the Suez Canal, decided he wanted to dig another ditch—this time across the Isthmus of Panama.

In the Fall of 1880, William Seligman in Paris proposed that the Seligmans associate with the de Lesseps Company. Jesse, who had struggled across the Isthmus on his way to California twenty-eight years before, asked William and Max Hellman to start negotiations. By October 4, 1880, the *New York Herald* was reporting:

"The Syndicate for the construction of the Panama Canal was definitely formed yesterday, Mr. Seligman and Messrs. Loubeyran and Denier are at the head of it . . . The American Committee . . . will consist of J. & W. Seligman & Co., Drexel, Morgan & Co., and Winslow, Lanier & Co. . . . 'It is a private undertaking altogether,'" Jesse Seligman said, "'and we have every confidence that an enterprise of this kind will pay.'"

Although Jesse thought the Panama Canal was a fine idea, the majority of his countrymen didn't. Public opinion opposed the construction of a canal under French control. Yet, stock issued to raise money for the canal sold easily.

The estimated cost of the canal had been $114,000,000; almost $400,000,000 was spent when the project failed in early 1889 after being only one-third completed. Ferdinand de Lesseps left Panama to return to France where he faced an investigation for corruption, of which the undertaking had been accused from the start. His honor was left intact.

There was also an investigation by the United States Congress into the purchasing of supplies and equipment. The Special Committee reported no wrongdoing, but it did bring out that an old friend of the Seligmans, Richard W. Thompson, had been persuaded to resign as Secretary of the Navy to become Chairman of the American Canal Committee because his name would give the project broader support among Americans. It also disclosed that Jesse Seligman had first tried to persuade former President Ulysses S. Grant to accept the Chairmanship at $24,000 a year. When Jesse was asked why by the Committee, he answered frankly, "General Grant was a bosom friend of mine, and I always look out for my friends."

Grant would have been better off if Jesse had been able to look out for him, for while the ill-fated

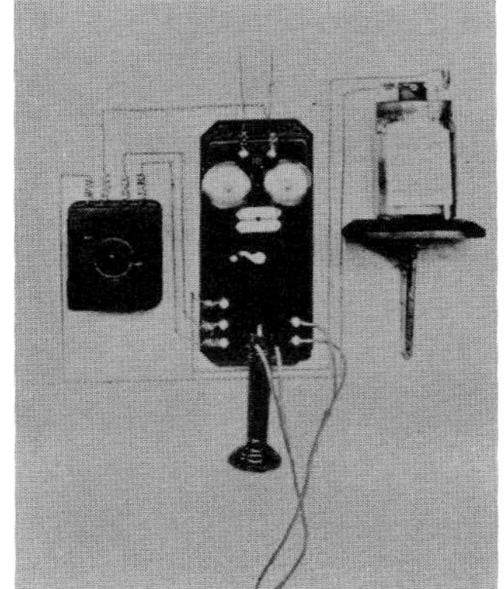

J. & W. Seligman & Co. had its first telephone in 1881; by 1899, the firm had two! The original number was "New 777"—a contrast to today's "HA 2-0400" with 135 extensions and multiple trunk lines in the offices at 65 Broadway.

Albert Strauss (top) was born in New York on August 26, 1864. His brother, Frederick (below), was born on August 11, 1865. Both enrolled at the College of the City of New York, class of 1884, but left for lack of means after three years. Many years later, the College conferred degrees upon them and they also were elected to Phi Beta Kappa. Albert joined J. & W. Seligman & Co. in 1882. His brother, for four years, worked at a small export company before joining the firm in May 1866. The pictures were taken in May of 1889.

A prospectus for the French Panama Canal venture announced "The public subscription" for 590,000 shares "will be opened in Europe and America the 7, 8 and 9 of December 1880." The firm's name is on the back page.

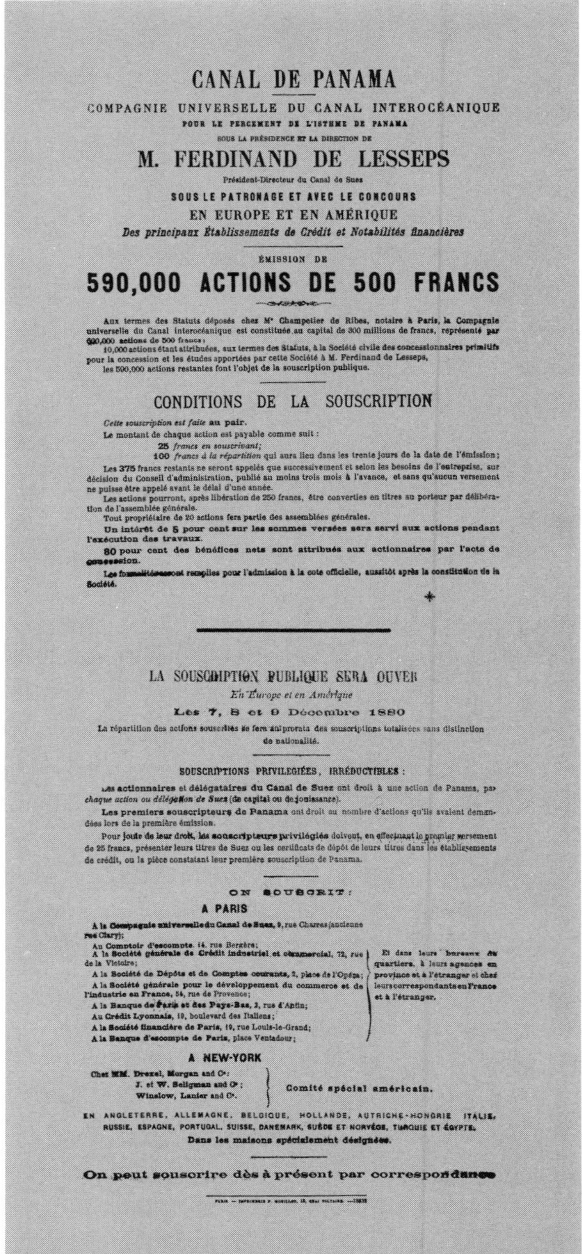

CANAL DE PANAMA

COMPAGNIE UNIVERSELLE DU CANAL INTEROCÉANIQUE
POUR LE PERCEMENT DE L'ISTHME DE PANAMA
SOUS LA PRÉSIDENCE ET LA DIRECTION DE

M. FERDINAND DE LESSEPS

Président-Directeur du Canal de Suez

SOUS LE PATRONAGE ET AVEC LE CONCOURS
EN EUROPE ET EN AMÉRIQUE
Des principaux Établissements de Crédit et Notabilités financières

ÉMISSION DE

590,000 ACTIONS DE 500 FRANCS

Aux termes des Statuts déposés chez Me Champetier de Ribes, notaire à Paris, la Compagnie universelle du Canal interocéanique est constituée au capital de 300 millions de francs, représenté par 600,000 actions de 500 francs;

10,000 actions étant attribuées, aux termes des Statuts, à la Société civile des concessionnaires primitifs pour la concession et les études apportées par cette Société à M. Ferdinand de Lesseps,

les 590,000 actions restantes font l'objet de la souscription publique.

CONDITIONS DE LA SOUSCRIPTION

Cette souscription est faite **au pair.**

Le montant de chaque action est payable comme suit :

25 *francs en souscrivant;*
100 *francs à la répartition* qui aura lieu dans les trente jours de la date de l'émission;

Les 375 francs restants ne seront appelés que successivement et selon les besoins de l'entreprise, sur décision du Conseil d'administration, publié au moins trois mois à l'avance, et sans qu'aucun versement ne puisse être appelé avant le délai d'une année.

Les actions pourront, après libération de 250 francs, être converties en titres au porteur par délibération de l'assemblée générale.

Tout propriétaire de 20 actions fera partie des assemblées générales.

Un intérêt de 5 pour cent sur les sommes versées sera servi aux actions pendant l'exécution des travaux.

80 pour cent des bénéfices nets sont attribués aux actionnaires par l'acte de concession.

Les formalités seront remplies pour l'admission à la cote officielle, aussitôt après la constitution de la Société.

LA SOUSCRIPTION PUBLIQUE SERA OUVER

En Europe et en Amérique

Les 7, 8 et 9 Décembre 1880

La répartition des actions souscrites se fera au prorata des souscriptions totalisées sans distinction de nationalité.

SOUSCRIPTIONS PRIVILEGIÉES, IRRÉDUCTIBLES :

Les actionnaires et **délégataires du Canal de Suez** ont droit à une action de Panama, par *chaque action ou délégation de Suez* (de capital ou de jouissance).

Les premiers souscripteurs de Panama ont droit au nombre d'actions qu'ils avaient demandées lors de la première émission.

Pour jouir de leur droit, les **souscripteurs privilégiés** doivent, en effectuant le premier versement de 25 francs, présenter leurs titres de Suez ou les certificats de dépôt de leurs titres dans les établissements de crédit, ou la pièce constatant leur première souscription de Panama.

ON SOUSCRIT :

A PARIS

A la **Compagnie universelle du Canal de Suez,** 9, rue Charras (ancienne rue Clary);
Au **Comptoir d'escompte,** 14, rue Bergère;
A la **Société générale de Crédit industriel et commercial,** 72, rue de la Victoire;
A la **Société de Dépôts et de Comptes courants,** 2, place de l'Opéra;
A la **Société générale pour le développement du commerce et de l'industrie en France,** 54, rue de Provence;
A la **Banque de Paris et des Pays-Bas,** 3, rue d'Antin;
Au **Crédit Lyonnais,** 19, boulevard des Italiens;
A la **Société financière de Paris,** 19, rue Louis-le-Grand;
A la **Banque d'escompte de Paris,** place Ventadour;

Et dans leurs bureaux de quartiers, à leurs agences en province et à l'étranger et chez leurs correspondants en France et à l'étranger.

A NEW-YORK

Chez MM. **Drexel, Morgan and Co;**
J. et W. Seligman and Co;
Winslow, Lanier and Co.

Comité spécial américain.

EN ANGLETERRE, ALLEMAGNE, BELGIQUE, HOLLANDE, AUTRICHE-HONGRIE, ITALIE, RUSSIE, ESPAGNE, PORTUGAL, SUISSE, DANEMARK, SUÈDE ET NORVÈGE, TURQUIE ET ÉGYPTE.

Dans les maisons spécialement désignées.

On peut souscrire dès à présent par correspondance

Panama Canal project was in full swing, he was having trouble looking out for himself. The General, after investing $100,000, had become a silent partner in Grant & Ward, an investment firm headed by Ferdinand Ward, a glib minister's son whose quick success in finance had led some to call him "the young Napoleon of Wall Street."

On Sunday, May 4, 1884, Ward went to General Grant and told him The Marine National Bank, in which Grant & Ward deposited large amounts of money, was in trouble and that to save the bank he needed $300,000 for one day only. Grant managed to get a personal loan for half the amount, which he turned over to Ward, who cashed the check and put the money into his pocket. By May 7, The Marine National Bank closed as a result of overdrafts by Grant & Ward, and when the investment firm itself failed soon after, it came out that Ward had milched the firm for more than $2,000,000.

These failures were a factor in the Panic of 1884. General Grant, ruined financially and dying of cancer, sadly remarked: "I have made it a rule of my life to trust a man long after other people gave him up; but I don't see how I can trust any human being again."

Jesse Seligman, according to family tradition, offered the General assistance, which was refused. Later, when Grant was in even worse financial straits, Jesse prevailed upon him to accept funds to enable him to live in comparative comfort while he raced against time to complete his *Personal Memoirs* to provide for his family. Death came July 23, 1885. In January of that same year, Abraham Seligman had died in Frankfurt.

That was the year cable cars first ran on Amsterdam Avenue in New York City. Democratic President Grover Cleveland took the Navy Department Fiscal Agency away from Seligman Brothers in London. And James Seligman, a member of the New York Stock Exchange's Governing Committee, was appointed chairman of the Committee on Government Securities in May. He later served on the Exchange's Finance and Admissions Committee.

Being a member of the New York Stock Exchange was serious business, but not all work and no play, as *Harper's Magazine* pointed out in November. "The nervous force necessarily expended in rapid reasoning and quick decision is often directed into other channels to relieve the overtasked brain." For the younger members of the "broker tribe," there was "an annual regatta of its rowing association . . . base-ball contests with the callow athletes of popular colleges, or . . . friendly struggles among themselves, in which the 'Good Boys' . . . pitted against the 'Bad Boys.' "

The biggest party of all took place during the Christmas season, when the membership "luxuriates in the blowing of tin horns and bugles, smashing of broker hats, pelting with blown bladders, wet towels, and surreptitious snow-balls, and in the sly insertion of the cooling crystals between the collars and necks of unsuspecting brethren. Hot pennies are sometimes substituted."

New York City grew fast in the mid-Eighties, and with new devices—telegraph, stock ticker, electric lights, telephone, fire warning systems, traffic signals, burglar alarms—came the ubiquitous utility pole to clutter the City's sidewalks. Robert Daley, the newspaper correspondent, declared that:

> *Some of the poles carried seven or ten or a dozen crosstrees, outstretched arms as closely spaced as railroad ties . . . Single poles were freighted with a hundred wires, or two hundred . . . In places a man could stand on the sidewalk peering up toward a sky he couldn't*

J. & W. SELIGMAN & CO.

Grant & Ward failed in 1884. A contemporary commercial artist of the late Nineteenth Century, Wu Yu Ju, made this picture showing the event. The writing says that "there is a terrible Panic among the general public."

READ THE SIXTH PAGE.
CIRCULATION OVER 100,000 EVERY DAY.
ADVERTISE YOUR WANTS.
Cheapest Rates in the City.

The World.

READ THE SIXTH PAGE.
CIRCULATION OVER 100,000 EVERY DAY.
ADVERTISE YOUR WANTS.
Cheapest Rates in the City.

VOL. XXV., NO. 8,472. NEW YORK, THURSDAY, OCTOBER 30, 1884.—WITH SUPPLEMENT. PRICE TWO CENTS.

THE ROYAL FEAST OF BELSHAZZAR BLAINE AND THE MONEY KINGS.

The poor went begging, insinuated The World, *while 200 "monopolists" dined at Delmonico's to honor Republican standard bearer James G. Blaine and "raise a corruption fund of $500,000." The 1884 campaign was one of the dirtiest. Jesse Seligman is caricatured third from right.*

First to ride a tricycle in Washington, D. C., she ran for President in 1884; lost. In 1888 with Alfred H. Love as running mate, she lost again. Jefferson Seligman may have voted for her; he supported woman suffrage. She was Belva Ann Lockwood.

COLLECTION OF CARL J. WHITE

see because the hundreds of wires were laced together as impenetrably as the canopy of leaves of a tree in summer.

A law passed in 1884 required wires to be placed underground. Nothing much happened. Then came the Blizzard of 1888. On March 11, it rained sixty-five hundredths of an inch; on the twelfth, it snowed sixteen and one-half inches. During the blizzard, Theodore Hellman, according to his son George, "walked all the way up to our house from Wall Street, stopping frequently at corner saloons to get drinks of whiskey to keep him going. He arrived exhausted . . . His frozen mustache broke off." On Tuesday, March 13, it snowed another three inches and on the next and final day of the storm, one and one-fourth inches. Wires strung above the City snapped, snagged, and sizzled to the street. Alarmed at the danger, New Yorkers made it a campaign issue which swept Hugh J. Grant into the Mayor's office that Fall. One of his first official acts was to tell the various utility companies if they didn't take down their wires and put them underground, the City would do it for them. In time, the City did.

Jefferson Seligman and his cousin, Henry, became partners of the firm in July, and Jefferson was admitted as a member of the New York Stock Exchange. Seats that year sold from a low of $17,000 to a $24,000 high.

Another storm took place in 1888 – New York's first ticker tape parade. It was "both humorous and picturesque, in the way of public demonstrations," *Frank Leslie's Illustrated Newspaper* maintained

Harper's New Monthly Magazine

"The activities of stock-brokerage involve exhaustive drain of vital energy," R. Wheatley wrote in Harper's New Monthly Magazine *in November 1885. "The nervous force necessarily expended in rapid reasoning and quick decision is often directed into other channels to relieve the overtasked brain." Harry Wolf sketched one of the other channels—Christmas Carnival at the New York Stock Exchange.*

on October 27. "The passing of a procession through Wall Street . . . was the occasion of . . . a veritable blizzard, of white 'tape' – those interminable ribbons of white paper which are run through the 'tickers' to receive the impress of the telegraphic stock reports. Roll after roll was unwound and sent streaming down from the windows upon the heads and shoulders of the enthusiastic promenaders, until they were as hopelessly entangled in white tape as litigants in court sometimes are in red tape . . . to the great hilarity of brokers and messenger-boys."

That Fall, Grover Cleveland received more popular votes than Benjamin Harrison, but lost on electoral votes; and Equal Rights candidate Belva Ann Lockwood, a female lawyer and suffragette who sometimes wore red stockings, did very poorly. The firm's London branch was reappointed Fiscal Agents for the Navy by the new President.

The Sherman Silver Purchase Act, passed in 1890, authorized the Treasury to purchase a specified amount of silver bullion monthly and to issue Treasury notes for payment as legal tender. This was followed by the highly protective McKinley Tariff Act and the dire predictions of opponents of the silver bill and protective tariff began to come true. Government revenues declined; gold exports increased. A period of depression began which would culminate in the Panic of 1893. Gold standard advocates urged currency reform. President Harrison, sympathetic to their views, commissioned Jesse Seligman to go abroad in the Fall of 1891 to arrange an International Bimetallism Conference "to secure

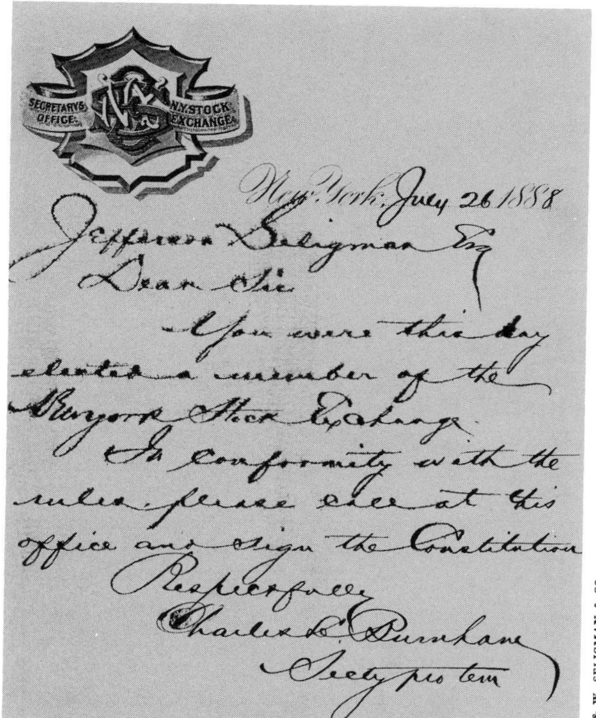

SECRETARY'S OFFICE — N.Y. STOCK EXCHANGE

New York, July 26 1888

Jefferson Seligman Esq

Dear Sir

You were this day elected a member of the Newyork Stock Exchange.

In conformity with the rules, please call at this office and sign the Constitution

Respectfully

Charles L. Burnham

Secty pro tem

J. & W. SELIGMAN & CO.

Jefferson Seligman became a partner in July 1888. He also was admitted as a member of the New York Stock Exchange on July 26. New Members, Harper's New Monthly Magazine *said, were somewhat prone to hazing. "If the welcome be peculiarly hearty, the novice may receive a free ride around the Board Room, the transfer of quotations from the blackboard to the back of his coat."*

Rain–.65 inch–on March 11 topped with 20.9 inches of snow during the next three days knocked down electrical wires and gave New Yorkers the Blizzard of 1888. New Street, looking toward Wall Street, was blocked by snow.

MUSEUM OF THE CITY OF NEW YORK

the establishment of a common ratio of value between gold and silver." Jesse conferred with German political and financial leaders and later with French leaders. William Seligman made speeches in behalf of the Conference. But their work came to nothing – Europe seemed too willing to use the United States as a dumping ground for surplus silver.

While Jesse was in Europe in 1892, Prince André Poniatowski, a nephew of Poland's King Stanislaus, visited the United States and called on the Seligman firm. Writing about his experiences more than thirty-five years later, the Prince remembered that the offices of J. & W. Seligman & Co. were "very much like those of the bankers in the City of London, of great simplicity, located on the first floor of the Mills Building, in those days the largest building of that type in New York. It was of no special architectural style, but, as the British say 'substantial.' "

After opening a checking account, the Prince asked Isaac Newton Seligman to arrange for a number of introductions and the banker "responded with a rapidity of decision, characteristic of businessmen the first of this type I met personally. With a few words he outlined to me what course of procedure to adopt and which people to see. While I was trying to express my appreciation to him, he held in one hand the telephone through which he arranged a meeting for the same day . . . while with the other hand he was ringing the bell for a stenographer, to whom he dictated a letter of introduction accrediting me in Chicago to Mr. Lyman Gage, President of the Bank that was their correspondent in that city."

Isaac Newton took the Prince to lunch on the tenth floor of the Mills Building "where there was a sort of grillroom reserved exclusively for the tenants and the owner of the place," and he believed Isaac Newton's partners at the table could almost read each others' minds. They immediately "knew as much about me as he did himself. They had watched him the moment we sat down and from his demeanour . . . if it had been a question of a bank statement, each partner would have been able to scribble right down on the tablecloth . . . the amount involved."

Some American customs left Poniatowski cold. He went with Isaac Newton by ferryboat to spend a weekend at Seabright, New Jersey. "As soon as we left New York," Prince André said, "the iced drinks circulated on the deck, and with more avidity than prudence I accepted the offer Seligman made me of a large tumbler of sarsaparilla, a hygienic drink, something like a cross between beer and a mouthwash." Guests of today's commuters to New York may feel similarly disappointed with ferryboat coffee.

While Poniatowski made notes on Americans, Grover Cleveland was elected President. He took office for the second time in March 1893, and in April, he took the U. S. Navy Fiscal Agency away from Seligman Brothers in London again. Cleveland was almost immediately faced with the Panic of 1893. Commerce and industry were at a low ebb, agriculture was depressed, and Government revenues declined sharply. To raise money, the Government sold bonds, and J. & W. Seligman & Co. participated in underwriting two issues the next year.

Jesse Seligman, having turned over control of the firm to his nephew, Isaac Newton, as his health began to fail, received a blow which George S. Hellman says "darkened his declining years." It came from The Union League Club in New York which he served for many years as Vice-President. Theo-

Transfers of Navy funds to Seligman Brothers typically were handled by letter which required the Navy Secretary's signature. Benjamin F. Tracy signed one dated January 12, 1892, which was received, noted, and filed.

Navy Department,
OFFICE OF THE SECRETARY,
Washington, Jany 12, 1892.

Gentlemen:

A requisition has this day been issued in your favor for Two hundred and fifty thousand dollars ($250,000), the proceeds of which you will please credit the Department by draft on London at sixty days sight.

Very respectfully,
B. F. Tracy
Secretary of the Navy

Messrs.
Seligman Brothers,
Care J. & W. Seligman & Co.,
New York.

J. & W. SELIGMAN & CO.

Prince André Poniatowski visited the firm in 1892 and said the partners "received me immediately and with a courtesy that demonstrated to me on what complimentary terms their Paris house had written to them about me."

D'un Siecle à L'autre

dore Seligman, his son, was proposed for membership and was blackballed because he was a Jew. Jesse Seligman resigned and never entered the Club again. The City's press made much of the affront, just as it had protested the incident at Saratoga Springs sixteen years earlier, and the next week, New York City made a point of showing the esteem in which it held him. The Duke of Varagua was planning a visit to the City and a drive to City Hall to be received by the Mayor. The committee in charge of arrangements asked Jesse to lend his carriage. In the Seligman carriage, the Duke and Duchess were driven through the streets, attended by bands, troops, and mounted police. The Seligman horses, coachmen, and footmen wore rosettes in tribute to a Spanish noble, while the people of New York paid tribute to Jesse Seligman.

Jesse failed visibly after the Union League affair and the following April, he left for a six-months' "trip across the continent." En route to California, he contracted pneumonia. He died on April 23, 1894, at Coronado Beach, in the State where he had been a pioneer in his youth.

"Two thousand people turned up for his funeral" at Temple Emanu-El in New York City, Geoffrey T. Hellman, Jesse Seligman's great-nephew, wrote for *The New Yorker* on October 30, 1954, "Among them, besides a raft of Seligmans, were Seth Low, General Horace Porter, Carl Schurz, John Wanamaker, John Crosby Brown, William M. Evarts, Oscar S. Straus, Cornelius N. Bliss, Bishop Henry C. Potter, Moritz Rodenburg, and James Back. Messrs. Low, Porter, Schurz, Wanamaker, Brown, Evarts, Straus, Bliss, and Potter went inside, but Messrs. Rodenburg and Back remained outside and mingled with the crowd on the street. They were presently arrested as pickpockets by detectives and identified as Nos. 23 and 2018, respectively, in the Rogues' Gallery."

The New York *News,* May 2, 1894, said, "It took twenty policemen . . . to keep people at the Temple from getting in when the gates were opened to ad-

COURTESY, MRS. JOSEPH L. SELIGMAN

Slender, pale, and gray-bearded, Isaac Newton Seligman looked older than he was. His typical dress in the office was a black frock coat with striped pants, fancy waistcoat, and lemon-colored spats. He was Joseph's son.

The firm had offices in the Mills Building, 1882-1907, built on the site of 59 Exchange Place. In 1893, the partly shade-drawn second floor window read "J & W Seligman & Co. Bankers." The building was torn down in 1926.

J. & W. SELIGMAN & CO.

mit people who had a right to enter earlier . . . The last delegation to arrive was sixty members of the Union League Club, headed by President Porter."

Although the firm was well-known for its international connections, the character of J. & W. Seligman & Co.'s business began to change rapidly after Isaac Newton became the dominant partner in New York. Financial needs of corporations and the cities expanding within the Nation absorbed Wall Street's attention, and J. & W. Seligman & Co. was a leader in raising capital for industrial and urban growth. In addition to its contributions to the growth of railroads and urban transit systems, some of the security underwritings in which the firm participated during the early 1890's were for the Grand Rapids Gas Light Company, Boston City Park, Chicago Sanitary District, St. Paul Gas Light Company, and the City of New York. On April 15, 1897—forty-two days after becoming President—William McKinley reappointed Seligman Brothers Fiscal Agents for the U. S. Navy. The London branch was

WILLIAM McKINLEY,

PRESIDENT OF THE UNITED STATES OF AMERICA,

To all who may see these Presents, Greeting:

Know Ye, That reposing special trust and confidence in the Fidelity and Abilities of Isaac Seligman and Leopold Seligman, trading under the name, style, and firm of Seligman Brothers, at London, England, I do, by and with the advice and consent of the Senate, appoint them to be Special Fiscal Agents of the U. S. Navy Department, at that place.

They are, therefore, carefully and diligently to discharge their duties as such Special Fiscal Agents, by doing and performing all manner of things thereunto appertaining; and they are to observe and follow the orders and directions which they may from time to time receive from the President of the United States and the Secretary of the Navy.

Given under my hand, at the City of Washington, this fifteenth day of April, in the year of our Lord one thousand eight hundred and ninety-seven, and in the one hundred and twenty-first year of the Independence of the United States.

William McKinley

By the President:

John D. Long

Secretary of the Navy.

Seligman Brothers were reappointed the Navy Department's Fiscal Agents by William McKinley in 1897. John D. Long, who was Secretary of the Navy, and the President, signed the appointment.

to keep the appointment until 1913, and it also served as Fiscal Agents for the State Department at times during these years.

The branches of the firm continued to work together, but the community of interest, so strong during the early years, was weakening; death had loosened old family ties. Aware of the need for change, Isaac Newton Seligman went to Europe in the late Spring of 1897 to arrange to reorganize the firm and to divorce the New York branch from its European associates. A "Family Liquidation Agreement" of July 1, 1897—which was not put into effect entirely until 1900—provided for dividing assets of the firm which were held jointly by the eight founders or their estates.

Coming to a meeting of minds was not easy, but finally it was agreed the New York branch would be an independent firm, and each of the four Seligmans in Europe—William, Henry, Leopold, and Isaac—retained a personal interest in it. Conversely, partners of J. & W. Seligman & Co. in New York—James, Isaac Newton, Henry, and Jefferson Seligman—kept an interest in the three newly separated European firms. The agreement was not entirely satisfactory to Isaac Newton Seligman, however, and he referred to his uncle Isaac as "the London Shylock;" to William in Paris as "too greedy," and to Henry in Frankfurt as "too cautious to be a banker." Nevertheless, it stood until revised in 1905 when J. & W. Seligman & Co.'s capital was increased substantially.

During its first year on its own—July 1, 1897 to June 30, 1898—things went well, but, as there had always been, there were moments of sadness and anxiety for members of the firm. Soon after the separation from the overseas branches, Isaac Newton's brother, David J., died at Long Branch, New Jersey. And, if the United States was beginning to flex its muscles industrially, it also insisted that its power be felt internationally. Cuba's struggle for independence from Spain became acute. American sympathy, whipped up by the "atrocity" stories head-

Lyman J. Gage of Illinois refused Cleveland's offer of the Treasury portfolio; accepted it from William McKinley. Historian Margaret Leech relates Gage was "not a great Secretary of the Treasury but a responsible public servant."

LIBRARY OF CONGRESS

lined by the Hearst newspapers, clamored for war. McKinley believed there was no need to fight with Spain, but any hopes he had of arranging a peaceful solution were blown sky high along with the U.S. battleship *Maine* on February 16, 1898.

At the time, an old friend of Isaac Newton Seligman was Secretary of the Treasury. He was Lyman J. Gage, former President of the First National Bank of Chicago, a Gold Democrat – the man to whom Isaac Newton had introduced Prince Poniatowski. Gage often conferred with Isaac Newton, and the banker wrote to London on March 25 about what was going on at home. "The markets are declining daily and don't anticipate any panic or trouble if hostilities should be commenced," he said. "Secy Gage, who telephones us . . . informed us that conditions were unchanged altho' perhaps more 'strained.' " He went on to tell his London associates that "altho' I think it perhaps a wild goose chase, I may cable you early next week to consult Rothschilds (perhaps also our Paris folks to confer with the Rothschilds) & ascertain what pressure could be brought on Spain to put a stop to this inhuman warfare in some shape."

Whether this idea was ever pursued is not known, but on April 22, Isaac Newton reported, "War has practically begun & naturally everything out 'of joint' here." War was official April 24. Two days later, the New York banker was in Washington to discuss "many matters of interest . . . Gage has not yet quite made up his mind as to whether he will issue 100 or 200" million in bonds. Gage finally issued $200,000,000 in three per cent bonds, and J. & W. Seligman & Co. received an allotment of $5,000,000.

On June 2, 1898, Seligman Brothers, London, was appointed Fiscal Agents of the U. S. Navy at Manila and Honolulu to handle the Army and Navy payrolls. This was simply an extension of the London Agency's activities, but it led Isaac Newton to think about opening banks in the two cities – an idea later abandoned.

If the Spanish-American War was one of the Nation's least necessary, as McKinley believed, it was also, happily, one of its shortest. It ended with an armistice August 12, less than four months after it had officially begun. Within a week, Isaac Newton observed that the stock market "is absolutely rampant. All industrial undertakings now in demand & altho' we are doing well we should have made a great deal more money, but I was rather afraid to go in too heavily in these enterprises."

The Spanish-American War focused attention on the need for a quick passage between the Atlantic and Pacific for United States fighting ships. This revived hope for the dormant Panama Canal project, but Isaac Newton was aware that France's tendency to side with Spain was likely to be a fatal handicap for the old, French-dominated company. While fighting was still going on in May 1898, he wrote his associates, "It is my impression that the unfriendly attitude of France in our present conflict with Spain, will make it absolutely impossible to effect any satisfactory arrangements in Wash^{ton} . . . as to aiding the Panama Canal C^{o}. It is unfortunate & it is not . . . improbable that the Nicaragua will now be vigorously pushed, as the necessity of an interoceanic Canal has been vividly brought before the public attention by the 'Oregon' circumnavigating the Cape." The news of the ***USS***

Congress finally decided on a Panama route for the interoceanic canal and the United States purchased the holdings of the French company. After about a decade, much of the machinery was rusted; useless.

Oregon's steaming from the Pacific around the tip of South America to the Caribbean had been one of the highlights of the naval campaign.

By the time the War was over, the Seligmans understood that if the Panama Canal project was ever to be completed it would need help from the United States Government. Moreover, if the original Canal investors were to recoup any of the millions poured into the partly-finished ditch and the expensive equipment left rusting for ten years in the tropical jungle, the route for the waterway must be via Panama. But, to get the project going again, the Seligmans and their associates had to overcome more than public distaste for their company's French parentage and its empty treasury. They also were faced with competition from the Nicaraguan Canal Company of New York, a rival promotion started in 1895 to dig an all-American canal across Nicaragua, which had wide support, including that of most members of Congress.

Political and financial maneuvering to decide on a canal route was complicated and drawn out. An American Panama Canal Company was formed at the end of 1899 to raise money to continue work on the project under what appeared to be totally American auspices, but despite its efforts, and those of Senator Marcus Alonzo Hanna, who vigorously advocated the Panama route, a Congressional Commission reported in favor of Nicaragua. Before Congress brought the matter to vote, however, Philippe Bunau-Varilla, the energetic, visionary chief engineer of the Panama Canal arrived in the United States. Isaac Newton Seligman introduced him to Senator Hanna, and the colorful Frenchman, acting as a persuasive one-man lobby, set about changing the country's mind. On March 31, 1901, Isaac Newton commented to Max Hellman in Paris that, "Senator Hanna told me that there is quite a change in the views of the Isthmian Canal Committee, as the Committee is beginning to realize that there are serious disadvantages as to the Nicaraguan Canal. Senator Hanna is of the opinion that if the Panama Canal people can arrange among themselves for the sale to the United States for a lump sum . . . turning over the canal clear of all barnacles, there will be a fair chance of the committee favoring the Panama."

In mid-1902, Congress authorized construction of a Canal across Panama to be controlled by the United States and purchase of the company's holdings and right of way for $40,000,000. Theodore Roosevelt, the hero of San Juan Hill (whom Senator Mark Hanna called "that damned cowboy") was now in the White House. His first task in getting the interocean waterway completed was to make a treaty with Colombia of which Panama was a part. A treaty was finally signed, ratified immediately by the United States, but rejected by

"I took Panama when Bunau-Varilla handed it to me on a silver platter," said Theodore Roosevelt, the man who saw that the U. S. finally did build the Panama Canal. His maxim: "Speak softly and carry a big stick," worked.

New York Globe

Colombia, which wanted more money. The Panamanians, however, wanted independence from Colombia, and the problem was solved, probably with help from Bunau-Varilla, by a revolution.

On November 3, 1903, Panama declared its independence. On the eighteenth, Secretary of State John Hay and Bunau-Varilla, who had become Panama's first Minister to the United States, signed a treaty guaranteeing Panama's independence. It gave $10,000,000 and an annual annuity to the new Republic for the Canal Zone, and work on the Canal got underway again. The waterway was opened to traffic on August 14, 1914, just as Europe plunged into World War I.

While partners of J. & W. Seligman & Co. were still wondering which route the interocean canal would take, Herbert S. Bachman, just shy of sixteen, took an elevated train downtown, walked from the station to the Mills Building, and entered the office of the firm. Emil Carlebach, who handled such matters on January 16, 1899, looked him over and said, "We'll take a chance on you," and hired him as a runner at $5 a week. It was a good gamble; Bachman is still with the firm.

It was a time when horses still looked with disdain on the new gasoline buggy. Movies had just been invented; radio, television, aircraft, nylon, and most electrical gadgets were still in the future. The firm had two telephones in 1899. One was a direct line to the New York Stock Exchange, the other carried all other calls. Bachman had never used a telephone before, but he soon became the voice of James Seligman, one of the founders. Mr. James (as he was called) didn't trust the gadget, and whenever he wanted to make a call, young Bachman had to do it for him. In those days, runners cleaned desks, copied correspondence by the old letterpress method, filled inkwells, and ran messages. "Things were somewhat relaxed most afternoons," Bachman remembers, "and the head runner didn't stay until closing time. He would rush out in the afternoon to 'moonlight' in an undertaking establishment uptown."

Partners usually wore high silk hats and Prince Alberts to the office, while the staff wore "ordinary clothes", Bachman says, "with a stiff, removable collar, buttoned back and front." Most businessmen turned up in the morning in horse drawn carriages, but Henry Seligman walked to the office from the boat basin at the foot of Rector Street after a sail from his home in Atlantic Highlands.

Bachman recalls that about this time a shabbily dressed woman named Hetty Howland Robinson Green occasionally came looking for business in the office of J. & W. Seligman & Co. as she did those of many other leading investment bankers. "To us," he says, "she seemed a poor old woman you'd like to give a handout." Her disreputable clothes and the pail of oatmeal she carried for lunch to save money may have softened Bachman, but older men knew her as Hetty Green, one of the richest and shrewdest financial operators in Wall Street. When she died in 1916, she was worth between one and two hundred million dollars.

Bachman also can remember John W. "Bet-You-a-Million" Gates, who earned his nickname from a willingness to bet on almost anything. A former Illinois hardware store clerk, Gates, says Bachman, "was a very loud man and a good customer. It wasn't unusual for him to give us brokerage orders for 10,000 shares at a time. For a while, Gates

"It is not stretching things so terribly far," Eric Sevareid has written "to say that [Philippe] Bunau-Varilla virtually invented Panama." A one-man lobbyist, he was introduced to Senator Mark Hanna by Isaac Newton Seligman.

Munsey's Magazine

Henry Seligman, who was on the cover of the September 1900 The Successful American, *was a McKinley man. He said "the trouble this year is the apathy shown by the Republicans, who believe . . . they will have a walk over."*

COURTESY, MRS. JOHN D. GORDON

had his own special office at J. & W. Seligman & Co., and his own staff," – but only for a while.

The flamboyant financier organized the American Steel & Wire Company of New Jersey (now a part of United States Steel Corporation) which *The Iron Age* for January 12, 1899, said, "is in the hands of a group of bankers at the head of which are J. & W. Seligman & Co. of New York, and the Illinois Trust & Savings Bank of Chicago . . . The entire amount of capital to be furnished . . . will be $28,000,000." Henry Seligman and Frederick Strauss represented the conservative interests on the board of directors, while John W. Gates was chairman.

Trouble among board members began almost at once. One evening, the story goes, while attending a party at the Waldorf, Gates remarked: "We're going to close our steel mills tomorrow." Asked why, he said, "We're short of the stock." The following day the mills were closed. The stock fell from the sixties to the thirties and Gates covered his short positions. He reopened the mills and the stock rallied. Appalled, Henry Seligman commented in a letter April 23, 1900, "There is no doubt there has been an over-production and that [stock] prices have been too high; but had he gone about it in an honest and honorable manner, the company would have been able to work off the surplus stock . . . without affecting the securities. He, however, saw fit to notify the entire public that the company was going to the devil, and, in fact, that the whole iron business was going to pieces."

Henry demanded that a board meeting be called, and said, "I intended to raise a big row at the meeting, and would have done so, had not his lawyer told me to keep quiet and that Mr. Gates would resign the chairmanship . . . Should, however, he refuse . . . there is nothing left for me to do but to get out, as I can not afford to remain in the board, when such a man controls the affairs of the company."

Gates changed his mind about resigning, and the *New York Herald* of May 8 reported what happened. The Board met for two hours, after which Henry Seligman and Frederick Strauss "came from

LIBRARY OF CONGRESS

Peeling paint and cracked windows form an interesting backdrop for Mrs. Hetty Howland Robinson Green at her Bellows Falls, Vermont, home in 1913. A millionaire, all she apparently liked was money—to hoard; not spend.

On July 1, 1901, the first three non-family partners were admitted to the firm. One of them was Emil Carlebach who had long handled much of the foreign business.

COURTESY, HERBERT L. CARLEBACH

the meeting room and announced to the waiting reporters: 'Mr. Gates has not resigned. We have'."

It was during McKinley's first Administration that Washington began to be concerned about the concentration of economic power in the hands of big business "trusts," an area, which until that time, had been considered clearly in the private domain. Corporate executives and financiers throughout the country felt strongly that Government had no place in business, and Henry Seligman was no exception. Called to testify before a Congressional Industrial Commission "on the question of trusts," in November 1899, Henry declined.

Governmental and public attention received by the giant corporate structures being formed tended to upset the stock market. "The bears," according to Henry, "took advantage of the situation and attacked the Trust stocks." Within a few days Henry was writing "we have had quite a panic in Wall Street," which he blamed on "the tightness of money throughout the world." But by the year end in 1899, he could report, "The financial storm has blown over . . . We were in very good

"John W. Gates' refusal," said the New York Herald *of May 8, 1900, "to retire . . . as Chairman . . . while 'under fire' in the courts has resulted in the withdrawal from the directorate of Henry Seligman and Frederick Strauss, who have heretofore represented what Wall Street calls the conservative element in [American Steel & Wire Company of New Jersey] management."*

shape all through the panic, loaning out a great deal of money on the Stock Exchange and having no trouble whatsoever in keeping our margins in splendid shape. We profited very little by the severe break, and I was not very anxious to do so, for the reason that Jeff was very nervous."

In early 1900, the firm kept busy with a large variety of brokerage and underwriting activities. One issue that interested J. & W. Seligman & Co. was the Buffalo Gas Company. "The Company is earning more than its interest," Henry said, "and I believe the bonds to be good." Natural gas was "quite serious" competition, "inasmuch as they sell gas for fuel purposes, and, when once delivered to the houses, the people use it for illuminating purposes." But Henry, understandably oblivious to the future, minimized the competition because, "We are told . . . natural gas is not as abundant as it has been, and the gas experts tell me that it is only a question of time before the oil wells will give out."

He and his partners showed more prescience a year later when Isaac Newton Seligman wrote about "a large steel consolidation" – United States Steel Corporation – which was "enough to take one's breath away . . . We have taken an interest with Morgan in the underwriting . . . I think in the long run it will be a wise move, provided the intelligent and conservative management which is now proposed will continue."

New organization came for J. & W. Seligman & Co., too, during the hot early Summer of 1901, when Henry thought it "practically impossible to do any work." Emil Carlebach, Albert Strauss, and Frederick Strauss were made partners July 1. They were the first men from outside the Seligman family to enter the firm.

EIGHT

Thought once awakened does not again slumber.

—Thomas Carlyle, 1795-1881

J. & W. Seligman & Co. earned world-wide recognition as a leader in Government finance and in international banking during its first forty years. But the firm's greatest business successes came from the development of America's railroads and the transit systems in many of the country's most important cities.

In the final months of the Civil War and in the years that followed, railroad securities were the "wonder" investments of the age. Yet, nearly a year before the firm was founded, Joseph Seligman rejected James' suggestion that they invest in rails with the comment, "I consider this a speculation entirely out of our line, and as certainly none of us *know* enough of Erie, Central, etc., to keep them for an investment, we ought not to buy them at all – let the war once come to an end, and we can make money enough in a legitimate way without gambling or hazard."

His reluctance was short-lived, however, and before J. & W. Seligman & Co. was two years old, the firm had begun to trade in rails along with such master financiers as Commodore Cornelius Vanderbilt, famed for building the New York Central, and Rothschild's U. S. representative, August Belmont. As might be expected in New York's tightly-knit financial community, the partners of the firm also were exposed to the rogues of finance – Daniel (Uncle Daniel) Drew, the ex-cattle drover, James (Jubilee Jim) Fisk, a one-time circus roustabout, and former farmhand Jay Gould.

No record shows which railroad interested the firm first, but a letter dated April 11, 1866, contains an extract of a message to Seligman Brothers:

> *We have just now seen Mr. Drew and he requested us to write you to sell his 5000 shares of Erie in London . . . You will please use your judgement in the matter and endeavor to get the best ruling prices, as Mr Drew is a large operator and if satisfied will give us frequent orders in future.*

Drew was treasurer of the Erie and he forced the price of its stock up and down almost at will. Yet it remained a trading favorite. In March 1867, for example, Joseph told a client in Cincinnati that Erie "is now 59, but we have reason to believe that old Drew is at work and we should not be surprised to see it up to 65 or 66 before two weeks."

J. & W. Seligman & Co. bought and sold Erie Railway securities for years – for customers and for its own account. It even acted as one of Jay Gould's brokers in the first Erie "war" when Cornelius Vanderbilt tried to buy control of the road in January 1868. By that time, Drew had taken Fisk and Gould into the management, and the three willingly sold Vanderbilt millions of dollars worth of stock. The battle earned the Erie the name of "The Scarlet Woman of Wall Street" and failure to

Three infamous men of the 19th Century (from left) Daniel Drew, James Fisk, Jr., and Jay Gould, did not lose any money when they bought and sold Erie stocks. Of the three, Fisk met the most violent death—he was shot by his ex-mistress's boyfriend.

LIBRARY OF CONGRESS

Harper's Weekly

LIBRARY OF CONGRESS

win control of the road cost Vanderbilt $2,000,000.

Regardless of their opinion of Gould's tactics, the Seligmans were loyal to him as a client. When he was jailed for a short time in November 1868, as a result of his railroad manipulations – too sharp even by the liberal standards of the time – they guaranteed his bail.

Less than six months later, Gould stopped playing with trains to try one of the most audacious schemes in American financial history. With the help of political intrigue which embraced, among others, Abel Rathbone Corbin, President Grant's brother-in-law, he set out to corner gold.

Reasonably assured that his political cronies could keep Government gold off the market, Gould and his old friend Fisk quietly began to buy up the available supply in the Summer of 1869. In theory, according to historian Richard O'Connor, Gould soon "owned all the gold then circulating in the United States and held contracts . . . for twice again as much." Even when the gold market became erratic, the President was unaware that he was being used by Gould through Corbin, who urged Grant not to lower the price by putting any of the Government's $100,000,000 of gold on the market. But, eventually, Grant grew suspicious. His military secretary, General Horace Porter, may have told him of Gould's attempt to open an account in his (Porter's) name – which Porter refused. But it is probable he learned about Gould's scheme on Sunday, September 19, when Joseph Seligman talked with Grant at the President's home at Long Branch, New Jersey.

Grant queried Joseph about his activities in the gold market. Joseph told the President frankly. Grant's attitude told Joseph just enough to warn him to sell gold instead of buy it. The President also warned Corbin to get out of the market, and, of course, Corbin told Gould. Quick to see the game was up, Gould decided to sell his gold before the Government broke the price, and to let his confederates – including Fisk – save themselves as best they could.

September 24, 1869, was Black Friday, one of the most disastrous days in Wall Street history. While President Grant and General Porter played croquet on the summer White House lawn, gold sold for 150 at ten a.m.; by eleven it was 160. Finally, Grant ordered Treasury Secretary Boutwell to sell $5,000,000 of the Government's gold. However, it took Major General Dan Butterfield, the Assistant Treasurer in New York and a member of the Gould clique, "until a few minutes before noon," O'Connor claims, to tell the news to the Gold Exchange – "and every minute" after Butterfield learned of it at 11:25 from Boutwell "was probably worth a hundred thousand to Gould."

The market plummeted. Gould got out with a

The Seligmans, whatever their personal opinions of Jay Gould, were loyal to him as their client. On November 28, 1868, the firm even went so far as to guarantee his bail bond for $20,000 in a letter written to Moritz Meyer.

Black Friday, on September 24, 1869, had nothing to do with stocks. It was an attempt to corner gold not held by the Treasury. Pandemonium broke loose when the Government decided to put some of its reserves on the market.

J. & W. SELIGMAN & CO.

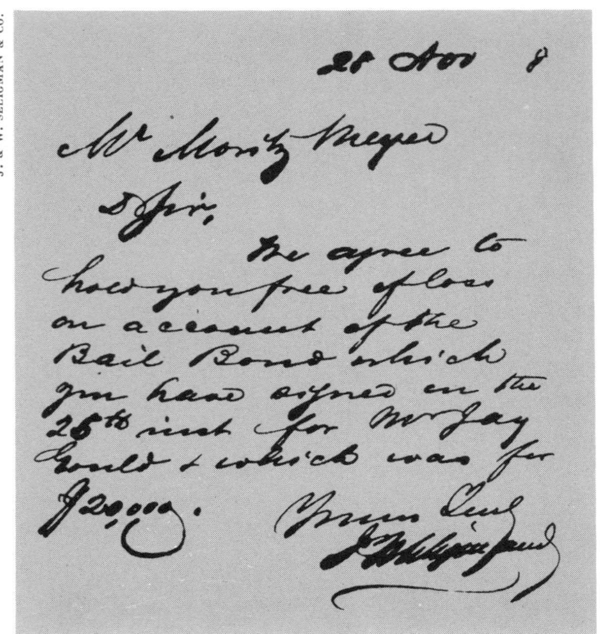

28 Nov 8

Mr Moritz Meyer

D Sir,

We agree to hold you free of loss on account of the Bail Bond which you have signed on the 25th inst for Mr Jay Gould & which was for $20,000.

Yours Truly

[illegible]

Menne-hatin, The Story of New York

profit of some $11,000,000. Jim Fisk repudiated his commitments. But thousands of more honorable men and hundreds of firms were ruined.

Gould was ousted from the presidency of the Erie in 1872, and a year later there was a long overdue investigation of the road's management. "Joseph Seligman, banker," *The New York Times* reported on April 9, 1873, "was the first witness called, and testified as to his connection with the market disposal of railway mortgages." The story pointed out the Seligmans acted only as brokers, and went on to make clear that their commission rate was no more than it should have been.

At first, as a broker, and then on a small scale for its own account, J. & W. Seligman & Co.'s involvement with rails was like a chain reaction. Its international banking connections attracted railroad promoters with dreams of linking city to farm and state to state, and with a need for more risk capital than the young American economy could possibly produce alone. The firm helped to raise capital in the United States and in Europe, and in the end, to protect its own and its clients' investments the Seligmans found themselves partially owning and on occasion actually operating railroads all over the country. Joseph Seligman's initial reluctance to take big risks was eroded gradually until it gave way to a severe case of railroad fever.

In 1868, the Pacific Railroad – which later became the Missouri Pacific – between St. Louis and Kansas City was crippled by poor connections with the East, the need for a bridge across the Mississippi, an out-moded wide-gauge track, and heavy debt. J. & W. Seligman & Co. advanced the road $400,000 and undertook to sell its bonds in Europe. The venture worked out well.

The Nation got its first transcontinental road the following year when California Governor Leland Stanford helped drive the famous Golden Spike connecting the Central Pacific and Union Pacific at Promontory, Utah, on May 10. Instead of ending the dream of transcontinentalism, the Union Pacific's success spurred rival efforts. Opportunities for growth seemed endless, and to share in them, J. & W. Seligman & Co. agreed to become fiscal agent for what was then called the South Pacific Rail Road Company of Missouri, a line authorized between St. Louis, via Pacific, Missouri, to the State line on the west.

J. & W. Seligman & Co. marketed an issue of mortgage bonds for the South Pacific "covering the road to the western state line and also 1,000,000 acres of land." The bonds were placed largely in Germany and Holland; American railroad securities were not popular in France and other bankers had the inside track in England. By September 1869, Seligman & Stettheimer, Frankfurt, had raised $1,675,000. Sales began to slow up by November. Joseph wrote the railroad's president, Francis B. Hayes, in Boston, the bonds were not selling well "in view of the fact that nearly 200 new railroads are being constructed within the borders of the United States, issuing 7%, 8% and even 10% bonds, and . . . the bonds of the old Missouri Pacific Railroad (a road fully finished and earning $70,000 a week) are being offered freely at 85." Nevertheless, he said J. & W. Seligman & Co. was prepared to go ahead as agent with another bond issue. But he insisted that someone from the firm be "elected to the directorate."

Joseph's terms were met. He was elected a director of the South Pacific Rail Road Company on March 8, 1870.

At about the same time the firm became interested in the South Pacific, Joseph Seligman decided to help to finance the Atlantic & Pacific – today a part of the Frisco and Santa Fe systems. Originally it was an ambitious project chartered by Congress in 1866 with a land grant of 42,000,000 acres and the right to lay track along the thirty-fifth parallel from the western part of Missouri near Springfield to the Pacific Ocean by way of Albuquerque, Territory of New Mexico, and Needles, California, a distance of 2,000 miles, and a westward branch from Van Buren, Arkansas. The firm agreed to become the road's fiscal agent, advanced it funds, and set out to sell three million dollars worth of mortgage bonds secured by half a million acres of land.

Before long it became apparent that the way to make a success of the Atlantic & Pacific was to consolidate it with the South Pacific Rail Road, and Joseph, with a group of other financiers, effected a merger on October 25, 1870. The new company, with headquarters in Boston, kept the name Atlantic & Pacific and elected Francis B. Hayes, presi-

THE HARRY T. PETERS COLLECTION, MUSEUM OF THE CITY OF NEW YORK

Currier & Ives were famous lithographers of the Nineteenth Century. Often, the prints of railroads would later be used for advertising; the railroad inserting its name on the locomotive, cars, and other equipment. An 1876 print, titled, "An American Railway Scene, at Hornellsville, Erie Railway," was one of those which became well-known.

UNION PACIFIC RAILROAD PHOTO

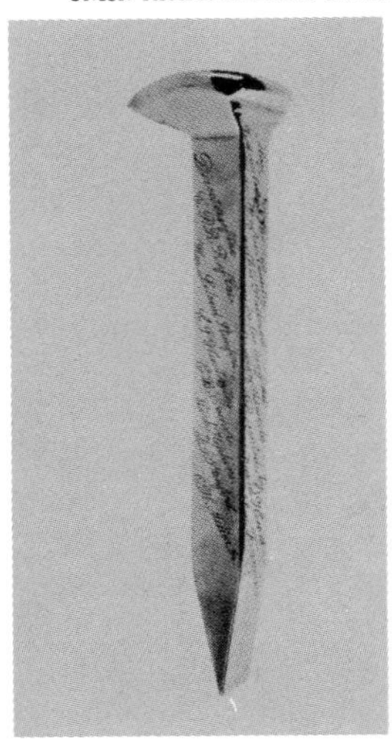

May 10, 1869 – the Central Pacific and Union Pacific joined to form the country's first transcontinental railroad. About 1,500 watched the ceremony when Leland Stanford, Governor of California, aimed the maul to drive the five and one-half inch Golden Spike (valued at roughly $400) to make the last link. Stanford missed!

dent; Uriel Crocker, vice-president, and Andrew Peirce, Jr., general manager. Joseph Seligman became a director. All of these men had been active in both predecessor roads. At the time of the merger the South Pacific had been completed as far as Seneca, about 292 miles from its starting point at Pacific, Missouri, and the old A & P was building through Indian Territory toward Vinita. The next year, J. & W. Seligman & Co. headed a group of Atlantic & Pacific financiers which gained control of the Pacific Railroad (Missouri Pacific).

While the A & P forged westward, the Seligmans sought more and more money to pour into its treasury. Favorable newspaper stories appeared, yet an 1871 bond issue was a failure. A delegation of St. Louis and Boston financiers sent to San Francisco in 1872 to raise working capital came back home empty-handed. But, not content with the railroad headaches it already had, J. & W. Seligman & Co. also became interested in the Union Pacific Railway Company, Southern Branch.

Organized in September 1865, to build a line from Fort Riley, Kansas, to New Orleans, the Union Pacific Railway Company, Southern Branch accomplished little until it was taken over by Judge Levi Parsons of New York in 1868. The Judge and a group of Eastern financiers staged into Emporia, Kansas, that October and held a "short and businesslike meeting with the befuddled directors of the line," according to historian V. V. Masterson. Parsons informed them, "Our object is to build your road and we come sufficiently endorsed to meet with no opposition." Actual construction began the next year when Parsons, says Masterson, "proceeded to let in on the ground floor such men as his illustrious namesake Levi P. Morton, President of Morton, Bliss and Company . . . Joe Seligman of the great banking house of J. & W. Seligman; the rising young financier August Belmont; and George C. Clark, partner in the Clark, Dodge Investment Company".

Parsons quickly got set to build the road to Indian Territory to win the race for the exclusive right to continue north and south through the area and to get the 3,100,000 acre land grant that went with it. He also changed the name of the road to the Missouri, Kansas and Texas Railway Company – the "Katy."

Judge Parsons apparently persuaded Joseph Seligman that investing in the newly-christened Katy was a good idea, for at the road's annual meeting at Emporia in 1870, Joseph gave a proxy for his one share of voting stock. J. & W. Seligman & Co., as a firm, gave its proxy for 1,900 shares of the 38,180 voted.

The Katy won the contest to build through Indian Territory. Then, in a short time, it was in bitter rivalry with the Atlantic & Pacific, a line with which the Katy shared Joseph Seligman as a director. While the Katy could build south through the Territory, the A & P had authorization to construct its line west. If A & P rails could be placed South of the Katy's tracks, the Katy's traffic would be reduced enough to hurt. Another race began to see who would be first to the crossing point of the two lines. Again the Katy won.

The A & P and also the Missouri Pacific went to great lengths to hinder the Katy's progress, and it was clear that Joseph Seligman's membership on the boards of all three roads created a conflict of interest. He resigned as a Katy director and his place was taken by J. Pierpont Morgan at the annual meeting on May 17, 1871. J. & W. Seligman & Co. continued its investment in the line, however.

Joseph Seligman was tough and a fighter, but he was fundamentally a peaceable man, and he tried to stop the battle between the lines through merger. This would have ended the friction – and would have enhanced the value of the A & P – but the Katy management refused to consolidate. So

LIBRARY OF CONGRESS

When the Missouri Pacific decided upon building a branch line between Kirkwood and Carondelet, Missouri, Joseph Seligman suggested the route go through Grant's farm because he had told the General it would. The cabin on the farm had been built in 1854 by Grant and a neighbor from logs the former had hewn and Indian cement. He lived there until 1858.

to make his own lines stronger, Joseph helped to negotiate a 999-year lease of the Pacific Railroad (Missouri Pacific) to the A & P on June 29, 1872, after resigning from the Pacific Railroad board to enable the directors to vote agreement of the plan.

About this time the Missouri Pacific was preparing to build the Carondelet Branch, a short line in St. Louis County from Kirkwood to Carondelet, which was financed by the Seligmans. Since they paid for it, they could dictate its route to some extent and on December 20, 1871, Joseph suggested to Andrew Peirce that "when the Pacific R. R. builds the Carondelet Branch, I would advise by all means to take the route through General Grant's farm, as . . . I have told Gen. Grant last summer such would be our route." The branch was built through the farmland where the President had lived for a time after resigning from the Army before the Civil War.

After six hectic years of dealing in rails, along with a host of other financial matters, Joseph, in effect, reported to his brother William in Paris on June 6, 1872: "Now as to our various investments in R. R. Bonds which have at present no market value I fully agree with you that we have too many of them for comfort . . . I agreed to advance \$200/m to a new road in Missouri (Memphis Carthage & Northwestern) as soon as they have completed and ironed 27 miles out of the 110 miles of their line, and have done so having \$1,900,000 of the entire Bond 7% gold in hand with a years

BY V. V. MASTERSON, COPYRIGHT 1952, UNIVERSITY OF OKLAHOMA PRESS

The Katy Railroad and the Last Frontier

The Atlantic & Pacific and the Katy may have shared Joseph Seligman as a director for a time, but amenities between the two railroads' construction crews were not always observed. In October 1871, a townsite battle at Vinita, Indian Territory (now Oklahoma), took place. A plan to consolidate the railroads was not successful.

option to sell them . . . But I have concluded not to go another Dollar on any R. R. or State or City Bond . . . and nothing will induce me hereafter [to put] another Dollar in any new enterprise until I have the moral assurance that the Bond is as good as sold in Europe."

He defended his investments in rails in the same letter in which he said he would get out of them. "We have made a fortune these past 6 years & made it principally out of new R. Roads, but I repeat my promise to you . . . and shall be satisfied hereafter with a balance sheet of one third the size as last year."

Joseph's comments to outsiders told a somewhat different story than his own activities. He wrote to a friend in Buffalo who had expressed an interest in investing in rails and becoming a director of one of them. "We wish to give you our experience. New roads want no end of money and directors are the very people who are asked to lend money or lend their name (by endorsement) to roads and when you are once in $25,000 they will draw you in for $100,000 and subsequently for half-a-million, and all with the best intentions; but it will take you many years to get your money back – and possibly never. This is our friendly caution."

Joseph knew what he was talking about, even though he failed to follow his own advice. On May 21, 1872, the Seligmans had invested over $1,000,000 in just *three* railroads. Firm records show that during the next forty years, the list rose to include more than one hundred different lines. As railroads stretched further and further West and South, J. & W. Seligman & Co. marketed increasingly large issues of securities to pay for them, and despite Joseph's frequent resolutions to the contrary, the roads continued to absorb much of his time and a good deal of the firm's money. Occasionally, the senior partner tried to solve a line's problems singlehandedly.

When the Memphis, Carthage and Northwestern Railroad found equipment hard to pay for in 1872, Joseph went so far as to buy a locomotive and to lease it to the line. "You will have learned

ST. LOUIS-SAN FRANCISCO RAILWAY (FROM: ASSOCIATION OF AMERICAN RAILROADS)

On November 8, 1872, Joseph Seligman wrote to M. Baird & Co. of Philadelphia (The Baldwin Locomotive Works), that he had "paid for the Locomotive 'Seligman.'" The company built two locomotives which were used by the Memphis, Carthage & Northwestern Railroad. The line was part of the Frisco system when this photo of the Seligman *was taken between Seligman, Missouri, and Eureka Springs, Arkansas, in the late Summer of 1882.*

from your correspondents in this City," he wrote to M. Baird & Co. in Philadelphia (a predecessor of The Baldwin Locomotive Works) on November 8, "that I have paid for the Locomotive 'Seligman' . . . in behalf of the Memphis, Carthage and Northwestern Railroad Company – The title to the Engine is in myself; but will be shipped to the Memphis Carthage, and Northwestern Railroad Co. St. Louis Mo. care Atlantic & Pacific Rl Rd Co – Please forward without delay & oblige."

The Memphis, Carthage and Northwestern agreed to pay Joseph seventy dollars a week rent for the locomotive. The arrangement, says railroad historian Lucius Beebe, "is the only instance of this set up I ever heard of, a sort of anticipation of today's equipment trusts." The Baldwin Locomotive Works' records show the *Seligman* was built under construction order number 2974 in October 1872. It was the second locomotive ordered for the railroad. The *L. P. Cunningham,* named for the road's president, was first. Even this unorthodox method of support failed to rescue the struggling line which Joseph originally termed "a short but very promising little road;" a "feeder" line to the Atlantic & Pacific and Missouri Pacific. And early in 1875, the Seligmans and their associates foreclosed the line's mortgages. The road eventually was reorganized as part of the Missouri & Western Railway Company which Joseph Seligman served as president until the line became part of the St. Louis and San Francisco Railway Company in 1879.

The Panic of 1873 very nearly persuaded Joseph to abandon the railroad business once and for all, and to sell out the firm's investments "no matter at what price. I am disgusted with all railroads," he declared, "and shall never again be tempted to undertake the sale of a railroad bond. I am daily engaged in two or three damned railroad meetings and, therefore, cannot attend to office business as much as I want to." But Joseph's moods of despair passed quickly, and as soon as the Panic ended he revived his dream of the "Great National, Atlantic and Pacific Railroad . . . a line never obstructed by snows, and of comparatively easy grades." In May

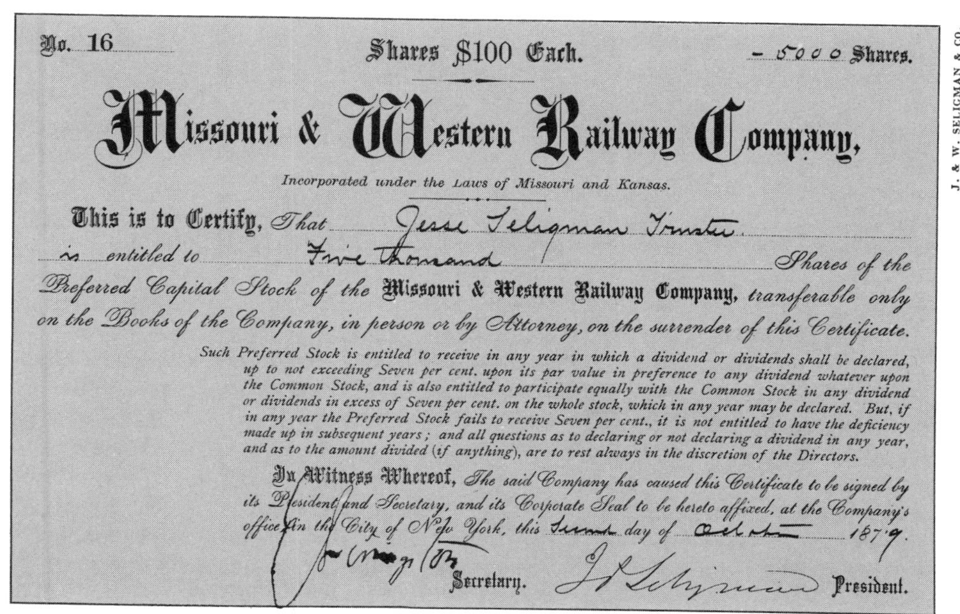
No. 16 Shares $100 Each. – 5000 Shares.

Missouri & Western Railway Company,

Incorporated under the Laws of Missouri and Kansas.

This is to Certify, That Jesse Seligman Trustee is entitled to Five thousand Shares of the Preferred Capital Stock of the Missouri & Western Railway Company, transferable only on the Books of the Company, in person or by Attorney, on the surrender of this Certificate.

Such Preferred Stock is entitled to receive in any year in which a dividend or dividends shall be declared, up to not exceeding Seven per cent. upon its par value in preference to any dividend whatever upon the Common Stock, and is also entitled to participate equally with the Common Stock in any dividend or dividends in excess of Seven per cent. on the whole stock, which in any year may be declared. But, if in any year the Preferred Stock fails to receive Seven per cent., it is not entitled to have the deficiency made up in subsequent years; and all questions as to declaring or not declaring a dividend in any year, and as to the amount divided (if anything), are to rest always in the discretion of the Directors.

In Witness Whereof, The said Company has caused this Certificate to be signed by its President and Secretary, and its Corporate Seal to be hereto affixed, at the Company's office in the City of New York, this Second day of October 1879.

Secretary. J. Seligman President.

J. & W. SELIGMAN & CO.

The Memphis, Carthage & Northwestern Railroad was reorganized as The Missouri & Western Railway Company before it became part of today's St. Louis-San Francisco system. Joseph Seligman was Missouri & Western's president.

As a director of the railroad, Joseph Seligman helped negotiate a 999-year lease of the Missouri Pacific with the Atlantic & Pacific. A newspaper ad, circa 1878, extolled the virutes of palace chair cars; said "Go West."

MISSOURI PACIFIC RAILROAD

and again in October 1874, Joseph persuaded a group of Eastern financiers to tour the A & P system and to subscribe funds to reduce the line's floating debt and to meet current expenses. It was no use, however, for the next year A & P directors were forced to announce that they could no longer meet the terms of their lease of the Missouri Pacific. The lines were divorced. The A & P's franchise and property were taken over by the newly formed St. Louis and San Francisco Railway, commonly called the "Frisco." The Seligmans retained their interest in the Missouri Pacific and Joseph became a trustee. He was also on the Frisco's executive committee.

INTERIOR VIEW OF THE CELEBRATED
PALACE CHAIR CARS
ATTACHED TO ALL EXPRESS TRAINS ON THE
Missouri Pacific Railway.
No extra Charge is made for Seats in these Cars. NO OTHER LINE runs these Cars between St. Louis and Kansas City.
Go West via the "MISSOURI PACIFIC."
F. E. FOWLER.
General Passenger Agent.

Although it was new in name, the Frisco's trouble was all too familiar—money. In 1880 it was forced to sell a half interest in the A & P to the Atchison, Topeka and Sante Fe, and the two lines continued to push the A & P route westward. Six years later, the Atlantic & Pacific entered California over Santa Fe tracks. But it was a Pyrrhic victory. By then, Joseph was dead and his Atlantic & Pacific was little more than a name.

The senior Seligman's efforts to complete the railroad were not unnoted, however. While the A & P

SANTA FE RAILWAY

By the time the Atlantic & Pacific reached California, the railroad, long troubled by financial difficulties, was little more than a name. In 1890, workers posed for Charles Battye alongside A & P locomotive number 95 in Needles.

COURTESY, GENOA E. WILLIAMS

COURTESY, BENNIE S. MC CANN AND EVERETT REDDICK

Seligman, Missouri, platted in 1880 for the Frisco, was incorporated on March 8, 1881, as "Seligman." Residents turned out en masse to watch a traveling acrobat perform on Main Street in 1900. The St. Louis-San Francisco Railway still goes through Seligman. Postmaster Genoa E. Williams photographed the depot in late 1963 and said it was located in what is now called "the old part of town."

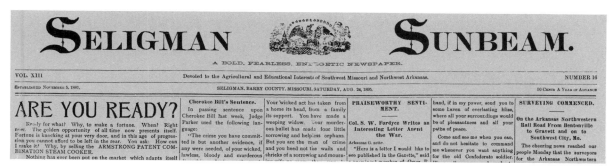

GENOA E. WILLIAMS

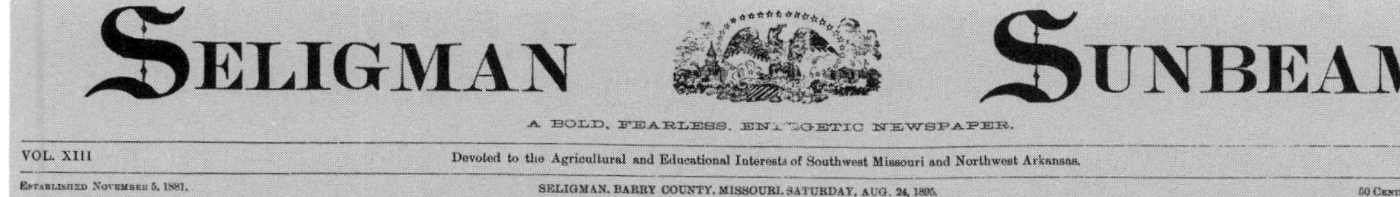

SELIGMAN SUNBEAM.

A BOLD, FEARLESS, EN[illegible]GETIC NEWSPAPER.

VOL. XIII — Devoted to the Agricultural and Educational Interests of Southwest Missouri and Northwest Arkansas. — NUMBER 16

ESTABLISHED NOVEMBER 5, 1881. — SELIGMAN, BARRY COUNTY, MISSOURI, SATURDAY, AUG. 24, 1895. — 50 CENTS A YEAR IN ADVANCE

ARE YOU READY?

Ready for what? Why, to make a fortune. When? Right now. The golden opportunity of all time now presents itself. Fortune is knocking at your very door, and in this age of progression you cannot afford to be left in the rear. You ask: How can I make it? Why, by selling the ARMSTRONG PATENT COMBINATION STEAM COOKER.

Nothing has ever been put on the market which adapts itself

Cherokee Bill's Sentence.

In passing sentence upon Cherokee Bill last week, Judge Parker used the following language:

"The crime you have committed is but another evidence, if any were needed, of your wicked, lawless, bloody and murderous

Your wicked act has taken from a home its head, from a family its support. You have made a weeping widow. Your murderous bullet has made four little sorrowing and helpless orphans. But you are the man of crime and you heed not the wails and shrieks of a sorrowing and mourn-

PRAISEWORTHY SENTIMENT.

Col. S. W. Fordyce Writes an Interesting Letter Anent the War.

Arkansas Gazette.

"Here is a letter I would like to see published in the Gazette," said

hand, if in my power, send you to some haven of everlasting bliss, where all your surroundings would be of pleasantness and all your paths of peace.

Come and see me when you can, and do not hesitate to command me whenever you want anything for the old Confederate soldier.

SURVEYING COMMENCED.

On the Arkansas Northwestern Rail Road From Bentonville to Gravett and on to Southwest City, Mo.

The cheering news reached our people Monday that the surveyors for the Arkansas Northwestern

COURTESY, EMORY MELTON

The History of Barry County *(Missouri) boldly declared in 1888 that the* Seligman Sunbeam *"was the first paper in the United States to nominate Cleveland for the presidency." It no longer exists. The front page of August 24, 1894 (partly shown), discussed pressure cookers and murder.*

COURTESY, FRED E. BROWN

A second Seligman, in Arizona, was named for Jesse. It had its first postmaster in November 1886. Seligman became a division point on the Sante Fe. The railroad still passes through the town, as the depot symbol shows. Mrs. Helen Pearson, now a newspaperwoman in nearby Williams, grew up in Seligman and says: "It has always been a railroad and sheep and cattle raising town, with these industries contributing almost exclusively to the town's economy—until the past 10 or 15 years when tourism began to play a major part." For years, all water for the town was "hauled in by train from Del Rio nearly 60 miles away." The Corner Bar, shown behind the Copper Cart sign, is "a meeting place for cowboys and railroaders [and] tourists." Most people pronounce the names of both towns differently from members of the firm or the Seligman family. The firm's way is SELL-ig-mun (sell as in tell; ig as in big, man as in money).

FRED E. BROWN

FRED E. BROWN

COURTESY, ROBERT A. HENNING

Holbrook, Arizona, was a small town in the 1880's—even after the Atlantic & Pacific Railroad made it, according to Jo Johnson, "the greatest shipping point in northern Arizona." After the Aztec Land and Cattle Company, Limited chose Holbrook for its headquarters, it still was not a large town.

had struggled along, the Frisco purchased the St. Louis, Arkansas and Texas Railway to develop a division from Plymouth (now Monett), Missouri, to Fayetteville, Arkansas. Along this route was a place once known as Roller's Ridge, located in the southern part of Barry County, Missouri, just about two miles from the Missouri-Arkansas line. Platted in 1880, it was named Seligman on September 27 in honor of Joseph, who had died the previous April.

Never very large, (in 1889 there were about 350 residents; about 400 in 1960), it still boasted in its first two years as Seligman a marshal, justice of the peace, farm implement store, meat market, druggist, stage line, livery stable, hay and grain house, lumber yard, billiard hall, barber shop, blacksmith, photographer, railroad agent, physician, attorney, postmaster, public school, academy, three saloons, four hotels, five trustees, and six general merchants, as well as one newspaper named the *Seligman Sunbeam* which termed itself "bold, fearless, energetic." Its motto was "The Union, the Constitution and the Enforcement of Law." Perhaps its singular claim to fame is that on November 4, 1882, it was the first newspaper in the entire United States to nominate Grover Cleveland for the Presidency.

Another Seligman, named for Jesse in the 1880's, is located northwest of Phoenix in Arizona and still serves as a freight division point on the Sante Fe. About 750 people live there today. The railroad, cattle and sheep raising, and tourism contribute to the town's economy. A third Seligman, once located in White Pine County, Nevada, no longer exists.

As A & P rails were pushed across Arizona Territory in the 1880's, the tiny town of Holbrook had just one restaurant – a greasy spoon operated by Louey Ghuey, a Chinese. His clientele included some of the town's 250 residents and the cowhands and drifters who patronized the Bucket of Blood Saloon down the street, or the four other saloons "which provided most of the local entertainment," according to writer Jo Johnson. Bloody knuckles and smoking six-guns climaxed fights over cattle, horses, and women – generally all rustled in the surrounding area. The St. Johns, Arizona, Salvation Army group was even planning a visit to Holbrook, which the local paper called "a good field of operation."

This was the spot, on a land grant held by the

Original Hashknife cowhands included, in 1886 (left to right), secretary Henry Kinsley . . . Roxy, George Smith, . . . Peck, Tom Pickett, Buck Lancaster, Don McDonald, I. M. Higgins, Billy Wilson, E. I. Simpson, and Fred Ames.

ARIZONA PIONEERS' HISTORICAL SOCIETY

Atlantic & Pacific, where J. & W. Seligman & Co. and a group of associates decided to enter ranching, a business the firm was probably least qualified to conduct. Nevertheless, the Aztec Land and Cattle Company, Limited was formed in the Mills Building in New York – very likely in the firm's offices – December 12, 1884, with a capital of $1,000,000. Capital Stock Certificate Number 1 for 1,475 shares was issued to J. & W. Seligman & Co. Additional funds were raised in Europe.

The Aztec bought 1,000,000 acres of land from the railroad at fifty cents an acre and stocked it with 33,000 Texas longhorns purchased from the Continental Cattle Company in West Texas. The company also acquired 2,200 horses. From that time on it is likely that neither the Seligmans, nor any of the other absentee owners in the East, knew quite what was going on in Arizona Territory.

The Continental brand which came with the cattle was generally known as the Hashknife, a once-common kitchen tool with rounded blades and a cross handle, and shortly the Aztec Land and Cattle Company, Limited was known as the Hashknife outfit. With offices at Holbrook, the Aztec was then the third largest ranch in North America. Its range spread eighty miles to the west to Mormon Lake, and forty miles to the south from the A & P track. Cowboys – many with shady reputations – came to work from all over the Southwest. Three

On April 8, 1855—a number of weeks after the "meeting of railroad men and capitalists" had been reported in The New-York Times, *Saturday, January 4, 1885—the first stock certificate for the Aztec Land and Cattle Company, Limited (commonly called the Hashknife outfit) was issued to the firm of* J. & W. Seligman & Co.

AZTEC LAND AND CATTLE COMPANY, LIMITED

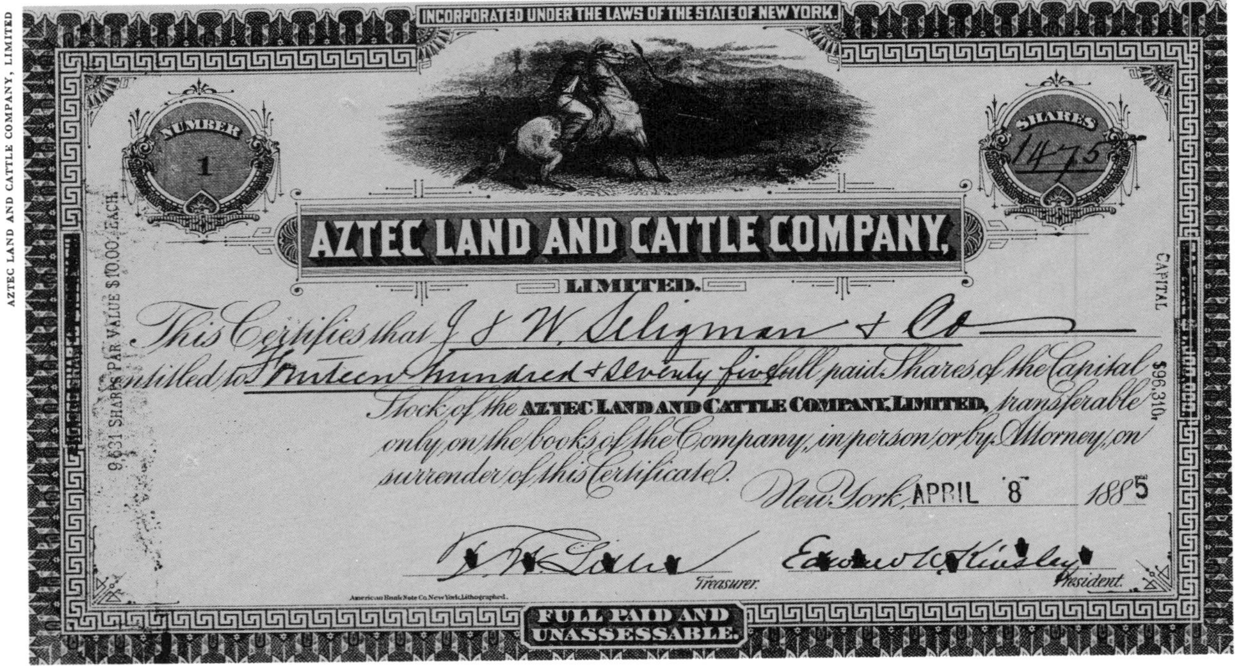

INCORPORATED UNDER THE LAWS OF THE STATE OF NEW YORK.

NUMBER 1

SHARES 1475

AZTEC LAND AND CATTLE COMPANY, LIMITED.

9,631 SHARES PAR VALUE $10.00 EACH.

CAPITAL $96,310.

This Certifies that J & W Seligman & Co entitled to Fourteen hundred & seventy five full paid Shares of the Capital Stock of the AZTEC LAND AND CATTLE COMPANY, LIMITED, transferable only on the books of the Company, in person or by Attorney on surrender of this Certificate. New York, APRIL 8 1885

Treasurer. President.

American Bank Note Co. New York, Lithographed.

FULL PAID AND UNASSESSABLE.

COURTESY, ROBERT A. HENNING

BRAND: COURTESY, JOHN J. BABBITT

Headquarters Ranch, the Aztec Land and Cattle Company, circa 1887 was located eleven miles west of Holbrook, Arizona Territory. Buildings (l to r) included the kitchen and dining house; grain house, and headquarters and office. Author Zane Grey mentioned the Hashknife (unfavorably) in some of his books, among them Arizona Ames; Under the Rim. *The Hashknife brand is superimposed, bottom right.*

of them had ridden with William Bonner, alias Billy the Kid, during the bloody Lincoln County, New Mexico, war in 1880-1881. Tom Pickett, an Aztec rider, always denied he was a member of the gang. He later opened a gambling hall in Winslow. Billy Wilson and Dave Rudabaugh were the other two. Gladwell Richardson of Flagstaff, Arizona, recalls they were hired to "guard the eastern line" of the Aztec's lands "against thieves." Wilson ended up as a sheriff named Doc Anderson in Terrill County, Texas. Others were professional gunmen who looked out for the company's interests "whether the company liked it or not," Jo Johnson said.

However, George W. Hennessey, who "went to work for the outfit in 1899-1900," and was no desperado, says, "It makes my blood pressure raise when someone comes out with the phrase, 'that Hashknife outlaw outfit.' I never worked with a better bunch of men [many of whom] became leading citizens . . . and some of them were elected to county office." Still, "the Hashknife no doubt had some poor characters as they worked from 25 to 30 men from April 1st to November 15th."

Each cowboy earned room, board, and twenty-five to thirty dollars a month—a few more dollars by breaking broncos—and in the early days usually spent it immediately on gambling and women in the ten saloons of Holbrook and neighboring Winslow. The Hashknife boys may have been trigger-happy at times, but one bartender in Winslow also "was

COURTESY, GEORGE W. HENNESSEY

George W. Hennessey visited the late Burton C. Mossman in Roswell, New Mexico, in 1945 and was told: "George, you and I are the last of the Hashknife cowboys left under my management, but Hell, there were lots of comers and goers." Hennessey, who was thirty-three in 1911 when this picture was taken, now lives in Phoenix, Arizona.

THE COLLECTION OF JOT STILES, COURTESY, MRS. J. B. STILES

In 1889, a photographer from Studio Grand in Winslow, Arizona Territory, went to the Fashion Saloon in that city and captured for posterity a group of Aztec cowboys. An original photo, owned by Mrs. Jot Stiles of Winslow, identifies the men as (from left): bartender Mike Oyster, Lucien Curley Cresswell, Frank Black, Cap Bagnal, Tom Williams, George W. Hennessey, Ed Bargman, Doug Johnston, Frank Dane, and Johnny Hoffman. One man, between the second and third from the right, remains unknown. But Hennessey, who also owns a picture, differs on some of the names. He says the bartender was Billie Burke, the saloon was Dick Barback's; Black is Flickncer.

Burton C. Mossman, Aztec superintendent, kept a six-shooter on his office desk (left side) and two rifles leaning against the wall in his office in 1900. Mossman later became the first Captain of the Arizona Rangers.

COURTESY, GEORGE W. HENNESSEY

hard on the life expectancy of Hash Knife men," Jo Johnson says. "He shot one cowboy just for getting roaring drunk and riding his horse into the saloon."

In the heat of Summer, sheepmen would drive their flocks onto Aztec range in search of grass, and one rider, John Paine, a Texan who hated sheep and sheepmen, combatted them with "simple and direct" methods, Lawrence Cardwell, has written. "He'd ride up to a sheep camp and say, 'Git!' Then the next morning he'd ride back with a couple of Hash Knife assistants to see if the herder had got. If not they'd charge the sheep and get them to running . . . It would be only a matter of time until the stampeding sheep would tumble pell-mell over the edge" of a steep canyon or deep cut-bank wash.

Just as in a modern television Western, all this led to reprisals against the Hashknife and often their line camps were burned. This alarmed the Aztec officers in New York, and they had the law firm of Seligman & Seligman (formed by Theodore, George Washington, and Eugene Seligman, sons of Jesse, Joseph, and James, respectively) write to their attorney, C. L. Gutterson, at St. Johns, Arizona.

Their complaint was that sheepherders were trespassing on Aztec land. The company owned 1,000,000 acres—but in alternate sections. Technically, every other section was public land open to anyone. It also meant, as Jo Johnson noted, "While the Aztec Company had the right to graze on public lands, the public did not have the right to graze on Aztec land." The lawyers said, "The Territory should give the Company all possible protection, since it is a heavy taxpayer, and *contemplates* spending money on improvements, such as wells, tanks and dams." The complaint was perfectly sound, and probably would have produced results in New York. It didn't in Arizona in 1887 when the Aztec Land and Cattle Company, Limited paid $407.94 in delinquent taxes to the county.

Rustling bothered the company as much as sheepmen. Employees often stole as much as the Indians, horse thieves,and Mexicans. Tom South, an Aztec cook, once decided to take some cattle and head for Colorado. He sold them, opened a saloon, went broke, came back to Arizona, and was rehired by the Hashknife.

The Aztec management, far away in the East, doubtless thought their western managers had the situation well in hand. But the ranch produced no income. According to author Frazier Hunt, some of the Aztec securities "were sold to German investors and when dividends failed to appear, Seligman Bros. [*sic*] of New York bought in the bonds at half price and with them went virtual control of the ranching company." The Sante Fe also owned a large part of the business. The Seligmans were patient, but finally in December 1897, Burton C. Mossman was hired as the Hashknife's superintendent and given orders to put the ranch on its feet.

One of Mossman's first acts as superintendent was to fire fifty-three of the eighty-four men then on the payroll. The Summer of 1898, his men put the Hashknife brand on some 16,000 calves, a record, and by year end, it looked as though the Aztec would be profitable at last.

T. W. Cabeen, now a vice-president of the Aztec, once learned from three of the company's old cowpunchers that it "was the easiest brand altered there ever was." Just "by two simple slashes with a hot iron," it could be changed to "a cow drinking out of a trough."

"Brand artists, droughts, and the 1893-1897 depression," Cabeen says, along with the harsh Winter of 1898-1899 "discouraged the Aztec people to the extent that they went out of the range cattle business in the early 1900's" and Mossman was ordered to liquidate the holdings. The Aztec retained its land, with the exception of 98,690 acres for which the Atlantic & Pacific never could deliver title because the Government designated the area a National forest.

In the Summer of 1952, the United States Court of Appeals held that this forest area belonged to the Aztec Land and Cattle Company and the acreage was then sold to Southwest Lumber Mills, Inc. Today the Aztec owns about 200,000 acres of Arizona land which it leases for grazing. Its corporate offices are still in New York's financial district. The Sante Fe and J. & W. Seligman & Co. both disposed of their shares of the company in 1928, but Francis F. Randolph, Seligman's senior partner, continues to serve as a director and Henry Holl, a Seligman staff member since 1920, is secretary-treasurer and also on the board.

While Arizona Territory suffered from growing pains in the 1880's, the Seligman's became involved in their last real railroad battle, and in the course of it learned, as many others had, that Jay Gould would turn on friend as well as foe for his own ends. The Frisco—controlled by J. & W. Seligman & Co. – wanted to build an extension of its line from Waldron and Hackett City, Arkansas, to Little Rock on the south side of the Arkansas River. Gould owned a railroad which operated on the north side of the river and when the Frisco started its survey, Gould started a fight. The "battle," as the *New York Herald* called it on May 22, 1887, raged for several weeks. Gangs of plug-uglies were thrown into the Frisco surveying camps. They attacked workmen, pulled up stakes, destroyed line levels. The Seligmans, ordinarily peaceful, retaliated. Finally, the two forces got together in New York and declared a truce. The Frisco abandoned plans for the extension and Gould conceded rights to another section of the Ozarks.

Just as the Atlantic & Pacific's had been, the Frisco's financial condition was weak. J. & W. Seligman & Co. exchanged its holdings in the line in 1890 for shares of the Sante Fe, and the Frisco continued to decline. It went into receivership in 1893. Even though J. & W Seligman & Co. no longer held an important interest in the road, the firm was selected to prepare a reorganization plan in 1896 with Isaac Newton Seligman as a member of the Reorganization Committee and Frederick Strauss as secretary. In 1913, the Frisco was again placed in receivers' hands. J. & W. Seligman & Co. became reorganization managers of a plan adopted three years later. Frederick Strauss was also named a director of what became the St. Louis-San Francisco Railway Company.

It is difficult to imagine that Joseph Seligman and his brothers had sufficient energy to spare, but by the time the firm really became involved in railroads it had also become one of the principal backers for New York City's transit system. This probably began on February 19, 1870, when Alfred Eli Beach revealed he had built the City's first subway, an experimental tunnel with one car that traveled 312 feet at up to ten miles an hour. Boss Tweed was furious, largely because the proposed subway threatened the flow of tribute he exacted from streetcar owners. Beach took his plan to the New York State Legislature and in 1871 the Beach Transit Bill was passed. But Tweed – also a State Senator—not only had a bill of his own, the Viaduct Plan Bill, he also had the ear of Governor John T. Hoffman. Beach's proposal was vetoed, while Tweed's became law.

The New York (Viaduct) Railway Company, formed in July, was hailed in *The Commercial and Financial Chronicle* as "one of the largest railroad enterprises of this country." Among the directors was Joseph Seligman. It seemed a wonderful plan, but it never came to be.

EDWARD B. WATSON COLLECTION

Trolley number 64, in 1893, was part of The Atlantic Avenue Railroad Company which had been sold to Seligman and three other firms by Deacon William Richardson of Brooklyn, "king" of the Nation's street railway owners.

His new interest in rapid transit led Joseph to resign from the New York Board of Education in 1875 to accept Mayor William H. Wickham's appointment as one of five commissioners of the first Rapid Transit Commission authorized by the Legislature. He was soon elected chairman.

The first line started under the eyes of the Commissioners was "Gilbert's Improved Elevated Railway," and James Blaine Walker, author of *Fifty Years of Rapid Transit, 1864 to 1917,* claims the major portion of the elevated railroads in Manhattan and The Bronx "owes its existence to the Board of Commissioners . . . which . . . also laid down 'connecting' routes for the New York Elevated Railroad Company." In October 1875, Walker says the Commissioners "caused the organization of the Manhattan Railway Company." Part of the $2,000,000 capital stock unquestionably was subscribed by J. & W. Seligman & Co., and General Horace Porter, a Seligman client, was one of the incorporators.

By the mid-Eighties, elevated railroads were in New York to stay, but even though the Seligmans had done much to make them possible, they reportedly had very little trust in their creation. A story in *The New York Sun* on June 26, 1936, declared there were reports at the time "that the Seligman brothers . . . would not . . . travel on the same train, fearing in case of accident that the whole family might be wiped out."

The firm's interest in transit companies was not confined to New York City. In 1890, it headed a syndicate to consolidate and to reorganize the street railways of Louisville, Kentucky. It also underwrote bonds for the Columbus (Ohio) Consolidated Street Railway Company in 1892, and a year later advanced $225,000 to the Crosstown Street Railway in the same city. Other transit issues handled by the firm ranged from those for London, England, to Portland, Oregon, and nearly from the northern to southern ends of the United States.

But New York's transit needs were greatest, and it was there the firm was most active. In 1892, the

EDWARD B. WATSON COLLECTION

Steam engines pulled elevated cars along the Third Avenue el, in the vicinity of Grand Street, New York City, 1896. The tracks, in those days, were built over the sidewalk. Cable and horse cars operated at street level. The firm maintained an interest in numerous transit issues in New York for many years.

Brooklyn Traction Company was formed to acquire The Atlantic Avenue Railroad Company. J. & W. Seligman & Co. joined in the underwriting, adding this interest to others it already had in the Buffalo City Railways, Rochester City Railway, the Lynn and Boston Railway Company, the Philadelphia trolley lines, and one or more lines in Pittsburgh.

The Atlantic Avenue Railway put its first electric car in operation in March 1892. In less than a year the entire line had been converted from horsecars and the company was running 200 closed and 200 open passenger cars over sixty-five miles of track. Three years later the parent Brooklyn Traction was in financial difficulty. A committee of reorganization, on which Henry Seligman and Frederick Strauss served, tried to put the company back on its feet by leasing the operating subsidiaries to Nassau Electric Railroad Company.

Nobody sets out in business to lose money and, although many of J. & W. Seligman & Co.'s transactions in the Nineteenth Century took years to work out, almost all of them, on balance, were profitable. However, there was one field – mining – in which all the evidence suggests the firm did poorly. It began almost as soon as the partnership was founded when Abraham Seligman in California became impressed with the proposal of a native Prussian named Adolph Sutro. His scheme was to build a five and one-half mile tunnel under the famed Comstock Lode which, in his own words, "at once insures drainage, ventilation, and facilitates the work of getting the gold and silver-bearing quartz above ground."

Sutro got a franchise from the State of Nevada in 1865 and the Federal Government, which held title to the Comstock district, awarded him a right of way for his tunnel a year later. At that point, all Sutro needed was about one and one-half million dollars to build his tunnel which, he estimated, would provide an annual revenue of between $2,300,000 and $6,000,000. Although few other bankers would support him, Abraham Seligman subscribed $3,500 to the Sutro Tunnel Company in 1867. When Joseph learned what his brother had done, he branded Sutro's plan a "visionary scheme doomed to failure," and insisted "it would injure J. & W. Seligman & Co. as bankers in foreign exchange to be known as investing money in speculations of any kind."

But Sutro—Joseph called him "the most persevering man I ever saw"—raised the capital he needed, and Abraham Seligman became a trustee of the Sutro Tunnel Company. The firm's interest must have warmed up, too, for by 1872 it held 95,500 shares in the company at an average cost of ninety-three cents each. Before long Joseph was writing, "I will do Brother Abm the justice that he was the only one who stuck through thick & thin to this scheme." Sutro finished the tunnel in 1879 and, shrewder than Abraham and many other investors, he sold his own stock before it became worthless. It was used for over fifty years, but the tunnel came too late to be of maximum aid to the Comstock Lode. The Sutro Tunnel Company went

COURTESY, ROBERT A. GRAHAM

Brooklyn Rapid Transit Company was reorganized as the Brooklyn-Manhattan Transit Corporation in 1923 with Frederick Strauss as one of the directors. A trolley built in 1905 for the B. R. T., was still in daily use in 1936.

through a number of reorganizations. The tunnel still exists but is no longer open or used.

The Sutro experience was the Seligmans' first failure to make money out of Western mines, but there were to be others. In 1870 the firm bought stock in the Oneida gold mine in California, later advanced funds to buy the Mahoney mine on adjacent land and, in the end, lost both investments. It was in the West also that Joseph Seligman made one of his rare errors in judging character and it cost the firm dearly in capital and embarassment.

The assay, purchase, and shipment of gold from Montana Territory looked profitable in the early days of the firm, and Joseph invested in the business of S. H. Bohm of Helena. To look after the firm's investment, Joseph sent the three Aub brothers – Michael, Philip, and Ludwig – who had been employed in the New York and New Orleans branches. Twenty-three-year-old Ludwig, and Michael Aub, became S. H. Bohm's partners in the banking house of Bohm & Aub. Meanwhile, F. Bohm, S. H. Bohm's brother, operated an assay office that was entirely separate from, but which did assay work for, the bank. His partners were S. H. Bohm and Philip Aub.

The bank opened October 25, 1867, and plans were made immediately to build a new office early

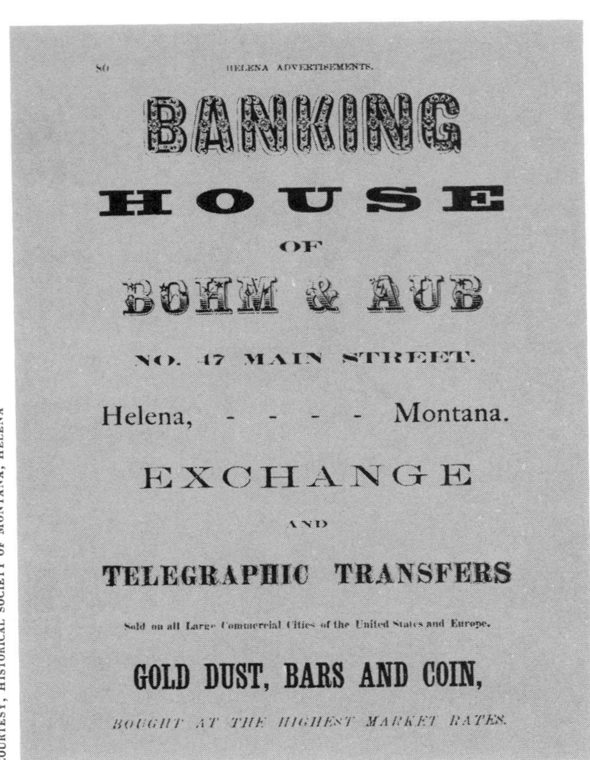

80 HELENA ADVERTISEMENTS.

BANKING

HOUSE

OF

BOHM & AUB

NO. 47 MAIN STREET.

Helena, - - - - Montana.

EXCHANGE

AND

TELEGRAPHIC TRANSFERS

Sold on all Large Commercial Cities of the United States and Europe.

GOLD DUST, BARS AND COIN,

BOUGHT AT THE HIGHEST MARKET RATES.

COURTESY, HISTORICAL SOCIETY OF MONTANA, HELENA

"Our Montana House," as Joseph Seligman called it, advertised in Historical Sketch and Essay on the Resources of Montana Including Business Directory Helena, *1868. Population of Helena, in the Census of 1870, totaled only 3,106.*

NEVADA HISTORICAL SOCIETY

Eight years after Adolph Sutro disposed of his interests in the Sutro Tunnel, in 1888, an elaborate façade – still standing – was built at the entrance. In 1872, the firm owned over 85,000 shares of stock in what developed into an ill-fated tunnel venture.

the following Spring. Before the $9,000 building was finished, however, Ludwig Aub died, and the firm sent Leopold Rothschild to Helena to take his place. S. H. Bohm urged Joseph Seligman to enter a formal partnership with him. When Abraham Seligman had made a similar suggestion the previous year, Joseph had been shocked. "No profit would induce me to lend my name to anyone where I or a brother of mine were not present to watch," Joseph told Abraham. But Joseph changed his mind by July 1868 and told Bohm, "We would in order to facilitate your business and to give your house an A-1 reputation, go in as special partners with a certain amount of capital."

"Our Montana House," as Joseph soon began to call it, shipped gold directly to New York—the shipments were insured "against Indians, et cetera" by Wells, Fargo & Co. for three per cent—and for several years the bank did a thriving business. On July 30, 1868, the *Helena Weekly Herald* reported the assay office "turned out, on Saturday evening last, a gold bar, the coin value of which was $24,772.58. This brick was cast for Messrs. Bohm & Aub bankers, and was shipped by them to New York by yesterday's coach. This is the largest brick, we believe, ever cast in Montana."

Leslie's Weekly

William Seligman, shown in his Paris office, 1903, was made an officer of the Legion of Honor on July 21 that year. Earlier, he had become a member of the Order after helping negotiate reciprocal trade treaties between France and the U. S.

HISTORICAL SOCIETY OF MONTANA, HELENA

Miners at the Gregory mine and works kidnapped Albert J. Seligman and held him hostage until two months' back wages were paid. An F. Jay Haynes photograph, circa 1886-1887, shows the mine (1), smelter (2), roaster (3), and boarding house (4).

J. & W. Seligman & Co., "one of the strongest and oldest American banking-houses," said King's Views of New York, *1908, built a "new $1,000,000 home" a year earlier. Architects were Francis J. Kimball and Julian C. Levi.*

Eventually, however, Joseph's initial assessment of S. H. Bohm proved prophetic. He began to lend the Seligmans' money without their knowledge and to overdraw funds, in spite of Joseph's threats to withdraw from the business.

Leopold Rothschild, supposedly a Seligman confidant, was told on May 20, 1871, "We are very much concerned about Mr. Bohm . . . Should there be any serious loss which has been kept secret from us we desire you let us know forthwith." Nothing happened, and to get at the facts, the firm in 1872 sent F. A. Benjamin, who had acted as a Seligman troubleshooter on other occasions, to take a close look at the Helena operations. By May the senior partner's patience was nearing its end and he wrote Benjamin:

> *Bro Ab^{m} telegraphs that you had discovered an additional indebtedness of $30,000. Now I am astonished at this discovery. I have lost all confidence in Bohm & his man Rothschild . . . Now you must stop this game . . . if not we must try to find places behind Keys & locks for all these chaps . . . these bad eggs.*

In a later letter, Joseph commented wonderingly "by what process they have made away with ¼ million of dollars or more in the space of less than one year in so small a place as Helena."

The Seligmans succeeded in getting rid of Bohm and reducing their loss. Benjamin ran the business and arranged shipments of bullion—which contained large amounts of silver—for several years and by the end of 1878 the firm was receiving about a half million dollars of silver monthly. This was sold to the United States Mint. But, by then, not yet having learned its lesson, the firm had purchased an interest in the Gregory Consolidated Mining Company located southwest of Helena.

This interest was maintained for nearly a decade, and Albert J. Seligman, a twenty-two-year-old mining engineer who was Jesse's son, went to Helena in 1881 to look after the family's interests. In 1887, the Gregory mine was in trouble. It was operating at a loss and the miners were due two months' back wages. Since they would not work for nothing, they kidnapped Albert Seligman and held him hostage until a settlement was made. Later, it leaked out that Harry W. Child, the mine's general manager, may have arranged the kidnapping as a way to keep the mine working. But almost as quickly as the miners got their back pay, the mine, whose ore was considered low grade, was closed and never worked again.

No record tells the full extent of J. & W. Seligman & Co.'s experience with mines. But the net result is perhaps shown by the firm's balance sheet for 1897 when Isaac Newton Seligman was running the business. Of sixteen mining holdings, there were shares held in six companies with a total value of six dollars.

Before the Twentieth Century dawned on January 1, 1901, it was decided to close Seligman & Stettheimer in Frankfurt and liquidation of the branch was completed in 1903. Henry Seligman, one of the founders and resident partner in Frankfurt, retired from active business and until his death February 20, 1909, spent his time in benevolent activities. Theodore Hellman, who had managed the New Orleans branch, died October 9, 1901.

During 1903 Isaac Newton Seligman wrote his cousin in London that "business is generally dull. I am pleased that I am not offered any interest in syndicates, as nine cases out of ten for the past six months or a year have turned out unprofitable." At least one unprofitable deal came along in 1906, too. It was an underwriting of gold bonds for American Telephone & Telegraph Company and it was a total failure.

Nevertheless, J. & W. Seligman & Co. still was growing in 1906. On Friday, April 13, *The New York Herald* reported the firm "filed plans for a new eleven story fireproof bank and office building to be erected in the block at the intersection of William, South William and Stone streets. It is to be of the Italian Renaissance type with façades of granite at the first story and limestone above, with decorative tower, crowned by a sculptured figure at the William street corner. The main entrance will be in South William street, adorned by a two story arched porch, flanked by engaged columns and bronze electroliers. The cornice above the arch will be decorated with four eagles of carved stone. The banking offices will occupy the basement and first stories with a mezzanine story and will be furnished elaborately. The building is to cost $500,000." It actually cost $1,000,000. Nearly fifteen months later, *The Herald* reported the firm would move July 8, 1907, "from their present quarters, the Mills Building, to their new bank building, No. 1 William

BOTH : LIBRARY OF CONGRESS

Photographers had a difficult time taking his photograph. He did not like it. In 1907, John Pierpont Morgan took charge of the Nation's economy and restored the people's confidence.

Pearson's Magazine *published what it called "the first successful attempt to catch in the camera the great . . . scene on the floor of the New York Stock Exchange . . . The scene is on a dull day. It would be impossible to photograph the frantic [activity] on a busy day." It all happened in 1907.*

Joseph Lionel Seligman, son of Isaac Newton, was born in 1877. On January 1, 1917, he became a partner; retired December 31, 1920. An Army officer in World War I and a Naval officer in World War II, he died in 1944.

COURTESY, MRS. JOSEPH L. SELIGMAN

street . . . The firm has been a fixture . . . on the corner of Broad street and Exchange place, many years before the construction of the Mills Building."

In March, before the move was made, stock prices broke. Isaac Newton Seligman and other bankers were summoned to Washington to discuss the situation with President Theodore Roosevelt. By October, the Panic of 1907 was upon the Nation. And it took J. P. Morgan, whom Frederick Lewis Allen called "a one-man Federal Reserve Bank," to save the country's financial system.

Morgan was semi-retired, but through persuasion and common sense he provided leadership at a time when thousands rushed to withdraw their bank deposits and the stock market was ready to collapse. One day, within five minutes, Morgan raised $27,000,000 to support the market, and when it closed for the day, cheers for him were so loud he could hear them across the street in his office. Yet, by evening, "there was almost no currency left for normal commercial life," author Walter Lord says. J. & W. Seligman & Co. got dollar bills, Herbert Bachman recalls, from The Anglo-Californian Bank which in turn were sold at a three or four cent premium. The bank got the bills, it was said, from frugal Chinese laborers on the Coast.

Morgan's iron will saved those institutions which were worth saving by raising millions to plug up first one weak spot, then another. During the conferences on what to do next, Isaac Newton Seligman was one of the bankers summoned to the Morgan Library on Manhattan's Thirty-sixth Street.

In an interview in 1907, Isaac Newton declared that "wealthy men are no longer satisfied with horses, they must have automobiles." He was, in fact, a little behind the times, for the automobile was already becoming more than a rich man's plaything, and one of the early geniuses of the new industry was William C. Durant. He had formed General Motors in 1908, only to lose control of it two years later to a group of bankers including J. & W. Seligman & Co.; Lee, Higginson & Co.; Kuhn, Loeb & Co., and the Central Trust Company. Albert Strauss was elected to the board and helped to run General Motors for five years. In 1915 the company declared a $50 dividend on each share of common stock—"the largest cash dividend ever declared on a stock listed on the Big Board up to that time," says Alfred E. Sloan, Jr., former board chairman of General Motors. Durant regained control of the corporation the same year and Albert Strauss left the board.

While the New York firm was involved with General Motors, William Seligman died in Paris on January 4, 1910. His brother Leopold died December 5, 1911, leaving only two of the original eight Seligman brothers alive—Isaac in London and James in New York. James died at ninety-two on August 20, 1916, having been the oldest living member of the New York Stock Exchange.

William Pyle Philips became a partner of the firm on October 1, 1912. A native of West Chester, Pennsylvania, he had been a partner in the law firm of Byrne & Cutcheon. Philips had helped argue a Metropolitan Street Railway receivership case and had impressed the Seligman partners.

During these years, the partners turned again toward Latin America. They entered into an agreement under which J. & W. Seligman & Co. and Brown Brothers & Co. of New York in effect became bankers to the government of Nicaragua. The relationship lasted until 1929, when both firms withdrew from their positions. At one time, along with helping to stabilize the country's fiscal affairs, the two firms held a controlling interest in a narrow-gauge steam railroad, the Ferrocarril del Pacifico de Nicaragua, and the National Bank of Nicaragua.

Meanwhile, when World War I began in Europe, Seligman Frères & Cie., like many French banking institutions, was in precarious condition and threatened with suspension. David Washington Seligman, William's son, then head of the firm in which Isaac Newton was also a partner, came to New York to seek a way to save Seligman Frères. It was agreed that at the end of 1914 Isaac Newton would withdraw. "We will say that the reason" he said, "is due to the fact that we are a neutral firm, and desire not to be involved in any possible eventualities." J. & W. Seligman & Co. advanced Seligman Frères the funds it needed. In November 1921, the French firm became Banque Seligman, which in 1935 became what is now Seligman & Cie.

Another wartime project was the Mercantile Bank of the Americas, Incorporated formed by J. & W. Seligman & Co. and Brown Brothers & Co. to conduct banking operations in several Central and South American countries, an area in which little had been done to establish direct banking connections with the United States. Even though Guaranty Trust Company joined the two founding firms the following year, and in spite of some initial success, the project was defeated by a combination of overexpansion and postwar inflation followed by severe deflation. The founders lost their investments and the bank was dissolved in February 1926.

J. & W. Seligman & Co. quickly felt the effect as soon as the United States entered the War. Henry Seligman was already a member of Governor Charles S. Whitman's New York State Defense Committee. Isaac Newton Seligman's son, Joseph Lionel, admitted to the firm on January 1, 1917, went off to France as a Lieutenant in the Army's 27th Division in April and came home a Major in December. The biggest blow came on Monday, October 1 that same year when *The New York*

William C. Durant was called a "genius" of the automobile industry. He founded General Motors, only to lose control. For five years, Albert Strauss was one of a group of bankers who helped to operate the company.

AUTOMOBILE MANUFACTURERS ASSOCIATION, INC.

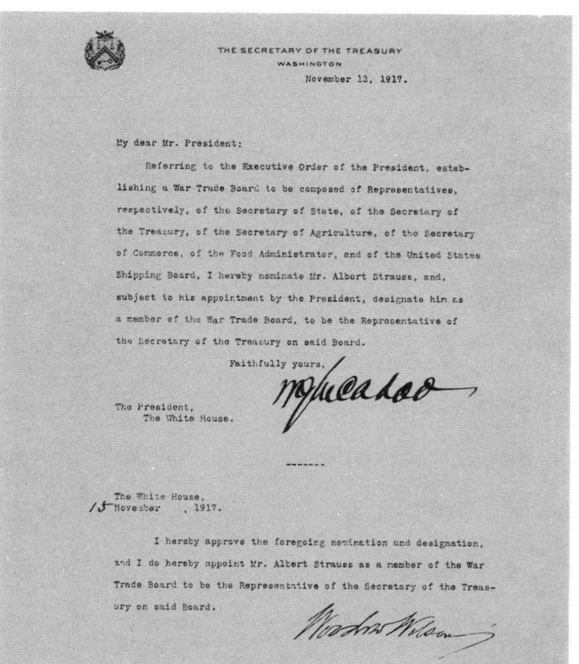

THE SECRETARY OF THE TREASURY
WASHINGTON

November 13, 1917.

My dear Mr. President:

Referring to the Executive Order of the President, establishing a War Trade Board to be composed of Representatives, respectively, of the Secretary of State, of the Secretary of the Treasury, of the Secretary of Agriculture, of the Secretary of Commerce, of the Food Administrator, and of the United States Shipping Board, I hereby nominate Mr. Albert Strauss, and, subject to his appointment by the President, designate him as a member of the War Trade Board, to be the Representative of the Secretary of the Treasury on said Board.

Faithfully yours,

WGMcAdoo

The President,
The White House.

The White House,
15 November , 1917.

I hereby approve the foregoing nomination and designation, and I do hereby appoint Mr. Albert Strauss as a member of the War Trade Board to be the Representative of the Secretary of the Treasury on said Board.

Woodrow Wilson

COURTESY, MRS. HENRY J. MALI

Son-in-law of President Woodrow Wilson, Treasury Secretary William Gibbs McAdoo nominated Albert Strauss to the War Trade Board, November 13, 1917. Wilson, two days later, wrote the date in ink and signed the appointment.

Times headlined a front-page story: FALL FROM HORSE KILLS I. N. SELIGMAN. The previous day, while riding near his summer home in Irvington, New York, Isaac Newton fell or was thrown from his horse. He was sixty-two.

Albert Strauss was the next to leave the firm. Secretary of the Treasury William Gibbs McAdoo asked him to advise the Treasury on matters related to international credit. In November 1917, he was appointed the Secretary's personal representative on the War Trade Board, and the following August became Vice-Governor of the Federal Reserve Board. He resigned all of his many corporate posts, gave up his partnership, and Frederick Strauss and Henry Seligman took over the active management of J. & W. Seligman & Co.

In January 1919, Secretary McAdoo sent Albert Strauss to Europe for the Treasury "in an advisory capacity in connection with the armistice discussions and other financial questions arising at the Peace Conference." Returning to Washington, he helped tackle the seemingly impossible task of untangling the Government's finances. On January 29, 1920, he delivered his resignation to Treasury Secretary Carter Glass, with whom he had worked and who was also planning to resign. But his Government service wasn't finished. Glass' successor in the Treasury, David F. Houston, told him "you are . . . appointed a Special Commissioner of the United States Treasury without compensation . . . to investigate all matters concerning currency and exchange in the Virgin Islands." Finally, on January 1, 1921, Albert Strauss was able to get his resignation accepted, and he rejoined J. & W. Seligman & Co.

Sixty-two days later, a former U.S. Senator from Ohio stood before the crowds at the Capitol in Washington and declared, "A regret for the mistakes of yesterday must not, however, blind us to the tasks of today." Warren Gamaliel Harding, the President, saw good times ahead and observed, "The forward course of the business cycle is unmistakable."

Members of the Federal Reserve Board, 1919, when Albert Strauss was Vice-Governor, and other officials joined him in autographing this picture. The men are (from left): Governor W. P. G. Harding, assistant secretary W. T. Chapman, Adolph C. Miller, Henry A. Moehlenpah, Secretary of the Treasury and ex-officio member Carter Glass, Strauss, Charles S. Hamlin, and Comptroller of the Currency and ex-officio member John Skelton Williams. The photo was taken in Washington, D. C.

COURTESY, MRS. HENRY J. MALI

NINE

Enthusiasm is that temper of mind in which the imagination has got the better of the judgment.

—Bishop William Warburton, 1698-1779

Americans came out of World War I sure of their country's power and feeling somewhat larger than lifesize. Politically, the Nation soon swore off strong drink, foreign entanglements, and Wilsonian idealism. Privately, this quickly came to mean moonshine and jazz, close concentration on business, and a surprising belief in the perfectibility of man.

The business community shook itself out of the short, severe depression which ushered in the 1920's and looked ahead confidently to years of prosperity. Since the world had been made "safe for democracy," people were once again free to be concerned with themselves. A good many fell under the spell of Dr. Émile Coué, a French psychologist who advocated autosuggestion for self-improvement—"Day by day in every way I'm getting better and better." Tin Pan Alley contributed *Yes, We Have No Bananas* to popular culture and the slogan and the song just about set the tenor of the times to come.

The effect of deep-seated social and business changes on J. & W. Seligman & Co. was not immediate. From 1915 through 1921, the firm, along with a large number of others, had participated in underwriting groups in raising billions for Great Britain, France, and Italy to finance the War. It had also marketed bonds and preferred stocks for a long list of companies, including Montana Power Company, Cuba Cane Sugar Corporation, Sinclair Oil & Refining, Cincinnati Gas and Electric, and a number of railroads. The deposit banking business, which provided commercial banking services to a long-established clientele, continued, and the firm, like others in Wall Street, had begun to feel the postwar upsurge in brokerage transactions.

In 1919, the Seligman Building at 1 William Street, which the firm had occupied since 1907, was sold at a substantial profit, and J. & W. Seligman & Co. moved into what had been the Central Trust Company building at 54 Wall Street. Roomier and more nearly in the heart of the financial district, the new quarters afforded a spacious partners' room on the second floor. There were ornate fireplaces at either end, over one of which was hung a painting of Joseph, Jesse, and James Seligman, the original resident partners at the New York branch of the firm. The bank tellers' cages were at street level and other activities were housed on the upper floors, reached by an old-fashioned cage elevator which gave a ponderous unity to the overall operation.

Emil Carlebach, who had managed the deposit banking business and the bulk of the firm's foreign correspondence, retired in 1919. Joseph L. Seligman decided not to continue with the firm and withdrew at the end of 1920. Albert Strauss' Federal Reserve Board term, followed by other Gov-

The partners' room, on the second floor at 54 Wall Street, was spacious and well lighted. A portrait of James, Jesse, and Joseph Seligman – residents in the New York branch from the day the firm was founded in 1864–hung over the fireplace.

COURTESY, FRANCIS F. RANDOLPH

ernment service, had been extended to 1921. Henry Seligman and Frederick Strauss found themselves with a major investment banking and brokerage business to run as the decade began with only one young partner–thirty-eight-year-old William Philips–to provide continuity. Jefferson Seligman, the other partner, had not been active in the firm for a number of years.

William Philips had worked in the field of railroad finance, first as a practicing lawyer and later under Frederick Strauss' tutelage. The contributions he had made convinced the senior partners that if the firm planned to continue to serve those railroads for which it had traditionally been investment banker, it was essential to find more men with backgrounds in law.

With eyes on the years ahead, Henry Seligman and the Strausses began to bring in new blood at a faster rate than it had ever been done before. They turned to Cravath & Henderson, then the firm's counsel, to get young lawyers, and invited Robert Vose White, Earle Bailie, and Francis Fitz Randolph, all of whom had worked on Seligman business at one time or another, to come into the firm. John C. Jay, Jr., former president of The Pierce-Arrow Motor Car Company and a widely-known industrialist, was brought in with the thought that his extensive business connections would attract new investment banking accounts. White and Jay were made partners in 1921. Walter Seligman, David J.'s son, became a partner in 1922 and Bailie and Randolph were admitted to the partnership in 1923.

The firm's present senior partner, Francis Randolph, was born in Elmira, New York, and since his father was a railroad man whose progress up the executive ladder usually meant a move for the family, he grew up in Boston, Massachusetts, and Baltimore, Maryland. He spent four years at Phillips Academy at Exeter, New Hampshire, and was graduated from Yale College with a Phi Beta Kappa key. Then he went to Harvard Law School during the normal school year and spent his Summers earning a Master of Arts degree in English literature from Yale. He was awarded both his M.A. and an LL.B. degree in law in 1914, the year he joined Cravath & Henderson. In 1916, Randolph went with Squadron A of the New York Cavalry to the Mexican Border, and then to France with the American Expeditionary Forces. He served in France as a Captain with the First Division's 6th Field Artillery and was awarded the Silver Star.

As it did to many young men, World War I gave Randolph a chance to think about his future. He spent a year with the U.S. Delegation to the Peace Conference and the Reparations Commission in Paris and London. By the time he returned to New York, he had pretty well decided that a career in

During its existence, J. & W. Seligman & Co. has always been located in the financial district, but only once was it literally on Wall Street. Offices were at 54 Wall from 1919 until 1940. The building still stands and is in use.

COURTESY, FRANCIS F. RANDOLPH

finance was more attractive to him than one in law. When the chance came along to go to J. & W. Seligman & Co. with White and Bailie, who had made the move from the Cravath firm a year or two earlier, Randolph says, "It looked to be a broad-gauged career, which didn't involve the drudgery of the law. It seemed to promise a chance for more originality and more reward, and I thought I was better fitted for it."

Randolph, Bailie, and White may have left the law to escape its uninteresting prospects, but they soon were involved in plenty of hard work for the Seligman firm. While Bailie set about learning the underwriting business and how to bring in new accounts, Randolph and White were put to work on the details of railroad finance under Frederick Strauss. All three were expected to take a hand in day-to-day administration and in helping run the deposit banking department. Randolph's first real assignment was to work under Frederick Strauss and William Philips on the detailed administrative work of a plan for reorganizing what is now the Missouri-Kansas-Texas Railroad Company. This was followed in subsequent years with work for such railroads as the Great Northern; Pere Marquette; St. Louis-San Francisco; Wabash; and Chicago, Rock Island & Pacific.

"Fortunately," Randolph remembers, "working conditions were pleasant enough, even though a

Paul D. Cravath of Cravath, Henderson & de Gersdorff once called Frederick Strauss (below) a "working phenomenon." In 1925, Strauss was a director of twenty-five companies and a Rockefeller Foundation trustee.

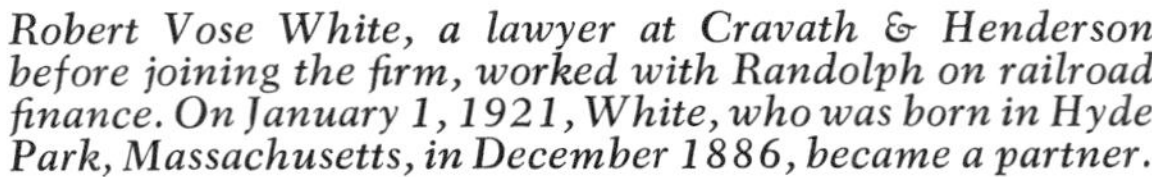

Robert Vose White, a lawyer at Cravath & Henderson before joining the firm, worked with Randolph on railroad finance. On January 1, 1921, White, who was born in Hyde Park, Massachusetts, in December 1886, became a partner.

COURTESY, MRS. HENRY J. MALI

COURTESY, MRS. ROBERT V. WHITE

little old-fashioned, for those of us who also were assigned to handling the routine details of the business were pushed pretty hard to keep up. We invariably started promptly in the morning and stayed until well after six in the evening, and, of course, everyone in the Street worked a full day, or at least a half day, on Saturdays."

Under the influence of the younger partners, J. & W. Seligman & Co.'s "old-fashioned" atmosphere gradually began to give way. Office procedures were modernized, the outmoded ledger copybook accounting system was brought up-to-date under the guidance of Samuel Nagler, who had been in the bookkeeping department since 1917. More and more young people joined the staff as business expanded. Historically, the firm's underwritings had been confined largely to bond and preferred stock issues of companies with which the Seligmans had maintained long-term investment banking relationships and of a quality which normally appealed to conservative clients with substantial portfolios. But as Earle Bailie began to get a grasp of the business, he realized that the bulk of securities to be issued in the postwar world would come from foreign countries planning to bring their economies up-to-date and from new companies looking for capital with which to expand. He also had the vision to recognize that the market for such securities would not be found only among traditional investors. They would be bought by the man in the street.

Bailie was a big, forceful man with almost limitless energy. He was determined to succeed, and men who worked with him during the 1920's remember that he seemed determined to make them succeed, too. Always impeccably dressed, down to the flower in his lapel, he insisted that all the staff, even the office boys, work in jackets and ties and wear hats when they ran a message outside the office. Hours meant little to him, and when he worked, people around him had to work to keep up, sometimes late into the night. Bailie had established a brilliant record at the University of Minnesota and Harvard Law School and had been marked as a young man to watch when he joined Cravath & Henderson. All of his driving energy and broad imagination came with him to J. & W. Seligman & Co.

His earliest efforts went into capturing a part of

Earle Bailie, says Francis Randolph, was "very hard working and a great asset for any business team." Bailie, who was born in Milwaukee in September 1890, was a lawyer before he joined Seligman. He died November 15, 1940.

COURTESY, MRS. EARLE BAILIE

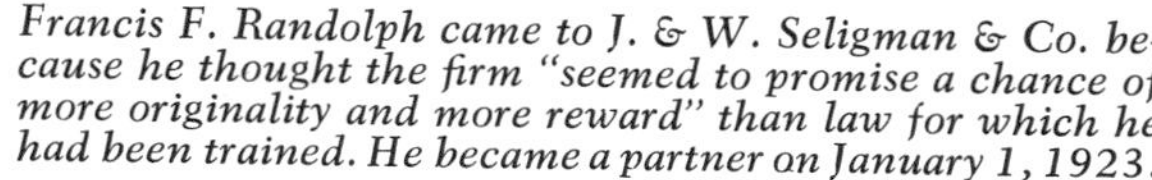

Francis F. Randolph came to J. & W. Seligman & Co. because he thought the firm "seemed to promise a chance of more originality and more reward" than law for which he had been trained. He became a partner on January 1, 1923.

COURTESY, FRANCIS F. RANDOLPH

the foreign financing the aftermath of the War had brought to the United States. Just as the country served as banker to the world after World War II, it was the major source of funds needed by almost all countries after the first World War. The difference was that in the 1920's financing foreign governments was still private enterprise. Like any other borrower, a government negotiated with a banker to underwrite a bond issue at the going rate of interest, and private capitalists or institutions invested in the bonds. And in the 1920's obligations of governments abroad seemed to be the most attractive, gilt-edged securities money could buy.

At first, true to its conservative heritage, when a foreign nation sought the Seligman firm's services, negotiations were begun slowly and cautiously. But as time went on, bankers competed more keenly for the underwritings, and clients demanded more and more foreign bonds for investment. As this business grew, Henry C. Breck, a young Californian with considerable experience abroad as well as in this country, was brought in to help with negotiations with foreign governments.

Breck, whose father was a banker, earned a Phi Beta Kappa key at the University of California where he majored in economics and later studied law. He left law school in 1914 to become the secretary to a member of the Federal Reserve Board in Washington where he served until the War took him overseas with the American Army as an Infantry Lieutenant in the 91st Division. Following the War, he was first an assistant to a member of the American Financial Delegation to the Paris Peace Conference, later worked with the Federal Reserve Bank in San Francisco, and then served as an aide to the Agent General for Reparations Payments in Berlin. He decided, in 1926, it was time to start making a permanent career, and since finance interested him, he came to New York and talked with partners of J. & W. Seligman & Co. at just the time they were looking for a vigorous man to help develop international new business.

But, it wasn't just high-yielding foreign bonds investors were seeking in the 1920's. Very early it was clear they wanted a direct share in the fabulous growth of American business which everyone thought was ahead. By 1924, common stocks, historically a businessman's risk, which could give investors that direct share, not only became respectable for even the more conservative investor to consider—they became fashionable. The great bull market of the Twenties had begun.

J. & W. Seligman & Co. never was a leading underwriter of common stocks—it was too conservative. But Bailie, Randolph, and White, with the approval of Henry Seligman and the Strausses, gradually began to offer the firm's services to a few corporations seeking equity capital. In 1924 the firm participated in a common stock offering for the first time in the postwar period—400,000 shares of Briggs Manufacturing Company. The next year brought underwritings of bonds and preferred stocks for such names as Dodge Brothers, Chicago Motor Coach, Cunard Steamship Company, and National Dairy Products.

Investor confidence continued to escalate, and the partners' new efforts to bring new business to the firm showed more noticeable results by 1926. William Philips, an aloof intellectual, highly respected, but all business when downtown, seemed to come to life after hours. Besides being a competent investment banker, he had a deep and serious interest in the theater. He made a point of knowing the leading lights on Broadway, and his friends included the prime movers of the legitimate stage and the burgeoning motion picture business. Philips' connection resulted in the firm's doing business for Shubert Theatre Corporation, United Artists Theatre Circuit, and other well-known names in the entertainment world.

With increasing public participation in the securities market, J. & W. Seligman & Co. decided to become a retail distributor, as well as an underwriter of new underwritings. This was a radical move, for it put the firm in contact with the general investing public for the first time since it was founded nearly sixty-two years earlier.

A retail sales department was launched in 1927 by hiring Kenneth C. Hanau, a securities salesman who had made an outstanding record of success at Redmond & Co., one of many firms with which J. & W. Seligman & Co. had participated in under-

GUY GILLETTE

Henry Breck was graduated from the University of California; attended law school there. After joining J. & W. Seligman, he worked under Earle Bailie on the "investigation of and negotiating loans for foreign countries."

HAVERFORD COLLEGE

William Philips, says Randolph, was "a very skillful lawyer. He was excellent on reorganization work which we did a lot of in the Twenties." Philips became a partner on October 1, 1912, and retired from the firm June 30, 1928.

writings. Personable, hard-working, and thoroughly trained in his craft, Hanau rapidly established branch offices in Albany, New York; Chicago, Philadelphia, Pittsburgh, San Francisco, Seattle, and Washington. He hired sales representatives and clerks by the dozens to man the new offices, and arranged for correspondents to handle Seligman offerings in other cities of the United States, Europe, and South America. As the staff grew, the firm took over one floor after another at 54 Wall Street until it occupied all eight floors.

It was a time of widespread optimism, willingness to spend money, and to take risks. But it was also a period of genuine business expansion needed to satisfy the Nation's growing population and rising standard of living. The automobile, for example, was changing Americans' way of life faster than it had ever been changed before. Mobility, provided by the family car and the spreading influence of radio, whetted appetites for more and more goods. Retail chain stores mushroomed, mass entertainment became big business, and the call for electric power and the conveniences it brought outran the utility companies' ability to supply it. Such massive business growth took money in undreamed of amounts, and as the economy's need for expansion capital began to reach a peak in the late Twenties, J. & W . Seligman & Co. was working hard to help raise it.

Henry Seligman was still active as the senior among the ten partners, and he always was looked to for advice and guidance. But his days were more and more devoted to private affairs. The Strausses, on the other hand—especially Frederick—were acknowledged leaders in the financial community. Albert had returned to the firm in 1921, and he continued to be sought out for his opinion on Government fiscal and monetary policies until his death on March 28, 1929. Frederick Strauss had been a trustee of the Rockefeller Foundation since 1916—he served until he was sixty-five—and he sat on the boards of a long list of railroads, transit companies, utilities, industrial companies, and banks. Despite his wealth and prominence, which Francis Randolph declared he earned "through sheer character and brain power," Frederick Strauss was probably closer to being truly loved by the staff than any other Seligman partner ever was. Gentle and soft-spoken, he is remembered by men and women who

The firm offered a convertible preferred stock issue for United Artists Theatre Circuit, Inc. in June 1926. William Philips was a director of the corporation whose business was "exclusively in the operation of theatres."

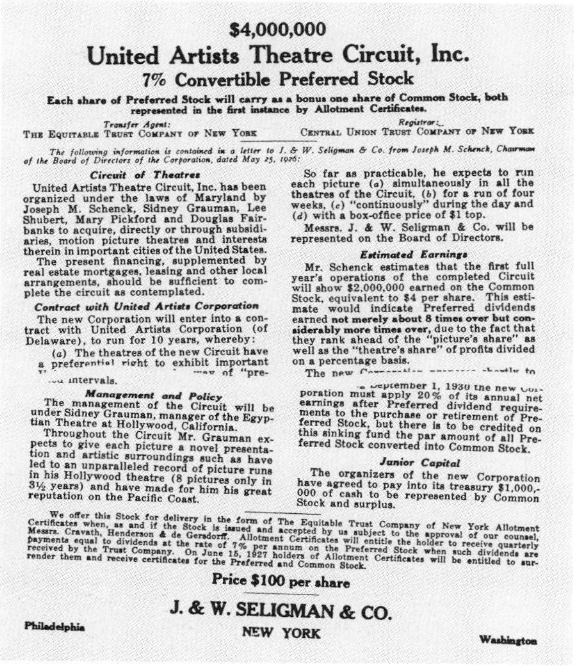

J. & W. SELIGMAN & CO.

$4,000,000

United Artists Theatre Circuit, Inc.

7% Convertible Preferred Stock

Each share of Preferred Stock will carry as a bonus one share of Common Stock, both represented in the first instance by Allotment Certificates.

Transfer Agent: THE EQUITABLE TRUST COMPANY OF NEW YORK

Registrar: CENTRAL UNION TRUST COMPANY OF NEW YORK

The following information is contained in a letter to J. & W. Seligman & Co. from Joseph M. Schenck, Chairman of the Board of Directors of the Corporation, dated May 25, 1926:

Circuit of Theatres

United Artists Theatre Circuit, Inc. has been organized under the laws of Maryland by Joseph M. Schenck, Sidney Grauman, Lee Shubert, Mary Pickford and Douglas Fairbanks to acquire, directly or through subsidiaries, motion picture theatres and interests therein in important cities of the United States.

The present financing, supplemented by real estate mortgages, leasing and other local arrangements, should be sufficient to complete the circuit as contemplated.

Contract with United Artists Corporation

The new Corporation will enter into a contract with United Artists Corporation (of Delaware), to run for 10 years, whereby:

(a) The theatres of the new Circuit have a preferential right to exhibit important [illegible] of "pre-[illegible] intervals.

Management and Policy

The management of the Circuit will be under Sidney Grauman, manager of the Egyptian Theatre at Hollywood, California.

Throughout the Circuit Mr. Grauman expects to give each picture a novel presentation and artistic surroundings such as have led to an unparalleled record of picture runs in his Hollywood theatre (8 pictures only in 3½ years) and have made for him his great reputation on the Pacific Coast.

So far as practicable, he expects to run each picture (a) simultaneously in all the theatres of the Circuit, (b) for a run of four weeks, (c) "continuously" during the day and (d) with a box-office price of $1 top.

Messrs. J. & W. Seligman & Co. will be represented on the Board of Directors.

Estimated Earnings

Mr. Schenck estimates that the first full year's operations of the completed Circuit will show $2,000,000 earned on the Common Stock, equivalent to $4 per share. This estimate would indicate Preferred dividends earned **not merely about 8 times over but considerably more times over,** due to the fact that they rank ahead of the "picture's share" as well as the "theatre's share" of profits divided on a percentage basis.

The new [illegible] to [illegible] September 1, 1930 the new Corporation must apply 20% of its annual net earnings after Preferred dividend requirements to the purchase or retirement of Preferred Stock, but there is to be credited on this sinking fund the par amount of all Preferred Stock converted into Common Stock.

Junior Capital

The organizers of the new Corporation have agreed to pay into its treasury $1,000,000 of cash to be represented by Common Stock and surplus.

We offer this Stock for delivery in the form of The Equitable Trust Company of New York Allotment Certificates when, as and if the Stock is issued and accepted by us subject to the approval of our counsel, Messrs. Cravath, Henderson & de Gersdorff. Allotment Certificates will entitle the holder to receive quarterly payments equal to dividends at the rate of 7% per annum on the Preferred Stock when such dividends are received by the Trust Company. On June 15, 1927 holders of Allotment Certificates will be entitled to surrender them and receive certificates for the Preferred and Common Stock.

Price $100 per share

J. & W. SELIGMAN & CO.

Philadelphia NEW YORK **Washington**

UNITED ARTISTS CORPORATION

The Circuit had a contract with United Artists Corporation, founded in 1919 by (front, l to r) D. W. Griffith, Mary Pickford, Charles Chaplin, and Douglas Fairbanks. Their attorneys were Albert Banzhaf and Dennis O'Brien.

One of the stars mentioned in the United Artists Theatre Circuit prospectus was Rudolph Valentino who, in 1926, appeared in a "sex-and-sand drama" called "Son of the Sheik" with Agnes Ayres. It was Valentino's last movie.

BOTH : UNITED ARTISTS CORPORATION

The "brilliant comic artistry" of Charles Chaplin, a founder of United Artists Corporation," was seen in "The Circus," a film of 1928 which was shown in various United Artists Theatre Circuit motion picture theaters.

worked with him for his genuine interest in each of them as individuals. In those days the firm sponsored an employees' baseball team for men and a basketball team for women, and "FS," as Strauss was fondly known, attended almost every game. His name, like his brother Albert's, on a charitable campaign committee – and they served on a good many – tended to attract funds. And his presence in the office attracted business.

There were times when the range of Frederick Strauss' business and social acquaintances was hard to believe. In the 1920's, for example, he was a friend of Governor Alfred E. Smith; he worked closely on many financial transactions with Elihu Root, Theodore Roosevelt's Secretary of State and a Noble Peace Prize winner, and he frequently gave advice to public utility pioneer Harrison Williams. One day, a newly hired and still brash receptionist walked up to "FS's" desk with the news that "there's a nut out there who claims he's John D. Rockefeller and wants to see you. What shall I do with him?"

Strauss was later amused, but at that moment he lost no time in getting to the reception room to greet his distinguished guest, who frequently conferred with the banker.

J. & W. Seligman & Co. helped to market sixteen new issues in 1926, and the figure totaled twenty-eight in 1927, most of which were managed or co-managed by the firm. Corporations then, as now, generally chose an investment banking house because of historical associations and its recognized competence. The prestige of Frederick and Albert Strauss, who, in effect, embodied the firm's integrity and experience, led to underwriting issues in 1927 for established clients that included the City of New York, Brooklyn-Manhattan Transit Corporation, Columbia Gas & Electric, Montana Power, and a number of railroads. Henry Breck's work resulted in the offering of a number of South American bond issues.

In addition to service provided for established customers, new business came into the firm in a variety of ways. Sometimes it was simply a matter of the firm's offer, or perhaps its ideas for a new capitalization were superior to those of its competitors, as in the case of the sale of securities for Victor Talking Machine Company in 1927. Sometimes it was a matter of imaginative banking, as it was with Minneapolis-Honeywell Regulator Company.

The Victor Talking Machine business was introduced to J. & W. Seligman & Co. by a promotor acting for the company's owners who wanted to sell out. When the firm learned that this widely-known and successful company was for sale, it sent John Jay and William J. Keary, a young assistant in the new business department, to Philadelphia to negotiate a purchase. It's offer was accepted; the firm co-managed issues of preferred and common stock for the company with Speyer & Co., an investment banking house which had been J. & W. Seligman & Co.'s friendly rival for many years. The sale of Victor Talking Machine, owner of the world-famous "His Master's Voice" trademark, gave the public an ownership share in a company whose product was making a lasting mark on American culture. Conservative James Speyer, head of Speyer & Co., was willing to sell the stock, but he had no illusions about what recorded sound had done to the country. When one lady client gushed about the wonder of records and asked him if he owned "a Victrola himself," Speyer answered, "Two." "Why two?" she asked. "So that I can have the pleasure of turning them both off."

A truly old-fashioned investment banker, Speyer resisted more than cultural change. Over the years, he was a thoroughly dependable but unusually fussy associate in the many transactions in which he worked with the Seligman firm. At times his insistent hairsplitting over every detail in a transaction tended to frustrate his colleagues and the Seligman partners once decided to teach him a lesson. In the late 1920's, Speyer was due payment on some railroad mortgages following a reorganization. When the time came for J. & W. Seligman & Co. to pay off the mortgages, the partners determined that Speyer would get no chance to quibble about the nature of the payment. They arranged for him to receive a shipment of gold. A heavily guarded armored car made the delivery, and, led by Seligman representatives, the guards marched into Speyer's office, some lugging the gold, others with pistols drawn. Speyer, perhaps with humor of his own, looked up in surprise and exclaimed, "Good heavens! More lawyers!"

The Minneapolis-Honeywell Regulator Company underwriting in 1927 is a good example of investment banking which benefited everyone con-

COURTESY, MRS. KENNETH HANAU, SR.

Kenneth Hanau joined Seligman in 1927; became a partner the following year. He had an "excellent knowledge of securities distribution," Randolph remembers. Hanau retired from the firm on April 30, 1931, and entered industry.

COURTESY, MRS. HENRY J. MALI

"Albert Strauss was a really great banker," Cyril Quinn says. He read law at night by himself and was admitted to the bar in 1890. Although he never practiced, he had a lifelong interest in legal matters. He died in March 1929.

COURTESY, MRS. HENRY J. MALI

Frederick Strauss (left) was interested in the welfare of East Side boys. At an outing, he was pictured with New York's Governor Alfred E. Smith, Police Commissioner of the City of New York Grover Whalen, Boys' Club trustee Frank Gulden, Judge John Freschi of the Special Sessions Court in New York and Club trustee, and Charles Sabin, chairman of the Guaranty Trust Company and also Club trustee.

COURTESY, ARTHUR A. WEINAR

Baseball players for the firm (the name is on the uniform) in 1937 included (l to r): Walter Dicke, J. Gardner (Doc) Lawlor, Arthur A. Weinar, Edward McSweeney. Years earlier (June 22, 1915) Seligman challenged the Central Trust Company. A program for the contest named the players and on the inside included songs to be sung.

Annual Base-Ball Game

Central Trust Company

And

J. & W. Seligman & Company

on Tuesday Afternoon, June 22, 1915

❀ ❀ ❀

The Teams

Central Trust Co.	J. & W. S. & Co.
Hernandez, 1 B.	Spencer, R. F.
Longua, L. F.	Wigand, C.
H. Vallely, 2 B.	Straat, 3 B.
Colton, C. F.	Selover, S. S.
Kottman, 3 B.	Snyder, 1 B.
Sticknoth, R. F.	Bush, L. F.
Walker, S. S.	Hamilton, C. F.
D. Hohman, P.	Richter, 2 B.
F. Hohman, C.	Curry, P.
Substitutes	*Substitutes*
Wilson	Ewing
Clancy	Hirch
Reimers	Bohstedt
Peck	
Kessler	

COURTESY, HENRY HOLL

cerned – almost immediately, and over the years. W. R. Sweatt headed the Minneapolis Heat Regulator Company of Minneapolis, Minnesota, while Mark Honeywell ran the Honeywell Heating Specialties Company in Wabash, Indiana. The concerns were strong competitors in the heating control field. Their products complemented each other and their markets were often in the same areas.

Out of conversation between Mark Honeywell and "W. R." in the Summer of 1927, emerged the idea of a united company better to serve the customers of both, to cover the whole field more widely and more economically, and more strongly to push the concept of automatic control of all heating. Earle Bailie was called in to help work out an equitable merger and to handle additional financing for the proposed new company.

As a sidelight, while Bailie was working up a plan, William Keary was sent to Wabash to learn the details of the business. On his arrival, Keary–

John C. Jay, Jr., a member of George W. Goethals & Co. before joining J. & W. Seligman & Co. as a partner on January 1, 1921, was born in New York City in 1880. His job included negotiations for new business; underwritings.

COURTESY, MISS AMY F. PHILLIPS

Victor Talking Machine Company

CAMDEN, N. J.

January 17, 1927.

MESSRS. SPEYER & CO.,
MESSRS. J. & W. SELIGMAN & CO.
New York.

Dear Sirs,

In connection with your offering of $6 Cumulative Convertible Preferred Stock of Victor Talking Machine Company, I take pleasure in furnishing you with the following information:

BUSINESS

Victor Talking Machine Company is the largest manufacturer of talking machines and records in the world. The business was incorporated in New Jersey under its present name in 1901 and its assets have been built up almost wholly from profits.

From the beginning the Company has maintained a position of leadership through the excellence of its instruments and records and through its success in securing the services of the greatest artists under exclusive contracts. The Orthophonic Victrola and Electrola, introduced in the latter part of 1925, and the Orthophonic Victor record, placed on the market in the fall of 1926, embody the latest developments in reproducing and recording sound. These instruments and records reproduce the human voice and instrumental music with a fidelity, range and volume never before approached, and thus represent the greatest advance in the industry since the invention of the talking machine. The Company also combines the Orthophonic Victrola and Electrola with the Radiola, manufactured by the Radio Corporation of America and its allied companies, in a single instrument which thus embodies the latest developments in the talking machine and radio receiver. The instruments range in price from $1,000 for the largest combination machine down to $17.50 for portable Victrola models. There is about to be placed on the market the Auditorium Orthophonic Victrola, which has the range and

J. & W. SELIGMAN & CO.

Nipper, a black and white fox terrier owned by Francis Barraud, stood listening to his master's talking machine and inspired the London artist to paint "His Master's Voice," trade-mark of Victor Talking Machine; now RCA Victor. J. & W. Seligman & Co. participated in three underwritings for Victor Talking Machine in 1927.

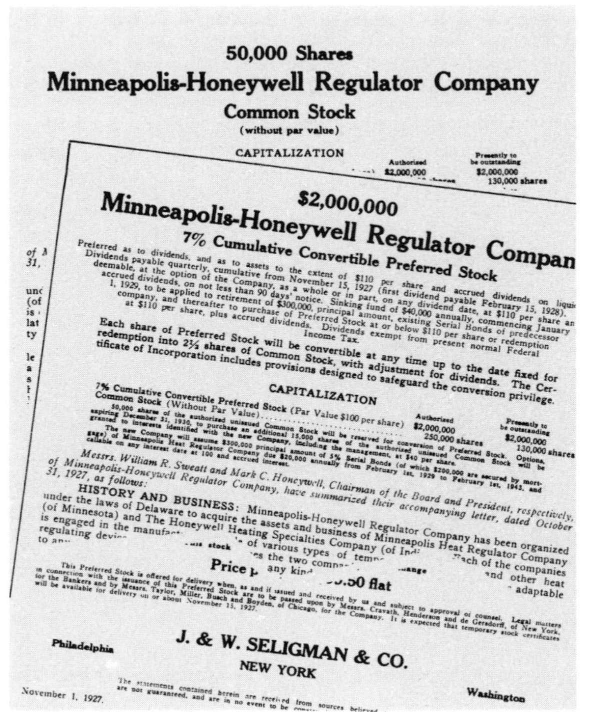

50,000 Shares

Minneapolis-Honeywell Regulator Company

Common Stock

(without par value)

CAPITALIZATION

	Authorized	Presently to be outstanding
	$2,000,000	$2,000,000
		130,000 shares

$2,000,000

Minneapolis-Honeywell Regulator Compan

7% Cumulative Convertible Preferred Stock

Preferred as to dividends, and as to assets to the extent of $110 per share and accrued dividends on liqui Dividends payable quarterly, cumulative from November 15, 1927 (first dividend payable February 15, 1928). deemable, at the option of the Company, as a whole or in part, on any dividend date, at $110 per share an accrued dividends, on not less than 90 days' notice. Sinking fund of $40,000 annually, commencing January 1, 1929, to be applied to retirement of $300,000, principal amount, existing Serial Bonds of predecessor company, and thereafter to purchase of Preferred Stock at or below $110 per share or redemption at $110 per share, plus accrued dividends. Dividends exempt from present normal Federal Income Tax.

Each share of Preferred Stock will be convertible at any time up to the date fixed for redemption into 2½ shares of Common Stock, with adjustment for dividends. The Certificate of Incorporation includes provisions designed to safeguard the conversion privilege.

CAPITALIZATION

	Authorized	Presently to be outstanding
7% Cumulative Convertible Preferred Stock (Par Value $100 per share)	$2,000,000	$2,000,000
Common Stock (Without Par Value)	250,000 shares	130,000 shares

50,000 shares of the authorized unissued Common Stock will be reserved for conversion of Preferred Stock. Options, expiring December 31, 1930, to purchase an additional 15,000 shares of the authorized unissued Common Stock will be granted to interests identified with the new Company, including the management, at $40 per share.

The new Company will assume $300,000 principal amount of 5% Serial Bonds (of which $200,000 are secured by mortgage) of Minneapolis Heat Regulator Company due $20,000 annually from February 1st, 1929 to February 1st, 1943, and callable on any interest date at 100 and accrued interest.

Messrs. William R. Sweatt and Mark C. Honeywell, Chairman of the Board and President, respectively, of Minneapolis-Honeywell Regulator Company, have summarized their accompanying letter, dated October 31, 1927, as follows:

HISTORY AND BUSINESS: Minneapolis-Honeywell Regulator Company has been organized under the laws of Delaware to acquire the assets and business of Minneapolis Heat Regulator Company (of Minnesota) and The Honeywell Heating Specialties Company (of Ind... ...ach of the companies is engaged in the manufa... of various types of tem... ...nd other heat regulating devi... ...es the two comp... any kin... ...ange ... adaptable to an...

Price ... .50 flat

This Preferred Stock is offered for delivery when, as and if issued and received by us and subject to approval of counsel. Legal matters in connection with the issuance of this Preferred Stock are to be passed upon by Messrs. Cravath, Henderson and de Gersdorff, of New York, for the Bankers and by Messrs. Taylor, Miller, Busch and Boyden, of Chicago, for the Company. It is expected that temporary stock certificates will be available for delivery on or about November 15, 1927.

J. & W. SELIGMAN & CO.

Philadelphia NEW YORK Washington

November 1, 1927.

The statements contained herein are received from sources believed ... are not guaranteed, and are in no event to be ...

J. & W. SELIGMAN & CO.

Honeywell Inc., as it's now known, was formed by merging the Minneapolis Heat Regulator Company and the Honeywell Heating Specialties Company in 1927. Two issues of the company's stock were underwritten by the firm. The Model 4010 Residential Thermostat (below, left) was a typical product at the time of the merger; the T86 Residential Thermostat is a widely-used product of 1964.

HONEYWELL INC.

who never allowed business to interfere with his sense of the appropriate–wired the Seligman office in New York: "This cannot fail to be a successful venture in the heat regulating field. The name of the boss in Minneapolis is Sweatt, and the chief engineer here is named Shivers." Keary's humor proved prophetic.

The plan Seligman produced proved sound and the new company became the Minneapolis-Honeywell Regulator Company. Shares of the two old companies were exchanged for shares in the new one, and J. & W. Seligman & Co. sold an issue of preferred stock and additional common stock to the public to raise added funds needed by the new company. The Honeywell underwriting was undoubtedly one of the most successful ever undertaken by the firm, both in terms of the company it produced, now known as Honeywell Inc., one of the Nation's leading electrical and electronics products manufacturers, and for investors who bought the shares. In the depths of the Depression the common stock which had been offered in November 1927 at $32.50 a share had declined to $11. But for investors who held on, every $1,000 invested in shares of Minneapolis-Honeywell common when it was first offered had grown in value to about $90,000 by October 1, 1964. In addition, the $1,000 had earned dividends totaling approximately $22,000 to the same date.

The Honeywell experience provides an excellent illustration of an investment principle which is basic in the investment management work of the modern Seligman firm. When fundamental values are sound, management is capable, and long-term prospects are good, a security should be held, without regard for intermediate fluctuations in market price.

As the great bull market moved up in 1928, so did J. & W. Seligman & Co.'s earnings. Kenneth Hanau was given a direct participation in them by being made a partner on December 1. Alexander I. Henderson, coming from the law firm of Cravath, de Gersdorff, Swaine & Wood, successor to Cravath & Henderson, which his father had headed and where he had been a close friend of Randolph, Bailie, and White, became a partner the same day.

Pressed for more efficient space as the staff continued to increase, the partners called in decorators to completely refurbish 54 Wall Street. Individual partners' offices—in addition to the partners' room on the second floor — were provided and furnished to each man's personal taste. A big, well-appointed library-sitting room was established on one of the upper floors, and above it—on "The Roof"—dining rooms and a kitchen were installed so that partners and staff could entertain visiting clients at lunch conveniently and in private.

Jefferson Seligman continued as a general partner of the firm until July 1934, but the fortune his father, James, had left him compounded by his own investments, helped subdue any desire he might have had to take on daily responsibilities. He came downtown regularly, however, and "somewhere along the line," Geoffrey T. Hellman wrote in the October 30, 1954, issue of *The New Yorker,* "he got off on a novel tack" and "began to establish himself as the fruit-and-ginger Seligman. He came to the office every day, or nearly every day, with a basket, from which he distributed fruit and ginger. He had a theory that if you ate fruit and ginger, you not only felt well but thought well and could make good decisions, so he would take his basket first to the partners' room, where the brains were supposed to be, and press his products on his cousins . . . and . . . other partners . . . 'On even the busiest days, the partners would accept the fruit and ginger Jeff offered,'" William Keary told Hellman. " 'He would then distribute the remainder to the lower echelons. One day, when I was talking to one of the partners in the partners' room, Jeff gave me a banana. I went back to my desk, in another room, and a little while later Jeff showed up and started to hand me an orange. He peered at me and withdrew the orange. "You've already had your fruit," he said.'"

"Mr. Jeff," as he was called, "was completely removed from the business," Francis Randolph explains. "He just had a capital interest and had no regular tasks."

But everyone else in the firm had plenty to do during 1928. Rising stock market volume and an increasing number of corporate and individual clients kept the firm busy day after day and often late into the night. About midyear, William Philips withdrew from the firm to become financial advisor to a group of motion picture companies. Henry Breck became a partner on December 1, and Cyril J. C. Quinn was hired to head the buying depart-

A World War I veteran, Alexander I. Henderson worked with the Peace Commission in France; joined a New York law firm; then became a Seligman partner on December 1, 1928. He withdrew in 1932 and returned to law practice.

COURTESY, MRS. ALEXANDER I. HENDERSON

FPG

Jefferson Seligman retired from the firm in 1934. An active equestrian, his lobbying for an improved bridle path in Central Park paid off and the Board of Estimate appropriated $100,000 for it. He died on June 18, 1937.

In the garden after a dinner given by the Council of Peoples' Commissars for the American Relief Administration in Moscow in 1923, Cyril J. C. Quinn (center) was seated with (from left) Vice-Commissar (later Commissar) of Foreign Affairs Maxim Litvinov, Acting President of the Council of Peoples' Commissars Leo Kamenev, leading Communist Party journalist Karl Radek, and Commissar of Health Aleksandrovich Nickolai Semashko.

COURTESY, CYRIL J. C. QUINN

Two stock issues for The Maytag Company were underwritten by the firm in 1928. Streamlining of the company's product has taken place from that time when the Model 90 wringer washer was manufactured to the Model A902 Custom Deluxe automatic washer in wide use today.

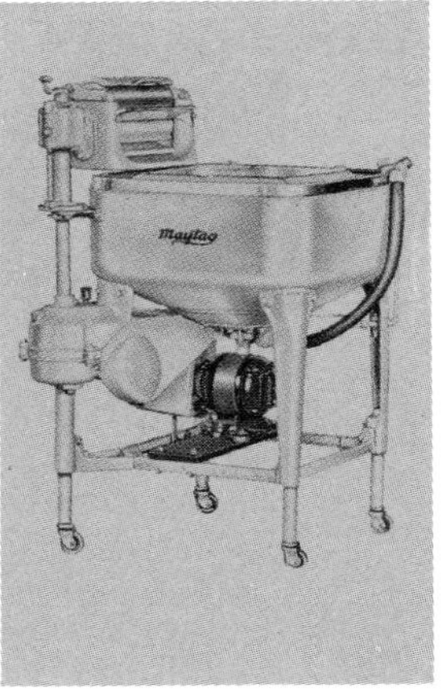

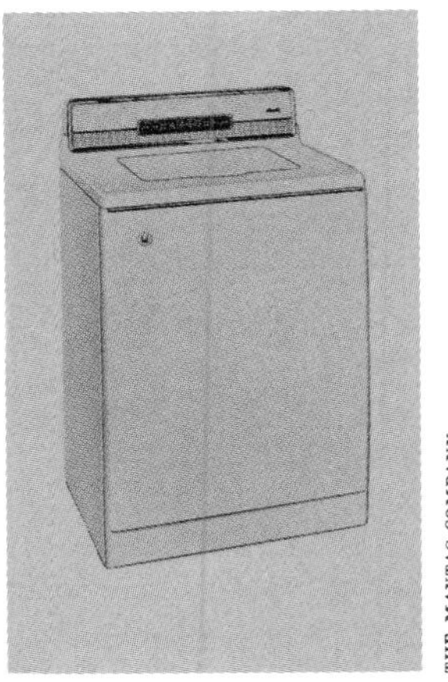

THE MAYTAG COMPANY

ment which was responsible for investigating new issues. New underwritings headed by the firm – American Re-Insurance Company, The Maytag Company, and Bristol-Myers Company among them – kept coming to the market until a total of twenty-seven had been offered during the year.

Quinn had turned to finance somewhat later than Randolph and Breck who today are his seniors, in years of service, at J. & W. Seligman & Co. But the experience he brought with him thirty-six years ago quickly proved to be just what was needed to work out complicated financial deals. He had learned about negotiating in a hard school after World War I when he worked for several years with the American Relief Administration – headed by Herbert Hoover – in Europe. Part of his time was spent helping to arrange relief programs for the Soviet Union with a group of high level Communist leaders, many of whom were liquidated in the Stalinist purges of the 1930's.

Born in Saginaw, Michigan, the son of a lumberman, Cyril Quinn was graduated from the University of Michigan in 1914. At college he earned the distinction of being a top scholar (he was elected to Phi Beta Kappa) while playing football for Michigan's immortal Fielding "Hurry Up" Yost.

After serving in France as an Infantry Captain at Second Army headquarters during World War I and his work with the American Relief Administration, Quinn was associated with the International Chamber of Commerce. In 1928, he was introduced to Earle Bailie and came to work for the firm. He became a partner in 1930.

When Herbert Hoover told the 1928 Republican Party Convention which had just named him their candidate for the Presidency that "given a chance to go forward with the policies of the last eight years, we shall soon, with the help of God, be in sight of the day when poverty will be banished from this nation," almost everyone agreed.

Francis Randolph viewed strong business and investor confidence as an opportunity to revive an old idea. As early as 1925 he had proposed to the partners that J. & W. Seligman & Co. sponsor an investment company. "One of the earliest examples of a successful closed-end investment company was U. S. & Foreign Securities Corporation which had been formed by Dillon, Read & Co. in 1924, and the idea interested me," the senior partner recalls. "I wrote what I thought was a good memorandum to the partners, suggesting that we form such a company, too. In those days I was very junior and my memo fell flat. It got no attention at all."

Three years later, when Randolph brought up the subject again, an investment company was scarcely a novel thought. While only a few had existed in 1925, American closed-end and open-end investment companies numbered about 300 at the end of 1927, and there would be an estimated 750 before the end of 1929. Almost every firm of any standing had formed such a company and the public seemed never to get enough shares. "Earle Bailie became interested in the idea," Randolph relates, "and the two of us convinced the senior partners that it was a sound thing to do. Henry Seligman and the Strausses were hesitant at first. They were used to taking risks on their own account, but taking risks for thousands of stockholders was something else again." But, finally, they decided to form a company. This was a decision which perhaps had more influence than any other on the subsequent evolution of the business of J. & W. Seligman & Co.

With a broad-gauged outlook typical of the times, and fully aware of the successful records such companies had made in England and Scotland, the partners envisioned a company that would invest its assets in the securities of companies on three continents–North and South America and Europe. The plan prompted Margaret Henderson Bailie, Earle's wife, to suggest the name Tri-Continental, which was adopted.

Basically, the new Corporation followed a familiar pattern. It was to be a closed-end company with a diversified portfolio selected to attain the most popular, middle-of-the-road objective–reasonable current income and growth of capital and income over the years–so that it would appeal to the maximum number of investors. To provide leverage or gearing, as the British call it, for the common shares, the Corporation's capitalization was to be half in senior securities and half in common stock. This meant, as similar companies were demonstrating dramatically as the market continued to climb, that when Tri-Continental's assets were invested in common stocks and the value of those investments rose, all of the rise would be reflected in the asset value of the Corporation's common shares, and hopefully in their market price. But it also meant that, if the value of the Corporation's investments fell, all of the decline would be reflected in the asset value of the common shares. Leverage was a valuable, but clearly two-edged, financial weapon.

In other respects, Tri-Continental was to be significantly different from most closed-end investment companies being formed in the United States at the time. Generally, these were sponsored by investment banking firms primarily interested in selling newly-created shares to earn underwriting and distributing commissions. Perhaps reflecting the optimistic tenor of the times, investment management ordinarily was left to one or two staff men who handled this chore routinely in addition to their regular work. But not at Tri-Continental.

With characteristic thoroughness, the Seligman firm resolved from the beginning that if it were going to be in the investment company business at all, it was going to be in it properly. Even before Tri-Continental began operations, the partners began to build up a staff of competent investment analysts, and these people were assigned exclusively to finding sound investments to recommend for the new company's portfolio.

Henry Breck worked up the details of Tri-Continental's incorporation with Alfred Jaretzki, Jr., then a young lawyer with Sullivan & Cromwell, and Carl W. Painter, of Cravath, de Gersdorff Swaine & Wood. Through his acquaintances,

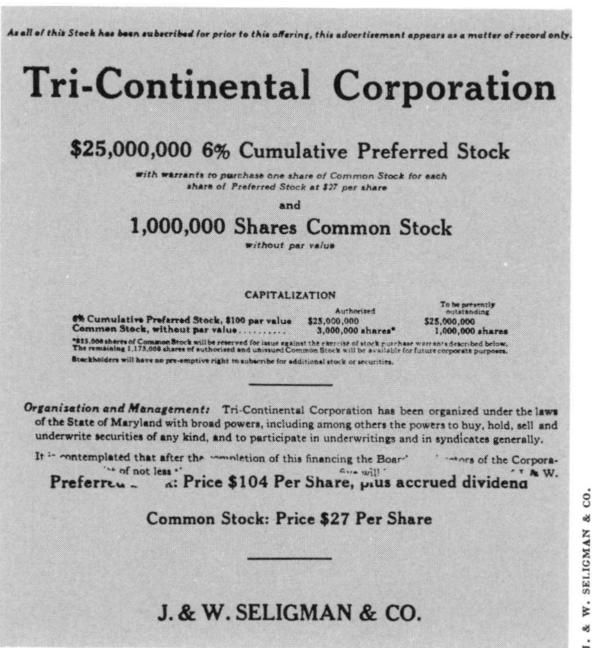

J. & W. SELIGMAN & CO.

The first advertisement for Tri-Continental Corporation appeared in The New York Times, *January 19, 1929. By then, all the stock had been subscribed, and the ad for the Seligman-sponsored Corporation was only for record.*

Breck also sought out Homer Bews Vanderblue, a widely-known economist on the faculty of the Harvard Graduate School of Business Administration who had established an outstanding record in his studies of the business cycle in connection with the Harvard Economic Society. Vanderblue was hired to gather together a staff of university-trained investment analysts capable of studying business conditions and seeking out promising investment opportunities on a full-time, professional basis. This was a challenging assignment, almost without precedent in Wall Street, and to get his new group started, Vanderblue invited Thurston P. Blodgett, a Harvard associate, to work with him at Tri-Continental. With Blodgett came Amelia E. Ohse, one of the first women in investment research, who was Vanderblue's statistician and later an assistant to Blodgett for many years.

J. & W. Seligman & Co. contracted with the new company to provide six directors from among its partners, three of whom—Bailie, Randolph, and White—also became officers. The majority of the fifteen-man Board was made up of prominent bankers and businessmen from outside the firm, including William S. Gray, Jr., vice-president of Central Hanover Bank & Trust Company; C. E. Groesbeck, president of Electric Bond and Share Company; David Sarnoff, president of Radio Corporation of America, and a young lawyer, Carl W. Painter, now a senior partner of Cravath, Swaine & Moore, and still on the Board. While a search was made to find a qualified business leader with extensive financial and investment experience to put at the head of the Corporation, Earle Bailie took the job as President and Chairman of the Board on a temporary basis and Tri-Continental was ready for business.

On January 12, 1929, the firm offered $25,-000,000 of Tri-Continental preferred stock with warrants attached, and 1,000,000 shares of common. The securities sold quickly. Herbert Bachman remembers that he helped to execute the order for the new Corporation's first investment—500 shares of United States Steel.

GUY GILLETTE

A Yale and Harvard Business School graduate, Thurston P. Blodgett joined Tri-Continental in 1929. He worked closely with Homer Vanderblue, and later became head of what is now the Union Service research department.

COURTESY, MRS. CHARLES BOUGHTON

Homer Bews Vanderblue (above), says Page, "was in charge of the economic work for Tri-Continental as well as general staff supervision until he left in 1937." Before joining Tri-Continental, he was on the faculty at Harvard.

With brisk demand for investment company shares, and following Tri-Continental's early success, J. & W. Seligman & Co. sponsored a second $50,000,000 investment company patterned on its companion corporation and to be operated in the same way. Tri-Continental Allied Corporation appeared on August 15, 1929. Scarcely eight weeks later, the great bull market of the 1920's plummeted. In days, what had seemed an insatiable demand for common stocks, turned into an almost limitless supply. The new investment companies were plunged into the problems of adversity.

J. & W. Seligman & Co. has never had a partner of the firm assigned to the floor of the New York Stock Exchange in its ninety-five years of membership. Yet on Black Thursday, October 28, 1929, the day of "The Crash," an interesting footnote to all the excitement went largely unnoticed. At the height of the panic, Jefferson Seligman, who held the firm's seat on the Exchange, decided to visit the floor "to see what a market crash was like," *Fortune* commented in August 1934. Impeccably dressed as usual in a frock coat, striped pants, with a bright flower in his lapel, he made an impressive appearance, and one of the afternoon papers commented on the calming effect induced by the sight of the well-known international banker coolly surveying the frenzy around him.

While Jefferson Seligman calmly sought local color, what had always been hard work in the back offices of every brokerage house became frantic, night and day drudgery. "Our job was to confirm trades made at the stock exchanges," one of the veterans of those days recalls, "and this was done on a next day clearance basis. Orders came in in bales. We were swamped. We couldn't keep up with them. No brokerage house could—and all of us worked until we literally fell asleep at our desks. Then we'd get a few hours' relief at a hotel and be back at it again. Finally, the market closed for a few days and we got a chance to catch up."

There were long hours in the partners' room, too. The firm had made it a practice to hold substantial blocks of shares of the companies whose securities it had underwritten—on the theory that if they were good investments for clients, they were good investments for J. & W. Seligman & Co. "We had large holdings in companies like Minneapolis-Honeywell, American Re-Insurance, and Tri-Continental," Francis Randolph relates, "and when the shrinkage came, we had our losses."

Yet, the partners' faith in the investment business, and in the investment company idea, was never shaken. They were determined to see Tri-Continental through. To simplify the operations of Tri-Continental and of Tri-Allied, the two companies were merged. And despite the nation-wide financial crisis, the partners vigorously maintained morale—their own as well as the staff's. Every employee was given a small bonus at year end, and on December 13, the entire staff was entertained at a formal dinner-dance at the Ritz-Carlton Hotel. It was the last party J. & W. Seligman & Co. ever held at the Ritz.

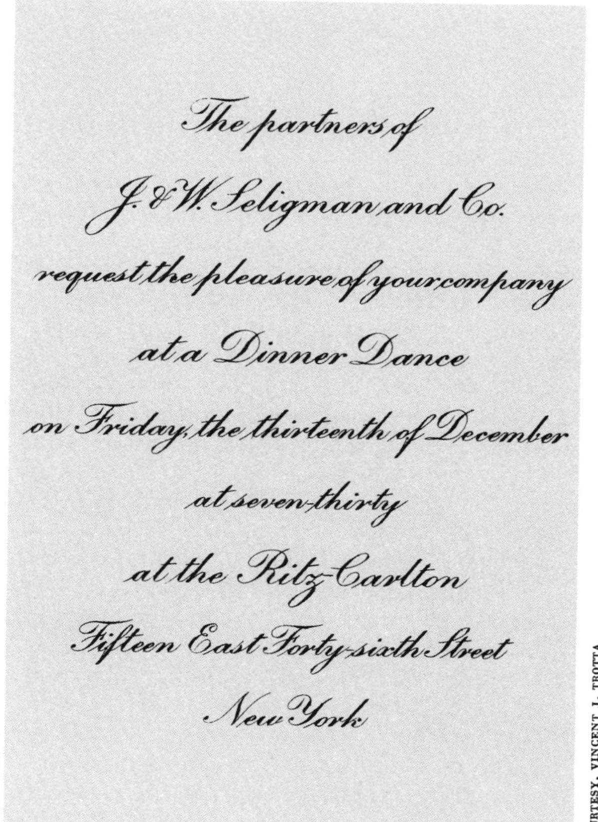

The partners of

J. & W. Seligman and Co.

request the pleasure of your company

at a Dinner Dance

on Friday, the thirteenth of December

at seven-thirty

at the Ritz-Carlton

Fifteen East Forty-sixth Street

New York

COURTESY, VINCENT J. TROTTA

Employees forgot the Crash, its aftermath, for a night in December 1929 when the firm held its annual Christmas Party. That year it was at the Ritz-Carlton Hotel. The date, coincidentally, was Friday the Thirteenth!

TEN

Those old Wall Street boys are putting up
an awful fight to keep the government
from putting a cop on their corner.

—*Will Rogers, 1879-1935*

In the retrospect of thirty-five years, the 1929 Crash was plainly a great divide in American economic and financial history—the end of one era and the beginning of another. But to businessmen in Wall Street as the 1930's began, history's meaning was by no means clear. Securities prices continued to fluctuate, although at increasingly lower levels, and every momentary upturn sparked hope that recovery might really be "just around the corner" as President Hoover bravely predicted. No one at J. & W. Seligman & Co., or anywhere else, could foresee the agony of depression and war they would all go through before the world's economies righted themselves nearly half a generation later.

By mid-1930, all Wall Street firms faced drastic retrenchment. Securities trading volume fell off, the underwriting business all but disappeared, and current income was too small to carry the overhead encouraged by the affluence of the 1920's. Like many investment firms and true to their heritage, the Seligman partners tightened their belts and resolved to carry on.

Henry Breck recalls that "Cy Quinn and I were given the unpleasant task of cutting the overhead sharply. We found that there were people being paid nine, ten, or twelve thousand dollars a year for doing jobs on which they could be replaced at a far lower going rate, and we had to tell them that if they wanted to stay, it would have to be at reduced pay. Others on the staff had to be let go."

Employees weren't the only ones whose lives were changed by the crisis. Two of the partners withdrew from the firm in 1931. Kenneth Hanau found little to sell. He left to build a new—and highly successful—career in industry. Alexander Henderson had experienced a bitter dose of the investment business in three years and returned to the practice of law. Other firms were worse off.

As the months went on, partners and employees of J. & W. Seligman & Co. began to realize that despite the blows it had taken, the firm was relatively strong. Instead of cutting the payroll further as the Depression deepened, some employees who had been laid off were called back to work. And, slowly, new members were added to the staff.

Seligman's surprising resilience was a product of three factors, two of which might have been expected of a firm nurtured in Joseph Seligman's tradition of independence. Even in the high-flying 1920's, the firm had never borrowed a dollar to buy securities. It had taken risks—but for cash—so that losses which came as prices tumbled were paid for the instant they were incurred. There was no burden of debt to repay. Secondly, true to its conservative heritage, the firm carried virtually no margin accounts and, as a consequence, no customers' debts had been assumed. The partners' determination to stick with the investment company idea and

The great prosperity ended on October 29, 1929, when 16,000,000 shares of stock were traded on the New York Stock Exchange. Crowds gathered in front of the building and mounted police kept order. The street was planked because of subway construction. A year later, the once prosperous sold apples on the street.

BOTH: WIDE WORLD PHOTOS

to bring Tri-Continental through the crisis was the third factor.

In this determination, Earle Bailie and Francis Randolph, the two partners most directly concerned with Tri-Continental, were backed by Henry Seligman and Frederick Strauss. But few investment company managements showed as much stamina. Among the more than 750 companies formed in the late 1920's, the mortality rate during the Depression was very severe. Most were forced or went out of business within a few months of the Crash. On the surface, the outlook for Tri-Continental scarcely seemed any better. It had been a latecomer. Its portfolio had been acquired at near the top of the bull market, and the asset value of its common stock, driven down faster than market prices in general by leverage working relentlessly in reverse, had fallen to a fraction of its original level. Before the Depression ended it was to sink temporarily to less than no value at all. But, if the firm had been slow in moving into the investment company field, when it had moved the partners had acted with characteristic care.

Tri-Continental's founders were thoroughly convinced of the soundness of the basic concept of a professionally operated investment company managed for the benefit of its security holders over the long term. The Seligman partners, helped by Homer Vanderblue and Thurston Blodgett with their highly-trained staff, had selected investments which, for the most part, represented sound values, and they were stubborn enough to back their judgment with patience. To men in Wall Street who looked at the investment company movement objectively, it was apparent the strong public demand for shares hadn't been all speculative fervor. To a considerable degree, it testified to a real desire to participate in a portfolio of diversified securities which would be managed by professionals who could do the job better than an individual could do it for himself. And in this, the firm recognized a clear responsibility to the security holders who had put both their faith and their money in Tri-Continental. There was self-interest in the firm's determination to make Tri-Continental succeed, too. The firm held a substantial number of the Corporation's shares and warrants, and if it were ever to make this holding valuable, it was going to have to work to do it.

Within a few months, the plan to invest in companies on three continents had been dropped. "When the outlook was obscured by conditions abroad," according to Tri-Continental's annual report for 1931, foreign holdings were sold, and the Corporation has concentrated its investments in the securities of American companies ever since. Thanks to careful research, however, the long-term outlook for most domestic holdings in the portfolio

COURTESY, SAMUEL RIPPS

Samuel Nagler (left) was in charge of the Seligman accounting department during the Depression. He vividly recalls the decrease in business activity which followed the Crash. Working with him in the Thirties were Vincent J. Trotta (center) and Samuel Ripps.

was promising, despite severe losses in current market prices, and the management stayed with them. Some are still held by the Corporation, and even after more than thirty-five years they have continued to grow and to produce good income.

For most other investment companies, the picture was vastly different. Many of those not forced into liquidation soon found it impractical to continue. Formed at a time of rapidly rising optimism and markets, few companies had troubled to build a qualified investment team. After the Crash, when the need for expert management became self-evident, there was no time and the cost seemed too great even when the will was there. Consequently, as J. & W. Seligman & Co. was gradually deciding to concentrate a major effort in the investment company field, many sponsors were finding the business distinctly unattractive, and some of them turned to the firm for help in solving their problem.

First to come was Wedgewood Investing Corporation whose assets were purchased by Tri-Continental in 1931. Then the Corporation bought an interest in Selected Industries Incorporated and Capital Administration Company, Ltd., both leveraged closed-end companies, whose assets Tri-Continental agreed to manage in return for an annual fee. At about the same time, Maynard, Oakley & Lawrence, an investment firm which in 1929 had founded The Broad Street Investing Co. Inc., a mutual fund managed by Broad Street Management Corporation, sold Tri-Continental an interest in the latter company, and both this and the fund were taken into the fold. Nobody knew it at the time, but the acquisition of Broad Street Investing was to have a very significant influence on J. & W. Seligman & Co.'s subsequent role in the investment company field.

By 1933, three closed-end companies were being operated by Tri-Continental and, in addition, the Corporation purchased an interest in Globe & Rutgers Fire Insurance Company, an organization which had run into difficulty when the stock market declined, and undertook to manage its investments with a view toward rebuilding their value and thereby reestablishing its insurance underwriting ability. And Tri-Continental's Directors ventured into an entirely different field. A subsidiary called Park Properties Corporation was formed to invest in choice parcels of real estate, largely in New York City, which at the time were selling at depressed prices and which, by any reasonable judgment, could be expected to recover their market value when business conditions improved.

With the base of investment assets broadened to help carry operating expenses, Tri-Continental was well-established. The partners had concentrated on getting the Corporation back onto the sound foundation on which it had started. A decision had been made to provide management and other essential services on an internal, at-cost, no-profit basis, an arrangement which continues today to be unique in the investment company field. Fees earned through the management of the investments of subsidiaries and from other companies which contracted for investment research services – Massachusetts Investors Trust was one of them for a time – provided the Corporation with enough extra income to cover about half of its operating expenses during the Thirties. Interest charges and preferred stock dividends were being met – no payment was ever missed – and Tri-Continental was rapidly building one of the largest and best-trained staffs of professional investment men in the business.

The philosophy within which the staff operated was unusual for the times, too. Unlike most investment research organizations, in which each member might be expected to pursue an investment idea in any area, Tri-Continental had decided to develop specialists. The investment research organization was divided into two sections. One – the economics department – was assigned to study and to forecast broad developments within the economy which might have an effect on business and finance, and to make regular reports on which investment policies could be based. The larger section was made up of investment research and analysis teams. Each senior investment analyst was assigned a specific industry, or group of industries, to which he devoted his full time. A junior analyst, a statistician, and, perhaps, a trainee worked with him. This team kept abreast of developments in its industries, took frequent field trips to develop contacts and gather first-hand information on specific companies, and was expected to produce meaningful investment recommendations in the light of its findings and current policy.

Tri-Continental was a pioneer among major investment institutions to adopt this type of organization for investment research developed under the direction of the Seligman partners. It is still the pattern followed today and it has been widely adopted throughout the industry.

J. & W. Seligman & Co. was making progress in other areas, too. Brokerage business from individual and corporate clients, although down in volume, was recovering, and the deposit banking business was a stable, if small, source of income. Underwriting profits, however, had virtually disappeared. "There just wasn't any significant amount of risk capital left with the public," Francis Randolph explains. "Investment banking found few investors with new funds and it had become an unattractive business almost overnight."

Stayman L. Reed (left) worked in the firm's foreign department in the 1930's. He is now the managing partner and as such, much of his time is spent making sure all rules concerning the brokerage business are complied with. Raymond J. Monahan, a staff member since 1925 and now in charge of the tax department, often is called upon to furnish legal interpretations on technical questions.

GUY GILLETTE

Banking weakness in early 1931 characterized the second phase of the Depression. As long as deflation had been confined mainly to the prices of common stocks, most banks could sustain themselves. Their investments were in fixed income obligations. But when American investments abroad were reduced after the Crash, the financial balance of most countries was upset. J. & W. Seligman & Co. had held substantial investments through European banks, but it was largely unhurt by the secondary crisis. Shortly before real trouble began, Frederick Strauss, with that rare intuition which made him an extraordinary banker, persuaded his partners to get their money out of Europe. He was just in time. In 1931, bank failures in Europe reverberated throughout the world and American banks were in trouble. Many failed. Soon the economy was caught in a renewed decline.

At the same time, Wall Street was hit with a new and unwelcome phenomenon—foreign bond defaults. In quick succession, one foreign government after another stopped interest payments on their debts, and altogether well over a billion dollars of American held foreign bonds were defaulted in 1931 and 1932. Henry Breck with Stayman L. Reed, now managing partner who was then a member of the firm's foreign department, went to work with other investment firms to reach settlements with foreign governments on behalf of Americans who held their bonds.

Stayman Reed had lived a good part of his adult life abroad, so that he was well-trained in foreign financial affairs, but his experience on Wall Street had included none of the prosperous times of the Twenties. When Reed left his boyhood home in Clearfield, Pennsylvania, where his father had been a lumberman and brick manufacturer, he planned to become a lawyer. By the time he was ready to be graduated from Princeton, where he earned a Phi Beta Kappa key, he was in officers' training at the Army's Fort Niagara in New York. His diploma came by mail. Following service in France as a Second Lieutenant in the 79th Division's 316th Infantry Regiment, he studied business for a few months at New York University, then was employed by the American Express Company in the Far East. Later he was sent to Western Europe.

"I was in Paris in 1928 and 1929," Reed remembers, "when I became interested in the stock market. I speculated a little by cable, and like everyone else, I made a little money. Since it looked easy, I quit my job and came back to the States."

Reed came to J. & W. Seligman & Co. in October 1929, a few days before the Crash, which, he says, "I prefer to think of as a coincidence." Considering his background, it was logical that he should have been assigned to the foreign department, and within a few years he became the department manager.

The work Breck and Reed performed in connection with foreign bonds involved extensive negotiations resulting usually in settlement of defaulted interest payments by the issuance of funding bonds. After formation of the Foreign Bondholders Protective Council, Inc., they cooperated with that institution in reaching acceptable agreements with several governments whose dollar bonds previously had been underwritten by J. & W. Seligman & Co.

The election of Franklin Delano Roosevelt to the Presidency, heralded by his eloquent appeal for forceful action, seemed in 1932 to promise a way out of economic disaster. But the new Administration soon declared the famous banking "holiday" and Wall Street learned that its problems had only begun. Investigations into the causes of the Crash and the ensuing Depression started with the support of nearly every faction in the financial community. Before long, however, investment men were appalled to discover that the methods of business which had served the economy for generations were to be challenged as improper, ethical standards were called into doubt, and bankers and brokers were, in effect, personally blamed for many of the country's difficulties. Resulting legislation —even when it was agreed that new regulations were desirable—was hard to welcome in the atmos-

TREASURY DEPARTMENT, BUREAU OF ENGRAVING AND PRINTING

Legislation enacted during Franklin D. Roosevelt's first Administration was like "a great big rock" thrown into the stream of business, Randolph recalls. "Our job," he declared, "was to figure out where the stream was going."

phere of the day, and it's little wonder that in financial circles Roosevelt soon became known as "that man" in the White House.

One day after the widely-touted National Recovery program got into full swing, Homer Vanderblue, a gruff but generally kindly man, demonstrated Wall Street's characteristic feeling toward the Administration to Adolf Juergensen, now Assistant Treasurer of the Mutual Funds in the Broad Street Group. Juergensen innocently had posted a print of the NRA's Blue Eagle ("We Do Our Part") on the office wall. Vanderblue promptly told him with unmistakable force to "Take that damned thing down! We're not in Germany!" And, says Juergensen, he meant it. Wall Street was willing to do its part to lick the Depression, but few firms were willing to advertise the New Deal's most flamboyant program in the process.

The Glass-Steagall Act of 1933 ended the private banking functions of J. & W. Seligman & Co. by compelling the firm and others like it to choose between the investment business and the deposit banking business. They could not stay in both. Francis Randolph, who feels the Act merely speeded up a process of evolution already well underway, says "there was never any question as to what Seligman would do. The firm's deposit banking business presented neither a challenge nor an opportunity for the kind of skill and knowledge the partners and employees had acquired in finance. Private banking was a routine function which had been carried on largely as a matter of prestige and convenience to clients."

J. & W. Seligman & Co.'s private banking business ended promptly. The firm stopped taking deposits and closed out checking accounts. The long-established network of correspondents abroad was notified that letters of credit would no longer be issued. Arrangements were made for depositors to change over to other banks. "We didn't sell the business," Randolph declares. "We made no reciprocal deals. We just wound it up and saw to it that our clients were taken care of."

In November 1933, Henry M. Morganthau, Jr., newly appointed Secretary of the Treasury and a friend of Earle Bailie's, invited Bailie to work in

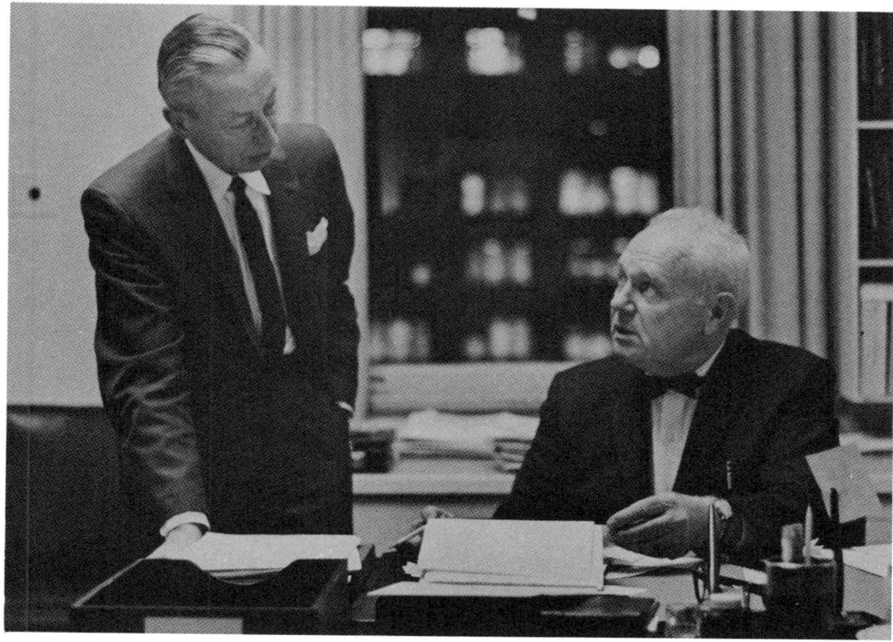

GUY GILLETTE

Adolf Juergensen (left), unknowingly upset Homer Vanderblue by posting the Blue Eagle. He's now an Assistant Treasurer of the Broad Street Group of Mutual Funds; works closely with William Renner, who has been Treasurer of the Funds since 1944.

The National Recovery Administration's Blue Eagle poster caused concern for more men than Homer Vanderblue. It's been said that when William Randolph Hearst, the newspaper owner, saw it, he often had to postpone dinner.

NATIONAL RECOVERY ADMINISTRATION, IN THE NATIONAL ARCHIVES

Washington as his assistant. Bailie jumped at the chance to serve the country in an area where his experience in economics and finance seemed likely to count. He withdrew from the firm and Francis Randolph became President of Tri-Continental. In the Capital, the Administration had started one of the earliest in a long series of monetary experiments designed to end the Depression. President Roosevelt had been persuaded the price of gold determined the general price level of all commodities and the quickest way to get inflation, which many thought was needed to start the economy upward, was to increase the price of gold.

Bailie's first task was to buy gold in the market at an increasingly higher price. Neither he, nor anyone else, had much faith in the theory, particularly after he learned that both the price of gold and the timing of purchases were set arbitrarily, virtually at whim. Before long the gold buying program was abandoned for a new experiment. For a man with Bailie's training, such actions seemed strange, but he was open-minded and wanted to be of service to the Government. He stuck out the job in Washington until June 1934 when he returned to New York and rejoined the firm.

In the next three years, the composition of the partnership changed markedly. Henry Seligman had died in 1933. Jefferson Seligman retired in 1934 and that same year, John C. Jay left to manage Globe & Rutgers Fire Insurance Company which was then controlled by Tri-Continental. He later became president of the Fifth Avenue Bank in New York. Robert V. White gave up his partnership to join another firm in 1935, and later to become president of Lehigh Coal & Navigation Company. Meanwhile, in Washington, as part of its determination to alter the nature of the financial business, Congress passed the Securities Act of 1933 and the Securities and Exchange Act of 1934, which meant revolutionary change for the investment community.

"The stream of business, as we knew it, had been flowing in a familiar channel for generations," Francis Randolph declared, "and suddenly the Federal Government had thrown a great big rock into the channel, diverting it radically. At first, the tendency was to curse the rock," he said, "but before long we realized that as investment men our job was not to belabor the diversion, but to figure out where the stream was going."

In effect, the firm had pretty much decided on where its business was going well before the Government changed the rules. One lesson J. & W. Seligman & Co. learned from the boom and bust of the 1920's was that the days of investing by guesswork were gone. Tri-Continental's experience with thorough research and careful selection of investments with a long-term objective in mind was a product of the partners' confidence in the future of the Nation and conviction that investment management had become a full-time job for professionals. If this approach was sound when applied to the management of an investment company's portfolio, it should be equally sound for individuals. Consequently, the firm decided to establish an Investment Advisory Service to provide custom-tailored, continuous investment advice for individual and institutional clients on a fee basis, along with its other services.

J. & W. Seligman & Co., like most established private banking houses, had long provided investment advice while attending to other business matters for its clients. But such service was informal in nature and usually was given in connection with

The Securities and Exchange Commission was created under authority of the Securities Exchange Act of 1934 and organized on July 2 that year. Members of the first Commission included (from left): Ferdinand Pecora, George C. Mathews, Joseph P. Kennedy, Robert E. Healy, and J. M. Landis.

SECURITIES AND EXCHANGE COMMISSION

stock exchange business. During the 1920's, as interest in common stock investments expanded, more and more clients looked to the firm for help with their financial affairs. The staff of the statistical department, then headed by J. Bernard Miller who later became Tri-Continental's first Treasurer and who is now a limited partner of Goodbody & Co., was increased. From this group of analysts an investment management department was formed to work closely with partners in handling accounts. But no fee was charged, and the amount of work which went into each account depended entirely on the arrangement the individual client had made with the partner involved. Frederick Strauss, to whom many clients looked for advice, made it a practice to note his suggestions for each of his accounts on little slips of paper each day. Then he would lay the papers out on his desk in the order of priority and call in members of the staff to give them instructions until all of the notes were disposed of. Strauss gave good advice, and his clients valued his judgment, but under the old system there was no way of assuring that such personalized service would be continued, if anything happened to him or to any of the other partners.

It was to provide for continuity—a prime requisite in any investment program—and equal treatment for all clients that is was decided to formalize the firm's investment management operations. A separate fee was charged so that the new Advisory Service would stand on its own feet, independent of brokerage and other activities of the firm. Since the idea of charging for investment advice was a sharp departure from the usual practice of Wall Street firms, none of the old accounts were transferred at first and the new undertaking started from scratch, so to speak. With Cyril Quinn as the directing partner, the task of organizing and promoting the Investment Advisory Service was given to Alfred M. Wilson, now executive vice-president of Honeywell Inc. Beverly W. Robertson, the partner who directs the Advisory Service today, was assigned to work with Wilson. When they got under way in 1932, they were backed by the full support of the firm, but getting the clients they hoped to serve was their problem.

Robertson started out from the very beginning to make a career in finance. He was born in East Orange, New Jersey, the son of a book publisher, and studied finance at New York University. Robertson says, "My next door neighbor, the president of a small New York City bank, got me a job as a

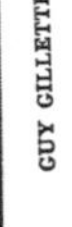

When Seligman analysts develop an idea on an existing or new holding, all angles are considered to make sure the proposal suits the needs of clients. Investment Advisory Staff members (from left) who work with Robertson (second from right) are Alan P. Fleming, Peter Quinn, and Frank Leighton.

trainee in the Bank of America (New York)." There he learned a good deal about bank procedures and also that he didn't like either commercial banking or large organizations. One day in 1929 he walked into J. & W. Seligman & Co. and was hired. "It was a matter of geography," Robertson claims. "The firm was right down the street at 54 Wall with a ground floor entrance, and it was a convenient place to try for a new job during my lunch hour."

He spent his first few months preparing reports on sales of new security issues in which the firm was participating. "Our salesmen were doing well," he recalls, "then came the Crash and when volume declined, I was moved to the accounting department, then into investment research which was my primary interest." For three years, Robertson worked closely with Frederick Strauss and Cyril Quinn, helping to manage a number of individual investment accounts, so that when the decision was made to start the Investment Advisory Service, it was logical that he would be made a part of it.

"We really did start from scratch," Robertson explains, "and it was not until August 1933 that we brought in our first account. We still have it."

When the Investment Advisory Service was first begun, efforts were made to attract new business through magazine and newspaper advertising. Nothing much happened. In 1935, the firm took on a number of salesmen to sell the Service with about the same result. "We began to realize, as we know today," Robertson explains, "that you can't promote a service as personal and as individual as ours with conventional advertising or sales presentations. In this business, it's the results you produce for your clients over the long term and the care you give to their affairs that attract attention. When Seligman's underwriting business began to revive after 1935, some of the salesmen in the retail sales department brought in a few new clients. But, generally, it's fair to say that our best advertising has been by word of mouth and our only real salesmen have been satisfied clients."

By 1936, the Advisory Service was firmly established. Its staff of account supervisors and of security analysts was growing and the firm began to transfer most of the individual partners' long-established investment management accounts into their care. Older clients, recognizing that experienced, professional advisors working with basic information were essential to succesful investment in a rapidly changing economic environment, were glad to pay a modest fee to get the kind of service the firm was ready to provide.

While the Investment Advisory Service was getting underway, Tri-Continental's investment staff continued to develop. Vanderblue, trained as an economist, was also an excellent administrator with a knack for attracting bright young men to the organization. With many acquaintances at Harvard Business School, he was in a particularly good position to pick and choose from among graduates who seemed qualified for the investment field. Frederick W. Page was one of those brought into the staff in this way. Page had gone to Dartmouth and later to Harvard Business School with the intention of entering his father's company. But by the time he was graduated as a Master of Business Administration in 1932, the family business had been closed and there were few jobs elsewhere.

"I started off from the Battery in downtown New York and kept dropping in on companies as I walked uptown," Page recalls. "It wasn't until I reached 42nd Street that I was offered any kind of a job at all." He worked with Mutual Life Insurance Company of New York in the actuarial department for fourteen months until Vanderblue needed a new staff member and Page was recommended by the people at Harvard.

Fred Page was assigned as a trainee to work with Gerard M. Ives in public utility research and analysis. By 1940 when Ives left—he is now a vice-president of Morgan Guaranty Trust Company—Page was given full responsibility for utility investments. Long before he became a partner of the firm in 1955, he was a nationally recognized authority in public utility finance.

While Fred Page was learning the intricacies of the public utility field, the winds of economic fate were readying the last—and perhaps the meanest—trick that was in store for Wall Street during the Thirties. Business started to pick up. Investor interest revived to the point where it was decided the time was ripe to begin actively offering shares of Broad Street Investing again for the first time since Tri-Continental had begun to manage the open-end company in 1932. Broad Street Management Corporation was renamed Broad Street Sales Corporation and was made general underwriter of the Fund's shares. District offices were opened in the Midwest and on the West Coast, and shares sold well for a few months after the new sales effort began on March 30, 1936.

Stock market prices, stimulated by general business optimism, had begun to rise and the Depression seemed ended. Industry, emerging from its long dormancy, looked more actively for expansion capital, and J. & W. Seligman & Co., along with most other Wall Street houses, revived its activities as an underwriter of new securities. During 1936, the firm managed an issue of Montana Power Company bonds which sold well. The next year, major participations were taken in groups formed to underwrite a preferred stock issue for Pure Oil and a bond issue for Bethlehem Steel.

"The Pure Oil and Bethlehem issues were correctly planned and correctly priced," Francis Randolph recalls. "But as they were offered for sale, stock prices broke and the issues were only partly sold. A substantial loss resulted for the underwriters."

In many ways, the decline of 1937 was harder to take than in 1929. At the end of the Twenties, businessmen could reason that all good things must come to an end. But after so many lean years there was no philosophical balm for a new wave of disappointment. At the end of 1937, after a year of generally poor underwriting experiences, the partners faced whether to continue in such an uncertain business, even though the long-established good will of the firm in the underwriting field was likely to lead to opportunities for large profits at some time in the future.

GUY GILLETTE

Frederick W. Page, a native of East Orange, New Jersey, is a Director, Vice-President, and member of the Executive Committees of the four investment companies and also President of Tri-Continental Financial Corporation.

Walter Seligman, a native New Yorker, became a partner November 1, 1922. "He had," says Henry Breck, "a great interest in the stock market and special investment opportunities." Now aged seventy, he retired August 26, 1937.

COURTESY, WALTER SELIGMAN

The composition of the firm had changed again. Frederick Strauss died in the Summer of 1937, and Walter Seligman, the last of his family in the firm, decided to withdraw the same year—just one hundred years after Joseph Seligman had come to the United States.

The remaining partners whose interests had turned more to brokerage and related services, financial and investment advisory work, and investment company management, decided to concentrate the firm's activities in those fields in the future and to transfer security underwriting activities with their special types of risks to a corporate basis.

Tri-Continental and Selected Industries, its largest affiliate, offered a logical channel into which to turn the firm's potentially profitable underwriting business. Homer Vanderblue left the investment companies in 1937 to return to academic work, and he spent the remainder of his working career as Dean of the School of Commerce at Northwestern University. But the staff he had built up, which was headed by Thurston P. Blodgett, was thoroughly capable of contributing importantly to the underwriting business, and all through the Depression, Seligman had held together a highly trained group with years of underwriting experience. So, to take advantage of the investment companies' large resources of capital and personnel and of the firm's existing investment banking contacts and experienced underwriting staff, a new venture was announced the following October. Union Securities Corporation was formed.

Jointly owned by Tri-Continental and Selected Industries, Union Securities was organized "to engage in the business of origination, underwriting, and distribution of security issues." The new company was capitalized at $5,000,000, and the investment companies each paid in $1,000,000 to get it started. The underwriting business of J. & W. Seligman & Co.—including all of the firm's long-established underwriting connections and most of its new business and sales staff—was transferred to the new Corporation without change and at no cost.

During the last four months of 1938, Union Securities won small participations worth only $4,239,085 in seven underwritings. The next year there were twenty-five, of which the Corporation's share was just $18,311,081, and Union Securities Vice-President Joseph H. King, who handled the new company's day-to-day business, and his staff were destined to handle small portions of twenty-one more issues before a chance came to manage an issue on its own. But when opportunity finally came, it was a big one.

Early in 1940, Everett Harris, an investment counsellor well-known in Los Angeles, informed his friend, Thurston Blodgett, that the Newport News Shipbuilding and Dry Dock Company was for sale to the highest bidder. Newport News Shipbuilding, founded by Collis P. Huntington, a railroading rival of the Seligmans in the Nineteenth Century, and still owned largely by his son, had long been a leading builder of all types of fine ships from tugs to luxury liners to aircraft carriers. Union Securities was interested, and one of the men assigned to look into the deal was Fred E. Brown, who had joined the Tri-Continental staff in 1936.

Fred Brown was born and raised in Muskogee,

Oklahoma, and was graduated from the University of Oklahoma with a degree in business administration where he was elected to Beta Gamma Sigma. Traveling East to Harvard Business School, he studied retail marketing and finance. He fully intended to go into retailing after he earned an M.B.A., but because of his graduate school record he was called to the attention of Tri-Continental.

"I was impressed with Homer Vanderblue," Brown recalls. "I had lunch with him, Thurston Blodgett, and some others. I liked all of them and a job with Tri-Continental looked interesting. The pay was $1,800 a year, which was about as much as I could get anywhere, so I decided to give it a trial."

Starting as an analyst-trainee, Brown made the mistake of reporting for work on the first day of the appointed month in the Summer of 1936 even though it was a Saturday morning. His first assignment by a righteously indignant Vanderblue was to ride the ferry boat to Staten Island and back—and to report on his trip on the following Monday.

By 1940, Fred Brown had developed an interest in shipping and shipbuilding "because they were industries no one seemed to pay very much attention and might offer me an opportunity." When the Newport News Shipbuilding opportunity came along, his extracurricular work in the field made him a logical man to be assigned to the job.

William Keary, then head of Union Securities' buying department, and Fred Brown were sent to Newport News, Virginia, to look over the shipyard property. Another firm, also planning to bid for the company, had made a tour of inspection earlier, and by the time the Union Securities group arrived, people at the shipyard were convinced, says Brown, that "Wall Street was moving in on them."

Armed with a favorable report, Keary and Brown returned to New York where Union Securities formed a group of seventeen purchasers, including Tri-Continental, Selected Industries, General Shareholdings, Adams Express Company, United States & Foreign Securities, Harriman Ripley & Co., and Massachusetts Investors Trust to make a bid for the company.

The task of developing a possible price to offer for the shipyard was given to Brown, an assignment that was enormously complicated by the fact

Fred E. Brown (left) helped with the initial investigation for developing the bid for Newport News Shipbuilding when it was sold in 1940. Francis Randolph became a director in 1940; Brown has been on the board since 1961.

GUY GILLETTE

that in all of Newport News Shipbuilding's history—it had started in 1886—there had never been an independent audit. After weeks of work, the purchasing group settled on a price at which it thought it could buy the company and later resell its securities at a fair profit considering the risk involved.

"When the bids were opened," said Brown, "we were told that we had bought a shipyard. The next day, Hitler invaded the Low Countries. We weren't sure whether to be happy or sad about our purchase."

The Newport News Shipbuilding purchase not only was the first major investment banking transaction headed by Union Securities—it set a pattern for the type of deal in which the company was to engage repeatedly and with marked success in the years to come. The transaction was also a first for the investment banking industry as a whole. Not since the Securities Acts of the mid-Thirties had become law had financial interests ventured into the unadjudicated areas of disclosure and public responsibility embodied in the new statutes to assume the unknown risks of the owner in registering and offering new securities to the public. These risks were not taken lightly, and Union Securities

BOTH: NEWPORT NEWS SHIPBUILDING AND DRY DOCK COMPANY

Newport News Shipbuilding and Dry Dock Company built the passenger liners United States *and* America *(shown in the foreground at the shipyard in 1962). The* America *was the Nation's largest passenger vessel in 1940. The* United States, *on its maiden voyage in 1952, set Atlantic speed records.*

proceeded carefully and cautiously, guided by the best legal advice then available. Financial statements for the shipyard going back twelve years—instead of only the required three—were prepared. An extensive appraisal of plant facilities was made by independent engineers. Meanwhile, a battery of lawyers worked day and night preparing necessary documents and papers that eventually filled two fat volumes.

Newport News Shipbuilding and Dry Dock Company was recapitalized with 71,550 shares of preferred stock and 796,998 shares of common. The registration of these securities with the Securities and Exchange Commission became effective on August 12, nearly four months after the successful bid for the company had been accepted. Two-thirds of the common was sold to the public by a Union Securities syndicate. The balance was retained by the investment companies in the purchasing group for long-term holding.

This imaginative transaction was profitable to both the buyers of the shipyard and to Union Securities, and investors who purchased Newport News Shipbuilding shares have had no reason to be sorry. Offered at $22 a share, the common has never fallen below that price. Dividends totaling $81.25 per share on the original stock have been paid in a period of twenty-four years. Each original share had a value equivalent to $90.75 at the end of 1963. The success of the offering broke the ice for Union Securities, and it went on to become one of Wall Street's leading underwriters in post-World War II years.

At Shipway Five, in Newport News, whirler cranes are silhouetted against a January sky while underneath the canvas covering, work progresses on another Polaris submarine, the Simon Bolivar, *in this B. J. Nixon photo.*

ELEVEN

Tomorrow to fresh woods and pastures new.

—John Milton, 1608-1674

For business in general, the Depression was over by 1940–a casualty of World War II. America's decision to build up its own armed forces and to become "the arsenal of democracy" fighting for survival in Europe released billions of dollars into the stream of commerce, created millions of jobs for people, and aroused the Nation's economy from almost ten years of lethargy.

In Wall Street, however, investor confidence was dampened by the uncertainties of war. And the Federal Government had not finished rewriting rules for the financial community.

Under the Securities and Exchange Act of 1934, the Securities and Exchange Commission had been given a mandate to study investment companies and to recommend legislation that would prevent practices believed to have contributed to the collapse of many companies after 1929. The Commission started its work in earnest in 1937. It probed every phase of investment company organization and operation. Representatives of virtually every company affected–Earle Bailie and Cyril Quinn among them–went to Washington for month after month of hearings. It was generally agreed that new rules were needed. But when the SEC presented a proposed bill to the U. S. Senate, it was clear that in its effort to make it impossible for unsoundly operated investment companies ever to exist again, the agency had put the entire investment company industry in jeopardy of being legislated out of existence.

In contrast to the relatively passive way businessmen had taken Federal reforms of the early Thirties–not all of which had worked out for the best–leaders of the investment company industry resolved to strive for a reasonable and workable law. A task force of company executives moved to Washington and prepared to speak for the industry before the Securities and Exchange Subcommittee of the Senate Banking and Currency Committee. These men included Cyril J. C. Quinn; Alfred Jaretzki, Jr., a partner in Sullivan & Cromwell and now a Director of the Mutual Funds of the Broad Street Group; Paul Bartholet, Tri-Continental's Treasurer, who later became the first head of the National Association of Investment Companies; Arthur H. Bunker and Dorsey Richardson of The Lehman Corporation, Paul Cabot of State Street Investing, Tudor Gardner of Incorporated Investors, Merrill Griswold of Massachusetts Investors Trust, and Raymond D. McGrath of General American Investors Company, Inc.

In preparation for the Washington meetings, Stayman Reed traveled to England to study investment companies in that country where they had been widely recognized as valuable and generally successful investment media since the late Nineteenth Century. Information on the British experi-

BOTH : GUY GILLETTE

The Investment Company Act of 1940 is an example of effective legislation produced by mutual efforts of business and Government. Cyril J. C. Quinn, a partner since 1930, was one of the investment company representatives who spent much time in Washington working on the legislation.

ence filling Reed's report when he returned provided effective background material for the investment companies' spokesmen in Washington.

When Cyril Quinn's turn to speak before the Subcommittee came, he forcefully stated what is still the industry's basic attitude toward regulation. "We are just as anxious as they [the SEC] are to see wrongs stopped," he contended, "but it is only natural that we should be more conscious of the fact that, in trying to cure a wrong, one may do a lot of harm that is unnecessary." He argued for a bill that would require full publicity of a company's affairs, which he believed would go as far "as it is feasible to go to accord protection to the investor." Calmly, he told the Senators, "I know you gentlemen are too experienced to delude yourselves with the thought that you can set up a bill which will stop wrong-doing. Certainly, one wonders, in considering the cases that have been cited in these hearings, if enactment of one more law

Stanley R. Currie (at right) directs the daily work of the investment research staff for the investment companies. He works closely with Raymond G. Fowler, veteran analyst of bonds, preferred stocks, and railroad securities.

Peter de F. Millard (left) and Laszlo A. de Mandy cover a wide range of industries as Union Service analysts. Millard, Paris born, was graduated from Yale and Harvard; de Mandy received a degree from Josef Nandor Technical University in his native Hungary and did graduate work in the U. S.

Phyllis W. Smith assists Robert L. Noddin, a specialist in public utilities securities. Miss Smith joined Union Service in 1960; Noddin came in 1961.

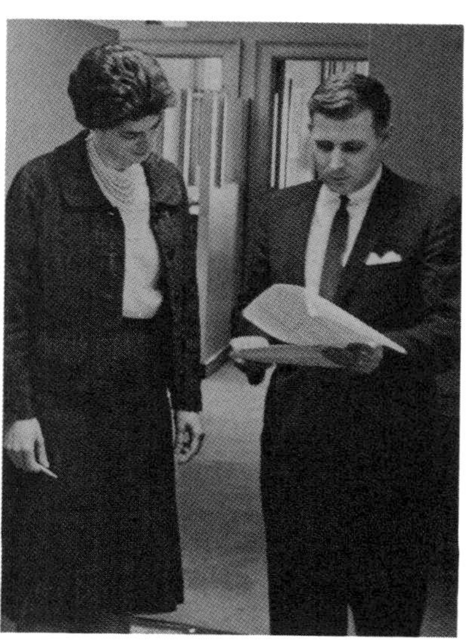

BOTH: GUY GILLETTE

will deter people from doing what they should not do. They certainly showed very little compunction about breaking existing laws in those cases. I also know that you gentlemen are too experienced to think that laws are going to prevent people from losing money, because no legislation that can be devised is going to endow people with good judgment and foresight."

Quinn's arguments, and those of others in the industry were effective, and then after a short time agreement was reached with the Securities and Exchange Commission to work out a bill that would be acceptable to both and in the public interest. The Subcommittee readily gave this cooperative effort its blessing.

"Producing a bill took time," Quinn recalls, "because we first had to consult with others in the industry, and then reach agreement with the Commission. But eventually we came up with a mutually acceptable proposal. Our combined ideas were presented to the Senators on the Subcommittee and they were incorporated in the Investment Company Act of 1940. I don't think the Act changed the nature of the business too much. The fundamental job of looking after funds that have been entrusted to company management wasn't touched very much. I don't think it ever should be. The Act is very sensible in that way."

The Investment Company Act of 1940 is undoubtedly one of the best examples of effective legislation produced by the mutual efforts of business and Government in which both sides were striving for the same basic objectives. No part of it was punitive. And, as intended, it provided safeguards for investors' interests without seriously impairing the freedom of investment action of the companies. It established the well-known "goldfish bowl" method of operation under which almost every phase of investment company activity is exposed to full public view.

Passage of the Act helped lay a foundation for investor confidence in investment companies and served as a stimulus for the rapid public acceptance of the companies and their growth in subsequent years. Significantly, the Act has stood the test of time. Recent extensive studies of the investment company business, more than twenty-five years after the first hearings, have prompted suggestions for various modifications of regulatory rules to bring them into line with modern conditions and methods. But no one has proposed that the Act of 1940 be altered fundamentally.

Union Service's Investment Committee reviews ideas for purchase and sale of securities; makes recommendations to the Executive Committee. Analyst James Ronan (r), presents an idea to the Committee (l to r): Stanley R. Currie, Frederick W. Page, and Thurston P. Blodgett, who is now retired.

GUY GILLETTE

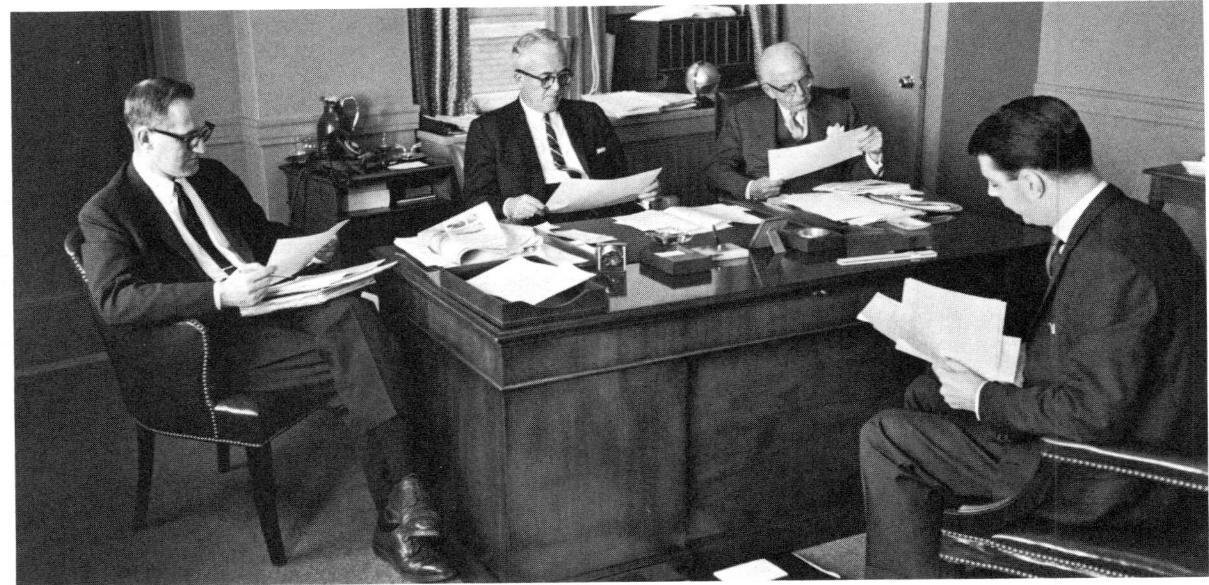

While new Federal rules were being worked out in Washington, partners of J. & W. Seligman & Co., along with the other Directors of Tri-Continental Corporation, were evolving a new organization for the investment companies to which the partnership had furnished officers for over a decade. Under the agreements drawn in the early Thirties, Tri-Continental's staff had been providing investment research and administrative services to the company's own security holders on an at-cost basis. At the same time, it had been performing these functions for associated companies for a fee. This arrangement had worked well, but as the companies grew in size, questions arose as to the fundamental soundness of having one group of security owners pay fees to another.

From the thought these questions provoked evolved a plan which retained the economics of at-cost, no-profit management and of spreading the costs of operating all the companies over the broadest possible asset base, and yet made it possible for the shareholders of each company in the group to share in the benefits proportionately. This plan took form in Union Service Corporation organized on January 10, 1940, and all inter-company fees were eliminated.

Union Service, new in concept when it was started, is still unique in the investment company field. Union Service is owned by the investment companies in the Tri-Continental-Broad Street Group and operated on a no-fee, at-cost basis for their benefit. Each investment company receives investment research and administrative services from it. Each shares its operating expenses in the proportion of the assets of the company to the combined assets of the four companies in the group. In this way, the largest company which requires the greatest amount of service pays the largest share of the costs; the smallest pays the smallest share. Each gets the full benefit of one of the country's largest and best-trained investment organizations at a cost which each can afford. All of the companies share the same officers, and officers' compensation is spread on the same basis as other expenses.

This concept of mutual ownership and mutual sharing, continued without basic change for more than twenty-four years, has made it possible for the Tri-Continental-Broad Street Group of investment

Dr. John W. Harriman, economist for the four investment companies since 1958, was also, until recently, Vice-Dean of the Graduate School of Business Administration at New York University. Ann L. Russell is his secretary.

GUY GILLETTE

Fred Y. Presley pioneered the growth stock theory of investing; founded National Investors Corporation. Early in 1942, the mutual fund became a part of the Tri-Continental group of investment companies. Presley died in 1964.

COURTESY, JOHN R. MCGINLEY

companies consistently to have operating expense ratios among the lowest in the industry. Shareholders of the companies have benefitted correspondingly from the unique Union Service arrangement.

J. & W. Seligman & Co. and the organizations associated with it were growing steadily toward the end of 1940. Quarters at 54 Wall Street–long in need of modernization–had become crowded and inefficient. The firm decided to move to 65 Broadway, a twenty-one story building just south of the corner of Wall Street, in which it is housed today. The offices in the top three floors were big enough to accommodate all partnership operations and the Union Service staff, and to provide extra space for Union Securities to grow into. Earle Bailie, with characteristic energy and attention to detail, helped to lay out the floor plan and to decorate the new offices. But he never really moved into them. He died unexpectedly on November 15, 1940, at fifty-one years of age.

Bailie's death could have been a severe blow to the firm. Many outsiders had the impression that he had been J. & W. Seligman & Co.'s driving force. But the firm was too seasoned not to be prepared for the unexpected. The three remaining partners were thoroughly grounded in all phases of its activities and the staff was organized in depth. Continuity was assured. Francis F. Randolph quietly assumed the chair at the head of the Board Room table and business continued without hesitation.

With World War II going badly for the Allies, investor uncertainty curbed brokerage volume, the Investment Advisory Service added few new accounts, and there were only a limited number of new issues for Union Securities to handle. Still, after the United States entered the War, the loss of many young men to the Armed Services and to Government work kept the remaining organization busier than ever. To take over the work of overseeing day-to-day administrative tasks, Stayman Reed, whose major activities had been in administration throughout most of his career, was taken into the firm and made managing partner on July 1, 1942.

Thurston Blodgett, who had headed the Union Service investment research organization since the Corporation was formed in 1940, had problems in keeping a full staff together during World War II. Nevertheless, the quality and professional stand-

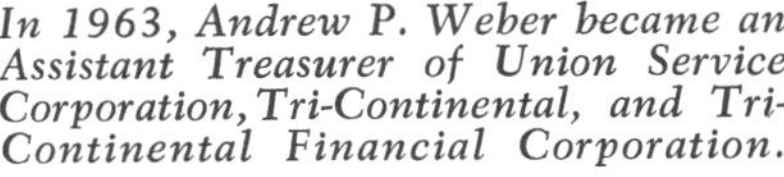
In 1963, Andrew P. Weber became an Assistant Treasurer of Union Service Corporation, Tri-Continental, and Tri-Continental Financial Corporation.

GUY GILLETTE

Franklyn R. Markey joined Tri-Continental in 1931; is an Assistant Treasurer of the company, of Tri-Continental Financial and Broad Street Sales.

ROY STEVENS - EXECUTIVE PORTRAITS, INC.

ards of the work done were maintained, and it was this plus the unique arrangement for sharing operating costs which brought National Investors Corporation within the Seligman orbit in 1942.

National Investors was the brainchild of Fred Y. Presley, an economist credited with much original thinking in the investment field. He spent most of the Twenties studying business cycles at the Harvard Economic Society, where Thurston Blodgett for a time worked as his assistant. Toward the end of the decade, Presley formed three associated closed-end investment companies dedicated to making capital grow by attempting to anticipate cyclical swings in stock prices.

However, the Crash and its aftermath persuaded Presley that there is no sure way of predicting the stock market's ups and downs with consistent accuracy, and he looked for a new approach to investing. He analyzed the history of a number of America's great fortunes. They had been built, he concluded, because the founders put their money into new and promising companies, gave them good management, and plowed back most of their earnings for expansion. They also had faith in their judgment and were patient.

Presley decided that a policy of investing in "growth stocks" would encompass these fundamentals and should work well for an investment company. The three closed-end companies were merged in 1937 to form National Investors Corporation, an open-end company, or mutual fund, which aimed to produce growth of capital by concentrating its investments in the stocks of companies which were expected to grow faster than the economy as a whole. Presley found before long that there were more problems to operating a mutual fund than he had anticipated, and this perhaps hastened a decision on earlier thoughts of retirement.

Through his friend, Thurston Blodgett, he approached J. & W. Seligman & Co. with the thought that the firm might take National Investors under its wing and bring it into the Tri-Continental-Broad Street Investing group. This was done in 1942 and Presley stepped aside to leave the developing and refining of the growth stock theory of investing to an organization in which he had confidence and which he thought would do the job well. National Investors has been one of the most successful mutual funds. And the policy of investing in growth stocks which it pioneered has been widely imitated.

The year 1942 was a turning point. Investor confidence began to return. J. & W. Seligman & Co.'s general business improved; Union Securities

Since 1956, Walter W. O'Connor has been Assistant Treasurer of the Mutual Funds: Broad Street Investing, National Investors, and Whitehall Fund.

WERNER J. KUHN

A reproduction of Federal Hall Memorial (once the Sub-Treasury) and J. Q. A. Ward's statue of George Washington in front of it in New York was first used as Broad Street Sales Corporation's service mark Sept. 11, 1958.

was more than holding its own in the investment banking business. Interest in mutual fund investment picked up, and Woodford A. Matlock, an experienced retail securities salesman from Denver, Colorado, was brought in to reorganize Broad Street Sales Corporation and revive sales of new shares of Broad Street Investing and National Investors to the investing public.

Slowly, through the War years, a distributing organization was built up. Sales results were modest, but the Funds gradually became known to leading investment dealers for their long-experienced management, their proven ability to meet sensible investment goals, and their unique, low-cost method of operation.

After the War ended, a number of retail dealers pointed out that while Broad Street Investing and National Investors covered a broad range of investment objectives, their shares were not suitable for one important group of investors. Neither of the Funds appealed to conservative investors who wanted to limit common stock risks by having a part of their funds invested in more stable, fixed income, senior securities.

To meet the goals of these investors, J. & W. Seligman & Co. decided to sponsor a fund that would maintain a balance of investments between bonds and preferred stocks selected for stability of capital values and income and common stocks chosen for their growth potential. The addition of a third mutual fund, it was thought, would serve a definite market and would enable dealers to offer a vehicle under the firm's sponsorship suited to every basic investment objective.

Whitehall Fund, Inc. began business in the Spring of 1947. The new mutual fund was included in the Union Service arrangement and became the youngest of what is now known as the Broad Street Group of Mutual Funds.

While the Seligman partners and the Union Service staff were building a foundation for the future growth of Tri-Continental Corporation and the Broad Street Group of Funds, they were perhaps even busier with Union Securities Corporation. Francis Randolph had become Chairman and President of the underwriting subsidiary when Earle Bailie died in 1940. Henry Breck and Cyril Quinn were Vice-Presidents from the very beginning. Because of their long experience and widespread contacts in both finance and industry, the partners were looked to for continuing advice and overall guidance. But many of Union Securities' most successful deals were brought in by Joseph H. King, an imaginative, aggressive Texan who

Joseph H. King (below left with Francis Randolph in December 1947) had been a bond salesman for the firm for many years. He was made President of Union Securities Corporation in 1945. The company became a leading underwriter.

COURTESY. WALTER W. O'CONNOR

Fred Brown says "had a remarkable talent for the underwriting business."

King had been a crack bond salesman for J. & W. Seligman & Co. in the Twenties and Thirties so it was natural for him to be made Vice-President in charge of sales when Union Securities was formed. By 1945, he was President of the company.

King was not only able; he was active. His business contacts spread to nearly every corner of the country and he seemed always to be "on the go." Under his aegis, and with the backing of Seligman's long-established reputation, Union Securities grew to be more than an ordinary underwriting house. It played a leading role in raising capital for industry during and after World War II, maintained a trading department in high grade corporate bonds and preferred stocks, bought and sold municipal obligations, handled Government bonds and equipment trust certificates, and placed millions of dollars' worth of securities privately.

Ten years after King became President, the Corporation had 160 employees including twenty-six officers and a staff of investment specialists as able as any in the Nation. It maintained branch offices in Boston, Buffalo, Cleveland, Hartford, Philadelphia, and Syracuse, and had correspondents in other financial centers. And, what is more important, Union Securities made money from the day it was founded.

In the pattern established by the purchase and resale of Newport News Shipbuilding and Dry Dock Company in 1940, Union Securities' greatest profits came from "carry financing" deals. None was ever to be quite so dramatic as the first, because it established a new approach to such business. But there were to be a number of others in which Union Securities, working with other financial houses, would buy a company, hold it for a few months or even a few years, make such internal changes as might be needed, recapitalize it, and then sell it to the public as a sound, going concern. Among the companies bought and later resold by the Corporation were Arkansas Louisiana Gas Company—one of the most successful ventures of them all—Colorado Interstate Gas Company, Mississippi River Fuel Company, Colorado Milling & Elevator Company, Pennsylvania Water Company, California Water Service, and San Jose Waterworks. In addition, the Corporation was a leader in underwriting the stocks of operating utilities offered by holding companies such as American Electric Power, American Power & Light, and others when those companies had to divest themselves of these properties under the Public Utility Holding Company Act.

As American business felt the great postwar surge of expansion, opportunities for Union Securities multiplied. Rising common stock prices were reflected in the asset value of Tri-Continental common shares, and in the value of securities of the Corporation's partially-owned, closed-end subsidiaries—Selected Industries, Incorporated, General Shareholdings Corp., and Capital Administration, Ltd.—which had come into the picture in the Thirties. For the first time, it became feasible to carry out a long-cherished plan to simplify Tri-Continental's organization and portfolio by exchanging its shares and warrants for those of the three subsidiaries, merging the smaller companies into the parent, and thereby eliminating what for Tri-Continental amounted to wheels within wheels. This was done, step by step between 1948 and 1953, giving the security holders of the four corporations an ownership in one big, soundly financed closed-

Union Securities was one of four firms that managed the underwriting of the Straits of Mackinac Bridge in the State of Michigan. The check, paid for the delivery of the bonds, was signed by Russell A. Tilton and Joseph H. King.

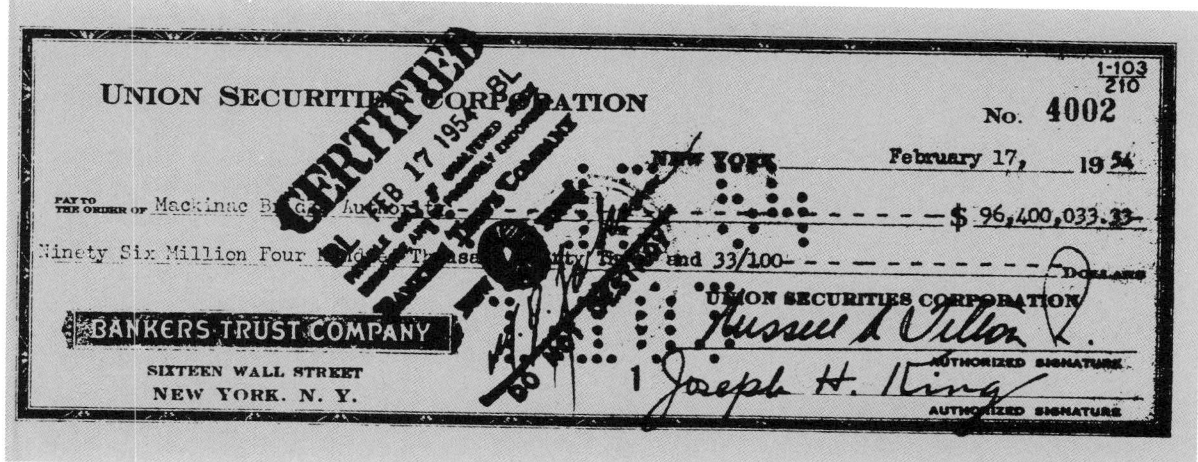

UNION SECURITIES CORPORATION

1-103
210

No. 4002

NEW YORK February 17, 1954

PAY TO THE ORDER OF Mackinac Bridge Authority — $96,400,033.33

Ninety Six Million Four ... and 33/100 DOLLARS

CERTIFIED FEB 17 1954 BL

DO NOT DESTROY

BANKERS TRUST COMPANY
SIXTEEN WALL STREET
NEW YORK, N. Y.

UNION SECURITIES CORPORATION
Russell A. Tilton
AUTHORIZED SIGNATURE
Joseph H. King
AUTHORIZED SIGNATURE

STATE OF MICHIGAN MACKINAC BRIDGE AUTHORITY

end company which was easy to understand, and which gave all of them an opportunity to participate in future growth on equitable terms. Tri-Continental's controlling interest in Globe & Rutgers Fire Insurance Company was sold in 1952.

Park Properties, the real estate subsidiary, had never really lived up to hopes for it. The idea of buying real estate while prices were depressed in the Thirties and holding it until good times returned had been sound enough. But rent controls, extended after the War, were a new, artificial factor which prevented normal expectations of profit from being realized, so the subsidiary was sold. By 1955, Tri-Continental, greatly simplified in organization and portfolio structure, was left with just one highly profitable offspring—Union Securities.

Within J. & W. Seligman & Co., the work load carried by Randolph, Quinn, Breck, and Reed began to increase in the postwar period in almost direct proportion to the improvement in the economy. Four partners had been able to direct the firm's varied interests during the wartime slowdown. But following the War, they were agreed that to provide continuity of purpose and management to the brokerage business, the Investment Advisory Service, and the investment companies, new men had to be brought into the firm. With Union Securities growing rapidly and demanding more of

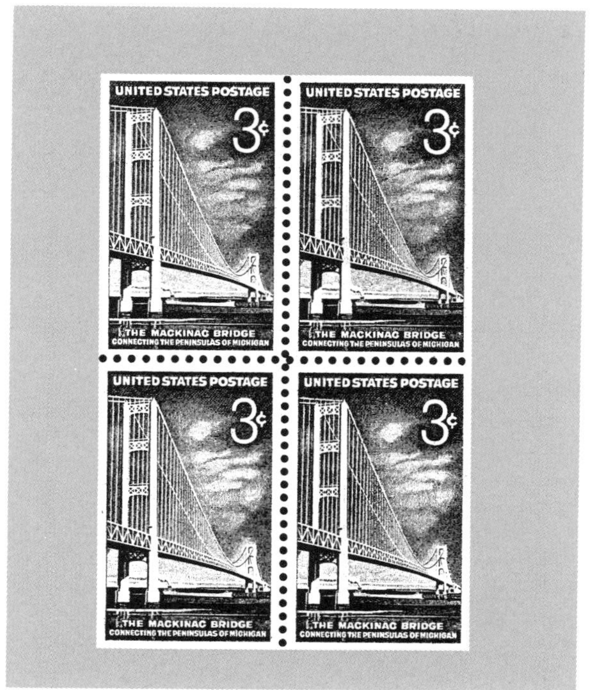

J. & W. SELIGMAN & CO.

A U. S. postage stamp was issued to commemorate the opening of the Straits of Mackinac Bridge in June 1958. The bridge, constructed at a cost of about eighty million dollars, connects Mackinaw City and St. Ignace, Michigan.

An advertisement, which appeared in the May 23, 1956, issue of the New York Herald Tribune, *pointed out that in 1955, Union Securities Corporation had "managed or co-managed securities issues approximating $665,862,000."*

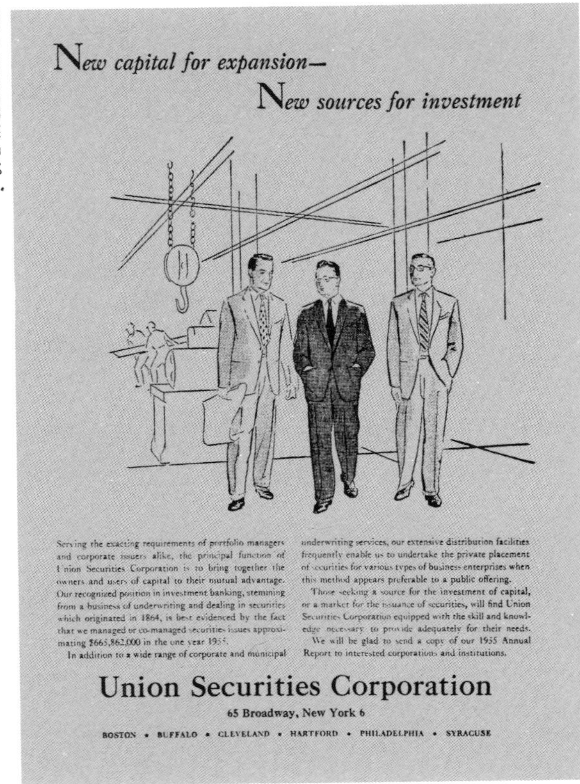

New capital for expansion—
New sources for investment
Serving the exacting requirements of portfolio managers and corporate issuers alike, the principal function of Union Securities Corporation is to bring together the owners and users of capital to their mutual advantage. Our recognized position in investment banking, stemming from a business of underwriting and dealing in securities which originated in 1864, is best evidenced by the fact that we managed or co-managed securities issues approximating $665,862,000 in the one year 1955.
In addition to a wide range of corporate and municipal underwriting services, our extensive distribution facilities frequently enable us to undertake the private placement of securities for various types of business enterprises when this method appears preferable to a public offering.
Those seeking a source for the investment of capital, or a market for the issuance of securities, will find Union Securities Corporation equipped with the skill and knowledge necessary to provide adequately for their needs.
We will be glad to send a copy of our 1955 Annual Report to interested corporations and institutions.
Union Securities Corporation
65 Broadway, New York 6
BOSTON • BUFFALO • CLEVELAND • HARTFORD • PHILADELPHIA • SYRACUSE

J. & W. SELIGMAN & CO.

their attention and time, they also gave increased thought to the future course of the firm and the various companies associated with it.

At the beginning of 1949, Charles P. Stetson became a partner, but in less than three years, he concluded that he preferred a different phase of the financial business. He withdrew from J. & W. Seligman & Co.

At the beginning of 1955, Fred E. Brown, Frederick W. Page, and Beverly W. Robertson were made partners. Robertson, of course, had been a Seligman employee throughout most of his career. And since he had helped to create the Investment Advisory Service and to oversee its successful development, it was natural that he continue directing it. Brown and Page, interestingly, had never been on the Seligman payroll. Both had started as trainees on the Tri-Continental investment staff and had gone over to Union Service when it was formed in 1940. They had progressed through the investment companies' organization from there.

Fred Brown returned from Washington in 1946 after having been awarded the Legion of Merit for his service during the War as a Lieutenant Colonel in the Fiscal Branch of the Army Quartermaster Corps. Starting as a senior investment analyst, he soon turned an increasing amount of his attention to investment company management and to the marketing of shares of the three Mutual Funds. These interests were, of necessity, superimposed on his research work, for before long Brown and Fred Page were assigned to guide the day-to-day activities of sections of the Union Service investment staff. By 1948, Brown was elected a Vice-President of Broad Street Investing and Page had been made a Vice-President of Tri-Continental. From then on their work was under the daily observation of the Seligman partners, and by the time Brown and Page entered the firm, both were Vice-Presidents of all four investment companies.

It is significant that the younger Seligman partners are investment men, rather than men trained in administration or sales. The firm's talents, the older partners recognized, were best employed in the more professional areas of managing investments, giving investment advice, and providing brokerage and related services to selected clients. And that was the direction in which the expanded firm planned to move forward. It had been decided that Union Securities, whose business was growing rapidly and becoming more and more time-consuming and demanding, basically did not fit into this long range plan. A search began for a way to dispose of this business to enable the senior men to concentrate on the primary interests of the firm and the investment companies.

The decision to separate J. & W. Seligman & Co. completely from all connection with underwriting —a function with which the firm had been identified for almost ninety years—was neither easily nor quickly made. For one thing, Union Securities' success had been remarkable. In the years it had been in existence, the company had raised capital for a wide variety of enterprises ranging from the Mackinac Bridge in Upper Michigan to major oil refineries. It had participated in more than

Charles P. Stetson was made a partner of the firm on January 1, 1949. He withdrew from J. & W. Seligman & Co. on September 14, 1951, to enter a different phase of the financial business and now operates his own organization.

COURTESY, CHARLES P. STETSON

1,000 corporate underwritings, which raised billions of dollars for companies all over the country and in virtually every important industry, in addition to selling other billions of dollars worth of local, state and Federal Government obligations. The two million dollars initially paid in by Tri-Continental and Selected Industries to form the subsidiary in 1938 had appreciated to more than $22,000,000 by the end of 1955. Moreover, dividends totaling $5,000,000 had been paid up to the parents. And Union Securities' future looked brighter than ever. Even so, risks inherent in the underwriting business were rising and it was agreed that these were out of place in the future envisioned for the Seligman organization and the investment companies.

Joseph King was completely committed to the underwriting business and determined to keep the organization going. He finally came up with a plan. He discussed the problem with Lloyd S. Gilmour of Eastman Dillon & Co. and together they proposed

MRS. AUDREY CASANI DE GROOT

Fred E. Brown (right), as President of Tri-Continental and the three Funds, and also Union Service Corporation, finds it important to have frequent conferences with William Renner, who is Treasurer for the five companies.

Olive Downie Beers, supervisor of the investment companies' marketing department, is in charge of the execution of all purchases and sales of securities. A native of Brooklyn, she joined Union Service Corporation in 1943.

ROY STEVENS - EXECUTIVE PORTRAITS, INC.

Percy H. Martins has been general maintenance man for over ten years. His job, keeping equipment in working order, is important to assure that the staff is able to perform its duties under the best possible working conditions.

GUY GILLETTE

to merge Union Securities into Gilmour's firm. Tri-Continental's Directors agreed, and the new firm of Eastman Dillon, Union Securities & Co. was formed in the Fall of 1956. However, as Francis Randolph has pointed out, "the transaction was not a sale, it was a transfer. All of the new issue business and all of the good will went to the new firm, with the proviso that profits on any new issue business which came up among a long list of companies would be shared for a period of time. Eastman Dillon agreed to take the entire Union Securities' staff and to give its members the same job security and employee benefits they had enjoyed with the old company."

"Beyond these terms," he adds, "full interest was kept in deals waiting to be worked out, and the right to continue the carry-financing transactions, which had produced by far the greatest part of Union Securities' profits, was reserved." All the capital stayed with Tri-Continental Financial Corporation, the new name given the subsidiary, and it was reorganized as a non-diversified investment company to carry on the business which remained.

Since 1956, J. & W. Seligman & Co. has concentrated on the task at hand. "These have been years of rapid growth for the investment community," says Fred Brown, who assumed the presidencies of the four investment companies in 1959, "and all of the firm's activities—the Investment Advisory Service, and brokerage and related services—have shared in that growth handsomely, as have the investment companies."

"Tri-Continental had a portfolio valued at about $550,000,000 at September 30, 1964, as compared to much less than half that ten years earlier. Easy to understand and widely respected, the big closed-end company provides income and a broad participation in American business to over 50,000 individuals and institutions in almost every part of the Free World. The Broad Street Group of Mutual Funds boasted only about $115,000,000 in combined assets and 28,000 owners in 1954. Today, ten years later, the assets of the Funds are worth over $780,000,000, and they have nearly 200,000 owners who look to us for the sound management of their investments. The Funds are still growing as their reputations spread."

Twice daily, vault custodians Henry Holl, Vincent J. Trotta, and Paul F. Volpe (l to r) visit the deep underground vault in which millions of dollars of clients' securities are safekept. To assure security, the vault staff works in pairs. Each man knows only half the combination to open the gate.

GUY GILLETTE

Tri-Continental Financial Corporation, successor to Union Securities, which Frederick Page has headed as President since 1959, has a good record, too. "In the eight years we have been out of the underwriting business we have participated in a number of interim financing deals and other short- or intermediate-term transactions, and we have taken positions in the securities of growing companies too small for Tri-Continental to invest in directly. These activities are interesting and they continue to be profitable."

All of this growth means that the Union Service staff, now directed by Page with the help of Stanley R. Currie, a Union Service Vice-President, is more active than ever. It has more than one hundred employees, its expenses are budgeted at over $1,100,000 for the year 1964. The investment men, who do the real work of Union Service, have had more securities to supervise as additional funds have been put to work in the companies, and the search for sound investments has become increasingly intense as business has grown more complex over the years.

Seligman's Investment Advisory Service, which scarcely twenty-five years ago had only a handful of accounts valued in the hundreds of thousands, now counts funds in its care in the many hundreds of millions. "This growth is no simple accident of economic expansion," Beverly Robertson will tell you. "Among the institutions we serve is a college fund of $60,000,000, a church which has investments of over $2,000,000, and trust, pension, profit sharing, charitable, and other institutional funds of almost every amount in between. Individual clients who came to us for advice on their own investment portfolios years ago have brought in their children, and then their children's children, until some of the family groups we serve are made up of as many as twenty different funds, each of which must be cared for on an individual, personalized basis."

"Over and beyond the actual managing of investments and giving advice, maintaining the spirit as well as the quality of service is one of our biggest day-to-day concerns," Robertson says. "The Seligman firm has lasted a long time only because it has

Robert H. Brown, Jr. (right), since 1961 President of Broad Street Sales Corporation, heads a nationwide sales network for shares of the three mutual funds. Russell A. Tilton, Jr. is Office Manager and Personnel Director for J. & W. Seligman & Co., Union Service, and Broad Street Sales.

GUY GILLETTE

had its own sense of direction and a deep commitment to its own special place in the financial world. We try to carry on this spirit by hiring the right men and women for the jobs that have to be done. Then the key to success is training and more training combined with years of experience. As time goes by, we will be able to ease the tasks done by using modern electronic office machines—a good deal of which we have accomplished already. But there is no way that I know that you can automate the kind of interest and personal concern that, in the final analysis, is what our clients need and expect and what we have been able to give them over the years."

"In the Investment Advisory Service," according to the partner in charge, "we have succeeded in maintaining standards of service by bringing in young people as trainees, then grooming them through training in investment research and analysis until they prove to be ready to supervise accounts and to meet clients face to face. The same basic approach to people learning to deal with people is applied, with obvious variations, in Raymond Monahan's tax department, Joseph Mendres' order department, Dominick Wolf's securities department, or Edward Pape's purchase and sales department. Monahan and his staff, for example, are keenly aware that when a client needs assistance with his tax returns, he wants the whole department to be vitally concerned with his personal tax situation. Few services are more sensitive to errors of any kind or more demanding in knowledge, skill, and accuracy. And, even though most clients never have and never will see the mechanics of buying and selling securities, or the great care that is given to securities in the Seligman safekeeping department, the firm's staff is keenly aware that behind every sheet of paper there are people, not just cold lists of numbers and valuations. In this respect," Robertson is sure, "we plan to provide for the future of this business by taking care of the present, training every employee thoroughly in the Seligman way of doing things. We like our clients, and we want them to go on liking us."

Fred Brown points out that all through the life-

Members of the staff of Broad Street Sales Corporation include (from back to front, left to right): Robert H. Brown, Jr., Ruth McKeel Goebel, Susanne Forch, Margaret C. Menke, Joseph J. Sicignano, and Linda Kihlstrom.

BOTH : GUY GILLETTE

William H. Hazen handles matters relating to regulation and rules affecting the firm and investment companies. Before joining the staff May 1, 1964, he was executive assistant to the New York State Superintendent of Banks.

time of J. & W. Seligman & Co. "we have been lucky in having active senior partners to whom all of us can look for advice and guidance. Investing is by no means a science, and mostly it scarcely seems to qualify as an art. But whatever it is, we are certain that there is no substitute for experienced, seasoned minds to which younger men can turn when advice in dealing with a client or a new situation is needed. I hope Seligman never gets so large that the youngest staff member can't be free to walk into any partner's office and get the help with his work that he wants."

"Sticking to the tested methods developed and proven over the years by our seniors and their predecessors is really a good part of our stock in trade. We have managed to stay young and vigorous enough to seize sound opportunities, but we are not opportunists. We shun the expedient and avoid chancy experiments which so often in the past have been the quickest roads to disaster for firms which seemed to move ahead so much faster, but haven't lasted nearly so long."

"When you look at Broad Street Sales Corporation, for instance, you will find that its basic organization and selling methods haven't really changed much since the days when shares of Whitehall Fund were first offered in 1947," Brown declares. "Sales of our Funds have grown because they have been offered through good dealers in the right way to investors who are genuinely in need of what the investment companies have to offer," he maintains. "We avoid sales gimmicks or pressures that may succeed for a little while, but which are bound to be self-defeating in the long run. It is significant," he believes, "that growth has come to every organization in our group without exploiting the momentary appeal of investment fads or fashions or playing on the fears and emotions of people who depend on us for help with their financial affairs. There is nothing flashy about our operations, and every Seligman partner earnestly hopes there never will be. We have succeeded because we are professionals. We try to do our jobs right. And we never lose sight of the fact that every one of our clients or shareholders has placed faith in us and that we have a high responsibility to each of them."

"Looking to the future, there is no way of knowing just how J. & W. Seligman & Co.'s activities may change. As we have in the past, we will

J. & W. SELIGMAN & Co.
ESTABLISHED 1864

INVESTMENT ADVISORY SERVICE

65 BROADWAY, NEW YORK, N.Y. 10006

ACCOUNT U/A 12/30/24

DATE OCTOBER 22, 1964

SUMMARY OF INVESTMENTS

	MARKET VALUE	% GROUP	% TOTAL	ANNUAL INCOME	CURRENT YIELD %
CASH & EQUIVALENT	$ 1,259		.2	$	
SENIOR SECURITIES — SHORT TERM					
SAVINGS DEPOSITS	$			$	
U. S. GOVERNMENT & AGENCIES					
TAX EXEMPT			4		
CORPORATE					
	$		5		
SENIOR SECURITIES — LONG TERM					
U. S. GOVERNMENT & AGENCIES	$				
TAX EXEMPT			32		
CORPORATE					
	$		32		
PREFERRED STOCKS	$				
MISCELLANEOUS	$				
CONVERTIBLE SECU					
TOTAL CASH & S			37		
COMMON STOCKS					
AUTOMOTIVE & EQUIP					
BUILDING SUPPLIES					
CHEMICALS					
CONSUMERS GOODS &					
DRUGS					
ELECTRICAL EQUIP. &					
FINANCIAL & INSURAN					
FOOD & HOUSEHOLD ITEMS					
METALS & MINING					
MISCELLANEOUS CAPI					
MISCELLANEOUS MAN					
OFFICE EQUIPMENT					
OIL & GAS					
PAPER & CONTAINERS					
RETAIL TRADE					
TRANSPORTATION					
UTILITIES - COMMUNIC					
UTILITIES - ELECTRIC					
UTILITIES - GAS					
SPECIAL HOLDINGS					
TOTAL COMM					
GRAND TOTA					

Periodically, J. & W. Seligman & Co.'s Investment Advisory Service clients receive an accounting of their holdings on the form over which photos of several account managers and analysts are superimposed. Shown clockwise, from twelve o'clock, are: Leonard A. Booth, Walter H. Baur, David Watts, Richard S. Palm, John F. Strauss, and George B. Stewart.

ALL: GUY GILLETTE, EXCEPT LOWER RIGHT WHICH IS BY MRS. AUDREY CASANI DE GROOT undoubtedly incorporate more and better services for shareholders of the investment companies as investors look more and more to professionals to handle their affairs. The world is becoming increasingly complex and the ordinary tasks which individuals automatically performed for themselves in years gone by are becoming the province of experts. We are bound to become involved in more of these tasks in time. But basically, an investment firm, like any other sound organization, makes progress almost imperceptibly, day by day, by sticking conscientiously to the task at hand and trying constantly to learn from new experiences and to better its work as a consequence. We hope never to become satisfied."

Perhaps the greatest tribute in recent years to J. & W. Seligman & Co. and the organizations associated with it, has been paid by the owners of thirty-one other companies—mostly private investment or personal holding companies—with assets totaling over $110,000,000, which since 1953 have elected to exchange those assets for shares of Broad Street Investing, National Investors, or Whitehall Fund.

These owners were knowledgable people whose fortunes were originally amassed in shipping, mining, advertising, and a host of other industries. For the most part, they were well-to-do, if not wealthy, and capable of hiring expert advice for the management of their capital. And many of them did before coming to a Seligman sponsored Fund.

"We have never solicited a transaction of this kind," Fred Brown has stated. "These investors came to us to put their assets to work in one of the Funds in the Broad Street Group purely on the basis of our reputation and record in the investment field. They have told us that our Funds were chosen because of sensible objectives consistently sought, good management organized to do the job today and in the future, steady records of performance, and economical low operating costs."

"This is the kind of recognition that has real meaning," Brown contends, "and we take pride in the knowledge that our heritage and our effort are such that people who need the services we can provide come to us with confidence. We look forward to the years ahead, not with visionary dreams of growing bigger or more widespread in our operations, but with the feeling that the future will be a time of opportunity for us to preserve and to

J. & W. Seligman & Co. partners, 1964

Francis F. Randolph

Cyril J. C. Quinn

Fred E. Brown

Beverly W. Robertson

Henry C. Breck

Stayman L. Reed

Frederick W. Page

ALL: GUY GILLETTE

strengthen the foundation on which the good names of our firm and companies rest as well as a time in which to grow. It is our job to make sure that all of our efforts are directed to doing each job we undertake as well as we know how, and to making sure the men and women in the organizations who will take our places some day are ready to carry forward when that time comes. The history of J. & W. Seligman & Co. indicates that we undoubtedly will move into new fields in years ahead. But, if our history is any guide, such moves will result from sensible evolution, related to the work in which we excell, and they will never be forced or hurried. If we give our full attention and our best efforts to the task at hand today, we need not worry about the next one hundred years. They will take care of themselves."

Francis Randolph, whose forty-four years of experience with J. & W. Seligman & Co. have taught him considerable patience—both in investing and in directing the firm—feels that whatever Seligman's destiny over the long term, a most important task is to provide continuity for the years ahead.

"We must remember," he says, "that ours is purely a service business. When investors come to J. & W. Seligman & Co. for investment management, or advice, or brokerage, or any of our related services, or when they come into the investment companies, they want to know that the service they get today will be available for them for as long as they may need it. They have every right to expect this, too."

"By bringing Fred Brown, Fred Page, and Beverly Robertson into the firm after they had years of intensive experience within the organization," Randolph declares, "and by putting even younger men into positions of responsibility where they can prepare to follow in our footsteps, we have assured continuity. Every client or potential client who comes into our offices or buys shares in the companies can have confidence that we are set to do the job he or she wants done honestly, conscientiously, and to the best of our abilities year after year."

"This is the tradition in which J. & W. Seligman & Co. was started one hundred years ago. We are determined that this tradition shall never change."

ACKNOWLEDGMENTS

"The next thing most like living one's life over again seems to be a recollection of that life," Benjamin Franklin wrote, "and to make that recollection as durable as possible by putting it down in writing." This book is the "life" of a firm which has existed for a century; a "recollection" of one hundred years. In writing this story, we have tried to make it "as durable as possible." In this effort, help came from many people and many sources. Each contributed a part which formed the whole. Our job was to combine the parts. We hope this is well done; any omissions or errors remain our responsibility. It is difficult to single out particular individuals or organizations which contributed most to our efforts. But several merit special notice. They are:

Linton Wells, a former staff member who, in 1931, completed writing nearly 1,000 invaluable manuscript pages - four volumes of information about the firm;

Geoffrey T. Hellman of New York, whose great-grandfather was Joseph Seligman and who furnished important papers, documents, and photographs, and

members of the staff whose personal contributions and whose continuing interest gave support and encouragement.

In addition, this story, in text and illustrations, could not have been told without the help of:

Alabama State Department of Archives and History, Montgomery–*Milo B. Howard, Jr.*
Harry P. Albrecht, Clifton Heights, Penn.
Alco Products, Incorporated, Schenectady, N. Y.
Miss Victoria M. Atkins
American Express Company, New York
Miss Gloria Mack
American Heritage, New York–*Mrs. Mary Dawn Earley*
American Home Assurance Company, New York
Max Debrovner
American Jewish Archives, Cincinnati, Ohio
Dr. Stanley F. Chyet
American Jewish Historical Society, New York
Dr. Nathan M. Kaganoff, Dr. Isidore S. Meyer
American Stock Exchange, New York–*John J. Sheehan*
American Telephone & Telegraph Company, New York
Miss A. Davis
Arizona Highways, Phoenix–*Raymond Carlson*
Arizona Pioneers' Historical Society, Tucson
Mrs. J. P. Moore
Arizona State Department of Library and Archives, Phoenix–*Mrs. Marguerite B. Cooley*
Arnhold and S. Bleichroeder, Inc., New York
F. H. Brunner
Association of American Railroads, Washington, D. C.
H. Stephen Dewhurst
The Atchison, Topeka and Sante Fe Railway System, Chicago–*Bill Burk*
Automobile Manufacturers Association, Inc., Detroit
Frederick A. Chapman
Aztec Land and Cattle Company, Limited, Albuquerque, N. Mex.–*T. W. Cabeen*
Babbitt Brothers Trading Company, Flagstaff, Ariz.
John G. Babbitt
Mrs. Margaret Bailie, New York
Baldwin-Lima-Hamilton Corporation, Philadelphia
John C. Kosky
The Bancroft Library, University of California, Berkeley
Cecil L. Chase
Ed Bartholomew, Toyahvale, Texas
Miss Carol Anne Bauer, New York
Lucius Beebe, Hillsborough, Calif.
Birmingham Chamber of Commerce, Birmingham, Ala.
Mrs. Sibyl R. McJunkin
Birmingham Public Library, Birmingham, Ala.
Fant Hill Thornley
Board of Governors of the Federal Reserve System, Washington, D. C.–*Miss Elizabeth L. Carmichael*
Mrs. Charles Boughton, Middlebush, N. J.
H. L. Broadbelt, Hershey, Penn.
Miss Hope Bunker, Waterville, Maine
2. Bürgermeister, Baiersdorf, West Germany
California Historical Society, San Francisco
James de T. Abajian, John J. Morris
The California State Library, Sacramento
Allan R. Ottley
Herbert L. Carlebach, New York
Carlton House, New York–*John D. Green*
Carthage Evening Press, Carthage, Mo.–*Robert S. Dale*
Bruce Catton, New York
Chamber of Commerce of the New Orleans Area, New Orleans–*Andres N. Horcasitas, Jr.*
The Chase Manhattan Bank, New York–*Francesco P. Cantarella, William J. C. Carlin, Robert E. Doran III, Ernest C. Grigg III, Miss Ann Hilden*
The Chase Manhattan Bank Money Museum, New York
Miss Barbara Deckard
Chicago Historical Society, Chicago–*Paul M. Angle*

The Children's Aid Society, New York
Mrs. Florence M. Brecht
The Condé Nast Publications Inc., New York
Paul H. Bonner, Jr.
Consolidated Edison Company of New York, Inc., New York—*Daniel P. Parker*
Cravath, Swaine & Moore, New York
Harold E. Beyea
Crocker-Citizens National Bank, San Francisco
Monroe A. Bloom
Dallas Historical Society, Dallas, Tex.—*Herbert Gambrell*
The DeGolyer Foundation, Dallas, Tex.
Everett L. DeGolyer, Jr.
The late J. Frank Dobie, Austin, Tex.
Eastman Dillon, Union Securities & Co., New York
William J. Keary, Miss Patricia Patten
Erie-Lackawanna Railroad Company, Cleveland, Ohio
George C. Frank
Adlai Feather, Mesilla Park, N. Mex.
Hill Ferguson, Birmingham, Ala.
Colonel George C. Fraser, New York
G. C. Haas & Co., New York—*William Moore*
General Aniline & Film Corporation, Binghamton, N. Y.
Philip M. Mikoda
General Services Administration, National Archives and Records Service, Washington, D.C.—*W. Neil Franklin, Victor Gondos, Jr.; Elbert L. Huber, Elmer O. Parker*
General Motors Corporation, Detroit
Miss Jean Houghton
Mrs. John D. Gordon, New York
Mrs. Kenneth Hanau, Sr., Montclair, N. J.
Harriman Ripley & Co. Incorporated, New York
Joseph P. Ripley
Haverford College, Haverford, Penn.—*Barclay M. Bollas*
Dr. Rudolph M. Heilbrunn, Kaiserslautern, West Germany
Mrs. H. E. Hellman, New York
Mrs. Irene Hellman, South Monsey, N. Y.
Mrs. Alexander I. Henderson, Fairfield, Conn.
George W. Hennessey, Phoenix, Ariz.
Robert A. Henning, Holbrook, Ariz.
Historical Society of Montana, Helena
Miss Mary K. Dempsey
Historical Society of New Mexico, Albuquerque
Victor Westphall
The Historical Society of Pennsylvania, Philadelphia
R. N. Williams 2d
Historical Society of Saratoga, Saratoga Springs, N. Y.
Mrs. Walter A. Britten
Mrs. Totsy Slaughter Hitchcock, Tucson, Ariz.
Honeywell Inc., Minneapolis
H. D. Bissell, Dean B. Randall
The Hoover Institution on War, Revolution, and Peace, Stanford University, Stanford, Calif.
Dr. Rita Campbell, Eileen W. Shaw
Jasper County Historical Society, Carthage, Mo.
Carl Kirchner
Mrs. Jo Johnson Jeffers, Holbrook, Ariz.
Jewish Child Care Association of New York, New York
Mrs. Frances A. Koestler
Kansas State Historical Society, Topeka
Robert W. Richmond
Lancaster County Historical Society, Lancaster, Penn.
John Ward Willson Loose
David F. Lane, Watertown, N. Y.
Lehigh University, Bethlehem, Penn.—*Samuel I. Connor*
The Library of Congress, Washington, D. C. .
Miss Virginia Daiker, Miss Alice Lee Parker, Mrs. Renata Shaw
Live Stock Sanitary Board of Arizona, Phoenix
Miss Elsie M. Haverty
Bennie S. McCann, Seligman, Mo.
Mrs. Henry J. Mali, New York
Marine Historical Association, Inc., Mystic Seaport, Mystic, Conn.—*Miss Alma Eshenfelder*
The Marine Midland Trust Company of New York, New York—*John R. McGinley*
The Mariners Museum, Newport News, Va.
John L. Lochhead
The Maytag Company, Newton, Iowa
Deane L. Markusch, George M. Umbreit
Emory Melton, Cassville, Mo.
State of Michigan Mackinac Bridge Authority, St. Ignace
Lawrence A. Rubin
Missouri Historical Society, St. Louis
Mrs. Ruth K. Field, Mrs. Fred C. Harrington
Missouri-Kansas-Texas Railroad Company, St. Louis
M. R. Cring
Missouri Pacific Lines, St. Louis—*Harry E. Hammer*
Model, Roland & Co., New York—*Irwin A. Brodsky*
Museum of New Mexico, Santa Fe—*Bruce T. Ellis*
Mrs. Jessie L. Murphree, Seligman, Ariz.
Museum of the City of New York, New York
A. K. Baragwanath, Mrs. Henriette Beal
National Cowboy Hall of Fame and Western Heritage Center, Oklahoma City, Okla.—*Glenn W. Faris*
Native Sons of the Golden West, San Francisco
Harold J. Regan
Nevada Historical Society, Reno—*Miss Marion Welliver*
Nevada State Library, Carson City
Mrs. Mildred J. Heyer, Walter T. McCauley
Bert Neville, Selma, Ala.
New Orleans Public Library, New Orleans
Miss Margaret Ruckert

New York City Transit Authority, Brooklyn
Walter L. Schlager, Jr.; Hal Wright
New-York Historical Society, New York
Miss Nancy Hale
New York State Historical Association, Cooperstown, N. Y.–*Miss Ruby M. Rounds*
The New Yorker, New York–*Milton Greenstein*
New York Stock Exchange, New York
Mrs. Ann Hoehl, George W. Lutes
New York Telephone Company, New York
Miss Ciel Christiana
Newport News Shipbuilding and Dry Dock Company, Newport News, Va.–*R. B. Hopkins*
Miss Catherine E. O'Hara, New York
The Ohio State University, Columbus–*James E. Pollard*
Oklahoma Historical Society, Oklahoma City
Mrs. C. E. Cook, Mrs. Dorothy Williams
Oregon Historical Society, Portland–*Miss Priscilla Knuth*
Mrs. Helen Pearson, Williams, Ariz.
Pennsylvania Historical and Museum Commission, Harrisburg–*Irwin Richman*
Pennsylvania State Library, Harrisburg
Miss Sally A. Weikel
Philadelphia Historical Commission, Philadelphia
Mrs. Charles J. Maurer
Miss Amy F. Phillips, Miami, Fla.
Mrs. Rhoda S. Prud'homme, Santa Barbara, Calif.
Railroads Magazine, New York–*Freeman Hubbard*
Railway and Locomotive Historical Society, Inc., Boston–*Charles E. Fisher*
Everett Reddick, Seligman, Mo.
The Rice County Historical Society, Lyons, Kans.
Mrs. John Sayler
Gladwell Richardson, Flagstaff, Ariz.
Miss Hattie Rosenstock, San Francisco
George E. Rowan, Seligman, Ariz.
S. G. Warburg & Company Limited (Incorporating Seligman Brothers), London, England–*G. C. Seligman*
St. Louis-San Francisco Railway Company, Springfield, Mo.–*C. H. Fairchild*
Securities and Exchange Commission, Washington, D. C.
Orval L. DuBois
Seligman & Cie, Paris, France—*Olivier Michel*
Mrs. Joseph L. Seligman, New York
Joseph L. Seligman, Jr., San Francisco
Walter Seligman, Farmingdale, L. I., N. Y.
The Selma Times-Journal, Selma, Ala.
Roswell L. Falkenberry
Seventh Regiment, New York
Colonel John J. Bellew, Colonel George Johnston
Smith, Barney & Co. Incorporated, New York
Russell M. Sanderson
Simmons-Boardman Publishing Corporation, New York
Miss Edith Stone
Peter F. Smith, Belmar, N. J.
The Society of California Pioneers, San Francisco
Mrs. Helen S. Giffin
Southwest Forest Industries, Phoenix, Ariz.
James M. Boyd
The State Historical Society of Missouri, Columbia
Kenneth B. Holmes, Miss Janet K. White
Charles P. Stetson, Fairfield, Conn.
Mrs. J. B. Stiles, Winslow, Ariz.
Tennessee State Library and Archives, Nashville
William T. Alderson, Miss Kendall Cram
Thomas De La Rue & Company Limited, London, England
Paul M. Gunn
Thos. De La Rue, Inc., New York–*Miss Valerie A. Spicer*
Thomas Gilcrease Institute of American History and Art, Tulsa, Okla.–*Mrs. H. H. Keene*
Trains Magazine, Milwaukee, Wis.–*David P. Morgan*
Treasury Department, Bureau of Engraving and Printing, Washington, D. C.–*J. R. Baker*
The Ulysses S. Grant Association, Columbus, Ohio
Dr. John Y. Simon
The Union League Club, New York–*G. Everett Hoyt*
Union Pacific Railroad Company, New York
Grant Burden
United Artists Corporation, New York–*Mori Krushen*
United Artists Theatre Circuit, Inc., New York
Mrs. Emma Jasin Reissman
University of Oklahoma Press, Norman
Savoie Lottinville
The University of Arizona, University Library, Tucson
John D. Gilchriese
Edward B. Watson, Brooklyn, N. Y.
Wells Fargo Bank, San Francisco–*Miss Irene Simpson*
West Tennessee Historical Society, Memphis
Buford C. Utley
The Western Union Telegraph Company, New York
Edward F. Sanger
Mrs. Robert V. White, Rumson, N. J.
Mr. Genoa E. Williams, Seligman, Mo.
S. R. Wood, Stillwater, Okla.

This book was printed by Photo-offset Lithography by Thos. De La Rue Inc., Westbury, Long Island, New York. Binding is by John M. Gettler, Inc., New York, New York. The cover is Arrestox Buckram cloth; text is Teton white and buff. Copy is set in ten point Fairfield with Bauer initial caps and Craw Modern. Design and layout was under the direction of Robert H. Whitehead who was assisted by Alex Berger and Michael J. Verderosa of Thos. De La Rue,Inc., as is David H. Bennett who coordinated the project.

Wall Street, 1964

J. & W. SELIGMAN & CO.

ESTABLISHED 1864

Members New York Stock Exchange

INVESTMENTS

65 BROADWAY **NEW YORK 6, N.Y.**

Cables : "SELIGMAN"

The Bankers' Almanac and Year Book, 1963-1964